Hidden Liberalism

Compared to rival ideologies, liberalism has fared rather poorly in modern Iran. This is all the more remarkable given the essentially liberal substance of various social and political struggles – for liberal legality, individual rights and freedoms, and pluralism – in the century-long period since the demise of the Qajar dynasty and the subsequent transformation of the country into a modern nation-state. The deeply felt but largely invisible purchase of liberal political ideas in Iran challenges us to think more expansively about the trajectory of various intellectual developments since the emergence of a movement for reform and constitutionalism in the late nineteenth century. It complicates parsimonious accounts of Shiism, secularism, socialism, nationalism, and royalism as defining or representative ideologies of particular eras. *Hidden Liberalism* offers a critical examination of the reasons behind liberalism's invisible yet influential status, and its attendant ethical quandaries, in Iranian political and intellectual discourses.

Hussein Banai is Assistant Professor of International Studies in the Hamilton Lugar School of Global and International Studies at Indiana University, Bloomington, and Research Affiliate at the Center for International Studies at MIT. He is coauthor of *Becoming Enemies: U.S.-Iran Relations and the Iran-Iraq War, 1979–1988* (2012) and currently serves as Associate Editor (for Social Sciences) of *Iranian Studies*, the journal of the Association for Iranian Studies. His writings on Iran's political development and foreign relations have been published in academic, policy, and popular periodicals.

Hidden Liberalism
Burdened Visions of Progress in Modern Iran

Hussein Banai
Indiana University, Bloomington

CAMBRIDGE
UNIVERSITY PRESS

University Printing House, Cambridge CB2 8BS, United Kingdom

One Liberty Plaza, 20th Floor, New York, NY 10006, USA

477 Williamstown Road, Port Melbourne, VIC 3207, Australia

314–321, 3rd Floor, Plot 3, Splendor Forum, Jasola District Centre,
New Delhi – 110025, India

79 Anson Road, #06–04/06, Singapore 079906

Cambridge University Press is part of the University of Cambridge.

It furthers the University's mission by disseminating knowledge in the pursuit of
education, learning, and research at the highest international levels of excellence.

www.cambridge.org
Information on this title: www.cambridge.org/9781108495592
DOI: 10.1017/9781108850445

© Hussein Banai 2021

This publication is in copyright. Subject to statutory exception
and to the provisions of relevant collective licensing agreements,
no reproduction of any part may take place without the written
permission of Cambridge University Press.

First published 2021

A catalogue record for this publication is available from the British Library.

ISBN 978-1-108-49559-2 Hardback

Cambridge University Press has no responsibility for the persistence or accuracy of
URLs for external or third-party internet websites referred to in this publication
and does not guarantee that any content on such websites is, or will remain,
accurate or appropriate.

To my family, and in memory of my grandmother,
Farahbanu Shoushtarian

Those days are gone,
the days of rapture and awe,
of daydreams and dreams,
days when each shadow bore a secret,
each box promised hidden troves,
each corner of the storeroom was a world
inside the silence of noon.
Anyone not afraid of the dark
was a hero in my eyes.

Forough Farrokhzad, "Those Days" (1962)

I believe in facts and very often the facts get abused, or left out, or embroidered or hidden or forgotten . . .

Edward W. Said, "Returning to Ourselves," interview
with Jacqueline Rose (1998)

Contents

Acknowledgments		*page* viii
1	Introduction: Hidden Liberalism	1
2	Aspects of Political Liberalism in Modern Iran	23
3	The Specter of Westernism	60
4	Liberation without Liberalism	102
5	Conclusion: (In)visible Liberalisms	142
	Bibliography	153
	Index	171

Acknowledgments

The writing of this book has been an education. As with any such process, the personal and professional debts accrued over time are too numerous and great to ever be acknowledged, let alone repaid, in full. Any hint of insight or value in this book is the result of enlightenments spurred by these engagements, just as any shortcomings, imperfections, or errors are my responsibility alone.

My education in liberalism continues to be influenced by the teachings and scholarship of my mentors and teachers at Brown University, where I completed my doctorate. My sincere thanks to Peter Andreas, Mark Blyth, Corey Brettschneider, Melani Cammett, James Der Derian, David Estlund, Sharon Krause, Charles Larmore, James Morone, Richard Snyder, Nina Tannenwald, and John Tomasi. Although the current book bears no resemblance whatsoever to the topic or contents of my dissertation – on the contextual basis of democratic legitimacy – the intellectual preparation that produced that work continues to enrich my understanding of liberal thought and Iran's political development to this day. Special thanks to the members of my dissertation committee – Corey (chair), Sharon, Charles, James Der Derian, and Nina – for sharpening my intellectual curiosities and always helping me out of dead ends. Since leaving Brown, Corey's unreserved encouragement and helpful advice have been both steadying and clarifying, especially during crucial moments of transition between institutions and cities. I very much treasure his friendship and mentorship.

My greatest intellectual debt in writing this book, and especially in charting an academic career at the intersection of Iranian studies and political thought, is to Ali Gheissari. We were first acquainted during my early days as a fledgling graduate student at Brown, where, as a visiting faculty fellow, he sought me out and instantly broadened my intellectual and professional horizons through introductions to active and fertile scholarly circles in Iranian studies. My education under his auspices continues to this day, and I am eternally beholden beyond measure to his generosity of spirit and intellectual example. I am especially grateful to

Acknowledgments

have had Ali's support and encouragement at each step of this book project. I have burdened him with various drafts and incoherent thoughts throughout the writing process, and should any of the arguments contained herein register as insights on Iran's politics or intellectual history, they are all entirely owing to his mentorship and close reading.

The central ideas of the book emerged and cohered during my time as a faculty member in the Department of Diplomacy and World Affairs at Occidental College. I am especially grateful for the critically constructive feedback and conversations (in the best Oxy tradition!) on aspects of the book with my treasured friends and colleagues Anthony Chase, Michael Gasper, Sanjeev Khagram, Malek Moazzam-Doulat, and Jennifer Piscopo. My sincere thanks to Derek Shearer, Director of the McKinnon Center for Global Affairs, and President Jonathan Veitch for their support and encouragement throughout. I would also like to thank Zach Abels, Calli Obern, and Danny Tobin for research assistance and conversations on early drafts of the project.

The writing of the manuscript began in earnest after I made the transition to the Department of International Studies in the Hamilton Lugar School of Global and International Studies at Indiana University, Bloomington. I am very fortunate to share a most rigorous, engaging, and congenial intellectual space with colleagues across a range of academic departments, area studies centers, and research institutes at IU. Early drafts from the book were presented at the Political Theory Colloquium, Islam in the Global Sphere Workshop, the Comparative Political Ethics and Theory Workshop, and the Center for Constitutional Democracy at IU. For their kind invitations and constructive feedback at these presentations, I am especially indebted to: Asma Afsaruddin, Aurelian Craiutu, Judith Failer, Russell Hanson, Jeffrey Isaac, Bill Rasch, Bill Scheuerman, Aaron Stalnaker, David Williams, and Susan Williams.

The Department of International Studies has been a most supportive, warm, and engaging intellectual home for me over the past four years. My deepest gratitude to the three department chairs who respectively hired, settled, and steadied me into a new academic environment: Bill Rasch, Padraic Kenney, and Purnima Bose. Special thanks to Barbara Breitung and Eric Weingarten for showing the way, every day. With their assistance, and the generous support of the department, the penultimate draft of the book was the subject of a manuscript workshop in November 2018, which enabled me to receive expert, constructive, and timely feedback and advice on how to best to advance the project to publication. I am most grateful for the participation of department colleagues and outside readers either at the workshop or through correspondence afterward. Profuse thanks to David Bosco, Gardner Bovingdon, Aurelian Craiutu,

x   Acknowledgments

Nick Cullather, Sarah Bauerle Danzman, Hamid Ekbia, Dean Lee Feinstein, Ali Gheissari, Emma Gilligan, Russ Hanson, Nur Amali Ibrahim, Jeff Isaac, Stephanie Kane, Padraic Kenney, Stephen Macekura, Jessy O'Reilly, Clémence Pinaud, Shruti Rana, Bill Scheuerman, Ron Sela, and Jess Steinberg. For close mentorship, professional advice, and institutional guidance, I am particularly grateful to Bill Scheuerman. For bibliographic and research assistance, I thank Carly Ball and Will Van Winkle.

Beyond formal academic venues, this book has been enriched immeasurably by countless stray and direct conversations – about Iran, liberalism, intellectual history, political thought, democracy, book writing, etc. – with colleagues, friends, family, and neighbors. Special thanks to Said Amir Arjomand, Ali Banuazizi, Jim Blight, Malcolm Byrne, Christopher Clary, Nilo Clary, Nader Hashemi, Jeremy Johnson, Hossein Khiabanian, Janet Lang, Andrew Lynch, Meysam Mobini, Jonathan Renshon, Stanley Renshon, Michelle Schwarze, John Tirman, Erika Wilkinson, and John Yasuda.

At Cambridge University Press, I am indebted to Maria Marsh, Daniel Brown, Atifa Jiwa, and Melissa Ward for their support, encouragement, and patience, in equal measure. For their utmost professionalism in steering the book through the production process and meticulous copyediting of the final manuscript, I owe an eternal debt of gratitude to Raghavi Govindane and Muhammad Ridwaan, respectively.

Since 2014, I have presented early drafts of various chapters from the book (and those that did not make it into the book, but which were instrumental in shaping its scope and arguments) at various conferences and workshops. My thanks to audiences and respondents at the annual or biennial conferences of the Association for Iranian Studies, the Association for Political Theory, the Middle East Studies Association, and the International Studies Association. I am particularly grateful to Nayereh Tohidi for the invitation to present perhaps the earliest gestation of ideas behind the book at the UCLA Center for Near Eastern Studies in fall 2014. My special thanks to her and Kazem Alamdari for their extremely helpful comments and feedback during that event and afterward. At the generous invitation of Michelle Schwarze, I presented a more developed version of the conceptual core of the book at the University of Wisconsin, Madison. The comments by participants at the Political Theory Workshop there were most valuable, and I am especially grateful to my good friend and colleague Jennie Ikuta for her incisive feedback and suggestions. Special thanks also to my dear friend Jonathan Renshon for graciously turning up at a workshop full of political theorists.

Acknowledgments xi

This book is dedicated to my family in Iran, Finland, Canada, and the United States, and to the memory of my beloved maternal grandmother, Farahbanu Shoushtarian, who left us too soon. She and my grandfather, Nosratollah Movasagh-Nekoonam, have set a high example for reflective understanding, compassion, and altruism. My heartfelt thanks to my parents, Reza Banai and Mitra Nekoonam, and my siblings, Azadeh and Sepehr, for their love and support. Also, special thanks to my dear aunt, Nazila Nekoonam, for procuring books and archival material for me in Tehran – she is a model of magnanimity and dedication.

Last and most important, this book would not have been finished without the unconditional love, caring support, forbearance, and limitless empathy shown to me by my wife, Tracey Wilkinson. As a first-rate physician and engaged academic researcher, she shows me the way every day, and is my ultimate resource for hope. Our daughters, Elyse and Eleanor, have lifted me up and cheered me on at every corner. For the light and vitality they all bring into my life and work, the words "gratitude" and "debt" do not begin to do justice.

1 Introduction
Hidden Liberalism

I knew that it was useless to attempt a remodeling of Persia in European forms, and I was determined to clothe my material reformation in a garb which my people would understand, the garb of religion.[1]

In 1861, Mirza Malkum Khan (1834–1908), a leading reformist in the Qajar court, presented the reigning monarch Naser al-Din Shah (1831–1896) with his treatise on political reforms entitled *Ketabcheh-ye Gheybi* [Booklet from the Unseen Realm].[2] The booklet's introduction reflected on Iran's perilous state of affairs: the ministerial ranks were plagued by incompetence and corruption; the treasury had been ransacked through mismanagement and plain thievery; the public's trust and its dignity were routinely violated; natural and human resources were massively untapped; and sovereign independence was a chimera in the face of ongoing and threatening foreign meddling in the country's internal affairs. These dire conditions, Malkum Khan contented, were chiefly caused by the absence of accountability and the rule of law (*qanun*), which the Shah could remedy by undertaking a series of legal and administrative reforms, akin to the *tanzimat* reforms undertaken in the Ottoman court. Malkum Khan deliberately used the term *qanun* to signal a departure from religious (*shari'a*) and customary (*'urf*) ordinances that derived their legitimacy from extra-civilian sources. *Qanun* was premised on the principle of free and equal citizenship, which Malkum Khan believed bestowed on the machinery of government (under the tutelage of the Shah) a measure of popular legitimacy in the fashion of

---

[1] Mirza Malkum Khan (Nazem al-Dowleh) in conversation with Wilfred Scawen Blunt in 1907. W. W. Blunt, *The Secret History of the English Occupation of Egypt* (London: T. F. Unwin, 1907), p. 83.

[2] Also known as *Daftar-e Tanzimat* [Book of Reforms]. Malkum Khan's writings are collected in Mirza Malkum Khan Nezam al-Dowleh, *Resaleha-ye Mirza Malkum Khan Nazem al-Dowleh* [The Treatises of Mirza Malkum Khan Nazem al-Dowleh], ed. Hojatollah Aseel (Tehran: Nashr-e Ney, 1381/2002).

2   Introduction

the European constitutional monarchies of the day. Although the Shah had initially been receptive to Malkum Khan's ideas and was even rumored to have become the honorary grandmaster of Faramoush-Khaneh (House of Oblivion) – a secret society Malkum Khan had established as a venue for cultivating European Enlightenment values and ideas among the ruling elite – he publicly disavowed both once religious authorities denounced Malkum Khan as an "atheistic heretic" and warned the Shah to affirm and fulfill his role as "protector of the faith." The bulk of Malkum Khan's career thereafter was spent in and out of exile, culminating in his founding of the highly influential London-based newspaper *Qanun* in 1890. The latter played a definitive role in the advent of the Constitutional Revolution in Iran (1906–1911) by shrewdly employing a parlance of righteous indignation that resonated with both lay and religious opponents of royal despotism.

Malkum Khan's intellectual odyssey and political career are not unique in the annals of nascent liberal thought-practices, especially in societies where non-liberal forms of rule and traditional customs predominate. Liberal beginnings often take the form of reformist undertakings; liberal beginners are more likely to be driven by narrow antipathies than coherent agendas; the preferred approach of the liberal is almost universally that of prudence over reaction; and persuasion is the liberal's favored method of conversion. Depending on one's definition of liberalism (a subject I address in the next section), since at least Niccolò Machiavelli's artful replacement of Christian ethics with a modern secular guide to moral action, these proclivities have accompanied the expression of forbidden, inconvenient, or unconventional thoughts the world over. Yet, Malkum Khan's example also poses a distinctive challenge in being representative of a particular kind of liberal thought-practice – especially in former (semi)colonial societies – that has not much evolved beyond these inclinations and modes of expression even as other attributes of Western modernity (e.g. secularism, nationalism, industrialism, capitalism, etc.) have proliferated. In the case of Iran, in more than a century following the birth of constitutionalism, liberalism has remained an embattled, taciturn, even shadowy thought-practice that is more readily detectable in the religious and nationalist doublespeak of vulnerable intellectuals than in any formalized intellectual program or political agenda.

Liberalism's tentative public standing in Iran is all the more remarkable given the essentially liberal substance of various social and political struggles – for greater rights, basic freedoms, and against arbitrary exercises of power – in the century-long period since the demise of the Qajar dynasty and the subsequent transformation of the country into a modern nation-state.

Introduction 3

To be sure, many Iranian intellectuals and political activists have been shaped by elements of liberalism in their thinking about such matters as representative government, civil and political rights, religious and ethnic toleration, gender equity, the plight of the poor and of the marginalized, and so on. Liberalism has never been alien to Iran's intellectual culture or its socioeconomic and political development. The oddity, rather, is in the lack of any self-proclaimed liberal project or movement dedicated to the advancement and defense of such ideals *as intrinsically and avowedly liberal ideals*. Liberalism is at once everywhere and nowhere to be found; it has formed the basis of many social and political struggles, yet it remains *hidden as a public standpoint*. This paradox is not peculiar to Iran, however; it is indeed evident in societies where (semi)colonial histories continue to define the substance and form of political debate. At its core, it is a conundrum about the ethics of taking on the ideology of an erstwhile system of exploitation (i.e. Western imperialism) that justified its practices through appeals to a "standard of civilization" rooted in liberal values. Unsurprisingly, while this ethical dilemma is an enervating burden on postcolonial liberals, it is also a crucial source of strength for a variety of anti-liberal ideologies vying for legitimacy on the basis of religion, class resentments, or claims to ethno-cultural authenticity and even superiority.

This book offers a critical examination of this paradox and its concomitant ethical quandaries through a conceptual engagement with currents of political thought in modern Iran. The deeply felt but largely invisible normative purchase of liberal political concepts in Iran challenges us to think more expansively about the trajectory of various intellectual developments since the emergence of a movement for reform and constitutionalism in the late nineteenth century. It complicates parsimonious accounts of Shiism, secularism, socialism, nationalism, and royalism as defining or representative ideologies of particular eras. The diffusion of liberal values and their subterranean influence upon political practices, as the following will attest, have played a major role in exposing the emancipatory limits of these competing ideologies and charted new paths in pursuit of more democratic social and political arrangements. In grappling with the oft-complementary legacies of Western imperialism and domestic despotism, moreover, Iranian liberalism has struggled to chart an authentic path toward a viable political vision that is not also viewed as a mere facsimile of Western liberal blueprints. As such, it has vacillated between high-minded, aristocratic paternalism and half-hearted, inconsequential reformism. It is a central argument of this book, however, that in between these zones of futility liberal thought-practices have achieved a measure of success as a repository of conceptual and theoretical

4   Introduction

knowledge, context-specific antipathies and prescriptions, norms-based practices, and politically unaffiliated identities that collectively make for a more self-reflexive variant of liberalism. This particular manifestation of liberal thought-practices has curiously been overlooked in contemporary Iranian studies as well as in theoretical considerations of liberalism in political theory.

It must be noted from the outset, however, that this book is not an exhaustive history of liberal thought in modern Iran. Nor is it in any way an attempt to will into being a hitherto overlooked cannon of political writings that could plausibly and coherently be classified as liberal. Such an endeavor – a remote possibility for a single volume, at any rate – is not my ambition in this study. Rather, the scope of my inquiry is confined to an exploration of *the reasons behind* liberalism's invisible, yet influential status, in Iranian political and intellectual discourses. This most modest contribution, I hope, will have the benefit of explicitly laying out a diagnostic that is merely hinted at – in terms of its impact and scope – in many existing intellectual and political histories of modern Iran. As such, my main objective is to slightly enlarge the space of scholarly inquiry into currents of thought behind Iran's political development through a recognition of the quite considerable set of intellectual and practical obstacles in the way of a more self-aware, confident, and capacious liberal discourse in the period between the emergence of constitutionalism at the outset of the twentieth century and the swift rise and eclipse of Islamic reformism at the close of the same century. Before expanding on the tortuous path of liberal ideas in Iran, however, it is important to clarify what exactly I do and do not mean by the term "liberalism" in this study.

Liberalism in Context

Liberalism is a vast and storied subject. "Anyone trying to give a brief account of liberalism," Alan Ryan has observed, "is immediately faced with an embarrassing question: are we dealing with liberalism or with liberalisms? It is easy to list famous liberals; it is harder to say what they have in common."[3] Similarly, as Jennifer Pitts observes, "Liberalism is notoriously and inevitably a complex ideology whose exemplars share family resemblances rather than any strict doctrine."[4] There are "classical," "modern," "social," "comprehensive," and "political" liberalisms; there is the literary "liberal imagination" and the practical "liberal

---

[3] Alan Ryan, *The Making of Modern Liberalism* (Princeton, NJ: Princeton University Press, 2012), p. 21.
[4] Jennifer Pitts, "Political Theory of Empire and Imperialism," *Annual Review of Political Science*, Vol. 13, No. 1 (June 2010): 214.

Introduction 5

pluralism."[5] The task becomes harder still when one has to account for liberalism's adaptations in various contexts: "liberal nationalism," "liberal internationalism," "liberal imperialism," the varieties of liberal toleration, and so forth.[6] As a recent historical study of liberalism laments, "we are muddled about what we mean by liberalism. People use the term in all sorts of different ways, often unwittingly, sometimes intentionally. They talk past each other, precluding any possibility of reasonable debate."[7] Indeed, these difficulties become further amplified in non-liberal settings, where liberal thinkers and practitioners, let alone variances among their positions, are not self-identified and publicly proclaimed.

Duncan Bell has insightfully offered three broad categories of answers that are typically given to the question "What is liberalism?"[8] There are "prescriptive" answers that "delineate a particular conception of liberalism, branding it as more authentic – more truly liberal – than other claimants to the title." "Comprehensive responses" (not to be confused with comprehensive philosophical *conceptions* of liberalism), in contrast, "seek to identify the *actual* range of usage, mapping the variegated topography of liberal ideology." Lastly, there are "explanatory" answers that seek to "account for the development of liberalism(s), whether understood in prescriptive or comprehensive terms."[9] In addition to these categories of answers, Bell identifies three "methodological strategies" that either "stipulate" a necessary requirement for an argument to be counted as liberal, appeal to "canonical" authorities, or aim to offer "contextualist" readings of liberal positions. Considering these positions, Bell then offers his own "summative conception" of what liberalism

---

[5] For a succinct summary of various prefixes, see Steven Wall, ed., *The Cambridge Companion to Liberalism* (Cambridge: Cambridge University Press, 2015); Freeden provides a comprehensive overview of liberalism as a twentieth-century ideology in Michael Freeden, *Liberal Languages: Ideological Imaginations and Twentieth-Century Progressive Thought* (Princeton, NJ: Princeton University Press, 2009); for a theoretical examination of modern varieties of liberalism, see Ryan, *The Making of Modern Liberalism*; for the most recent history of liberal thought-practices, see Helena Rosenblatt, *The Lost History of Liberalism: From Ancient Rome to the Twenty-First Century* (Princeton, NJ: Princeton University Press, 2018).

[6] Yael Tamir, *Liberal Nationalism* (Princeton, NJ: Princeton University Press, 1995); Michael W. Doyle, "Liberalism and World Politics," *American Political Science Review*, Vol. 80, No. 4 (December 1986): 1151–1169; Duncan Bell, *Reordering the World: Essays on Liberalism and Empire* (Princeton, NJ: Princeton University Press, 2016); and Chandran Kukathas, *The Liberal Archipelago: A Theory of Diversity and Freedom* (Oxford: Oxford University Press, 2003), chapter 4.

[7] Rosenblatt, *The Lost History of Liberalism*, p. 1.

[8] Duncan Bell, "What Is Liberalism?" *Political Theory*, Vol. 42, No. 6 (2014): 1–34. He also offers a corresponding set of "methodological strategies" employed by scholars to answer this question, but for the purposes of this chapter I shall only focus on the "types" of answers given. For a discussion of the former, see pp. 5–8 in his article.

[9] Ibid., p. 4.

6   Introduction

means: "the liberal tradition is constituted by *the sum of the arguments that have been classified as liberal, and recognized as such by other self-proclaimed liberals, across time and space.*"[10] This conception is particularly useful in its inclusion of a great variety of liberal thought-practices, even if its reliance on "self-proclaimed liberals" may reinforce the visibility bias in theoretical investigations of liberalism that I alluded to above. Regardless, it certainly infers, as Bell notes, a "sense of the discursive 'overextension' and elastic usage of the term, while avoiding unhelpful claims about pure essence or authentic form."[11]

In the pages that follow, my usage of the term "liberalism" is intended along similar lines as Bell's "summative" conception, even as my methodology is mainly of the "contextualist" variety. While the former is inclusive of a great variety of liberal thought, the latter makes it possible to trace the origins and evolution of liberal practices that correspond to the vicissitudes of time and place. The resulting approach, then, operates on the premise that liberal theory and practice are mutually constituted through a process of "morphological flexibility" that, in Michael Freeden's words, "reflects the readiness of liberals to organize their key concepts, employing a reflective commonsense that permits a modicum of pluralist adaptability, and that is prepared to contain a variety of views within the family of liberalisms."[12] A key but neglected instance of such "morphological flexibility," the present study contends, is the nonpublic espousal and embodied practice of liberalism in non-liberal societies where official ideologies of ruling regimes and reigning norms are especially hostile to liberal prescriptions for social and political change.

Why is hidden liberalism especially a feature of non-liberal societies? As William Galston has argued, central to understanding the practical manifestations of liberalism is the concept of "expressive liberty," which attests to "a presumption in favor of individuals and groups leading their lives as they see fit, within the broad range of legitimate variation defined by value pluralism, in accordance with their own understandings of what gives life meaning and value."[13] But expressive liberties merely attest to the existence of constitutional democracy, and are not necessarily indicative of the absence of liberal values in a given society. Galston's practical view is characteristic of a fairly entrenched *visibility bias* in standard accounts of

---

[10] Ibid., pp. 8–9 (emphasis in the original).   [11] Ibid., p. 9.

[12] Freeden, *Liberal Languages*, p. 260.

[13] William A. Galston, *The Practice of Liberal Pluralism* (Cambridge: Cambridge University Press, 2005), p. 2. He places this concept alongside those of "political pluralism" and "value liberalism," by which he means the existence of multiple sources of authority and visions of the good life, respectively. These concepts are explored in greater depth in William A. Galston, *Liberal Pluralism: The Implications of Value Pluralism for Political Theory and Practice* (Cambridge: Cambridge University Press, 2002).

Introduction 7

liberalism, which only look to the presence of constitutionally sanctioned and observed liberties such as freedom of speech, assembly, religion, and press. Indeed, the anti-liberal fascination with public expressions of liberal principles is what necessitates the circumspect expression or struggles on behalf of liberal values in the first place. As such, the invisibility of liberalism in non-liberal states is a testament to an acute sense of the limits to the public pursuit of liberal ideals based on practical experience.

Hidden liberalism, then, is neither solely the embodied practice of liberal principles in individual or communal acts (as would be the case in liberal-constitutional settings) nor liberalism embedded in socioeconomic, cultural, or political institutions.[14] Rather, *it is the judicious and circumspect thought-practice of liberalism articulated and carried out in a manner unfamiliar to would-be opponents of liberalism.* In this regard, hidden liberalism closely resembles some key attributes of what James C. Scott has called "hidden transcripts."[15] The latter differ from "public transcripts" in their discernible adherence to "patterns of disguising *ideological* insubordination" as a means to resisting domination.[16] As Scott explains, "Every subordinate group creates, out of its ordeal, a 'hidden transcript' that represents a critique of power spoken behind the back of the dominant."[17] As an analytical framework for understanding strategies of resistance, "hidden transcripts" certainly resonate with the experience of liberals in settings where they are subordinate to the ruling ideologies of the state, or to non-liberal social practices in society. However, as the case of Iran will show, hidden liberalism extends beyond a strategy of resistance into a particular mode of thought that differs substantively from its Western variants in its heightened awareness – for historical reasons (i.e. legacies of Western imperialism) – of the burdens imposed by context on the legitimacy of liberal principles. The substantive aspects of this conceptual difference will be explored further in the next section, and account for the bulk of the book's scope. In other words, although *Hidden Liberalism* certainly examines a range of hidden liberal

---

[14] Here I employ a definition of "practice" offered by Freeden, which nicely complements his emphasis on the "morphological flexibility" of political ideologies across time and space: "A practice is here understood to mean the performance of, and participation in, an identifiable regularity of action or thought, one replicated as well as shaped by other such practitioners. It is hence a communal activity taking place in social space and recurring over time. Practices and acts are not synonymous: many acts do not constitute practices, and some practices-cum-regularities of thinking do not constitute acts." Freeden, *Liberal Languages*, p. 239.

[15] James C. Scott, *Domination and the Arts of Resistance: Hidden Transcripts* (New Haven, CT: Yale University Press, 1990).

[16] Ibid., p. xiii (emphasis in the original).

[17] Ibid., p. xii. The dominant, in turn, also construct their hidden transcript "representing the practices and claims of their rule that cannot be openly avowed."

8 Introduction

practices, its main focus revolves around a critical examination of liberal thought as an "insubordinate" ideology.

It may reasonably be asked, however, if the conception offered here is ultimately a distinction without much difference. If hidden liberalism is still signified by its liberal traits or results, then is it not merely the practice of liberalism under inhospitable circumstances? There is little doubt that as a form of liberal *practice* hidden liberalism is indeed qualitatively different from its visible counterparts. As an embattled view, it is burdened by the dual challenge of articulating and acting on liberal principles using vocabularies and measures that broaden the domain of "expressive liberties" and expose the arbitrary foundations of monistic systems of thought and rule, without being perceived as promoting a liberal agenda. This entails not only constant vigilance as regards the terms of permissible political discourse, but more importantly also an almost Olympian capacity for rethinking the objective and subjective circumstances that, in Pierre Bourdieu's conception, condition its intellectual "habitus."[18] Although these burdens place considerable constraints on expressive liberties (as we understand them in the Western tradition), they can also engender more sophisticated means of articulating, disseminating, and acting on liberal principles – a fact too often ignored by Western liberal political theorists. Therefore, a core argument of this book holds that hidden liberalism is in fact a *reflexive* form of liberal practice. Bereft of any procedural or institutional support, it must always account for its own genesis and modes of justification, as well as being mindful of the contextual bases for reasonable disagreements, the effects of various inequalities and insecurities on social views and practices, and the fallibility of ideal-typical constructions informed chiefly by Western socioeconomic and political assumptions.

But can we also discern a qualitative difference to hidden liberalism as *a mode of thought*, given the widely accepted impression of liberalism as a universal creed? It is certainly evident that even as liberal struggles may have different referent objects and involve distinct vocabularies, the ideals they seek – for example, unencumbered individual expression, equal respect and dignity, equality of opportunity, fairness, etc. – involve the same set of substantive principles. The meaning and expression of individual liberty, for instance, may be relative to the obstacles placed in the way of individual rights in specific settings, but as a political matter it ultimately concerns the

---

[18] Pierre Bourdieu, *The Logic of Practice* (Stanford, CA: Stanford University Press, 1990), chapter 3.

Introduction 9

dynamic between the boundaries of sovereign (individual) agency and state coercion. Therefore, purely at the level of political thought, there is no qualitative difference between the substance of liberal theory and its hidden variants. Where there is a glaring difference, however, is in the historical context – that is, Western imperialism – that shapes how liberal ideas are understood and argued for in the former metropolitan and peripheral imaginations of liberal intellectuals, respectively. In postcolonial settings, as I will elaborate in Chapter 2, the referent objects of liberal antipathies and prescriptions are vastly more burdened by the limitations placed on state capacity due to imperial exploitation and foreign meddling than is remotely the case in Western societies. This historical burden significantly affects the conceptual and theoretical resonance of liberal principles among liberal thinkers and their detractors. For at issue here is not merely, for example, the affirmation and pursuit of individual liberties or equal recognition, but the institutional capacity of the state to meaningfully deliver on such guarantees. The judicious thought-practice of liberalism, therefore, entails the constant qualification, amendment, or revision of liberal concepts out of concern for feasibility and efficacy.

To be sure, the absence of institutional support also significantly hinders liberals' ability to coordinate or focus their efforts in the most optimal manner possible. Whatever the benefits of reflexivity, given the choice between operating in the shadows or engaging in public debate nary a liberal would opt for the former. Hidden liberalism is beset by inertia, inconsistency, and the lack of ability to coordinate political action. These difficulties become apparent especially in times of political crisis when the quest for more expansive domains for expressive liberties requires more visible forms of liberal self-assertion, as in moments of revolutionary upheaval when a particular regime attempts to impose even more restrictive social and political injunctions. Under such circumstances, long-simmering liberal commitments held in abeyance may reach a boiling point whereby the failure to act or speak out publicly in their favor would risk even their circumspect practice. These efforts may succeed or fall depending on the dynamics of political coalitions, the determination and capacity of ruling elites and their networks of patronage to fight on, or external factors such as foreign intervention. But, too often it is the inability of liberals to translate their fractured hidden practices into a coherent and unified political movement that leads to failure. Conventional accounts of liberalism in non-democratic societies tend to treat such instances as evidence of its tenuousness or newcomer status in these settings. Those seeking representative institutions and democratic rights, it is somewhat condescendingly argued, must recognize the priority

10   Introduction

of liberal political values to the exercise of popular sovereignty.[19] But as this study will demonstrate, the failure to gain public standing could paradoxically lead to the further diffusion of liberal values.

If the preceding observations render hidden liberalism, a deeply contextual thought-practice that is best understood through national or individual case studies, it must also be noted that, nevertheless, there are familiar lines of argument, strategies, and tactics that connect its disparate manifestations. The autonomous pursuit of rights under the guise of justice and through appeals to fairness, for instance, is a familiar approach adopted by embattled liberals the world over. The same modus operandi can be gleaned in instrumental calls for law and order, transparency, equal representation, and the general recognition of the inherent dignity of human life through self-expression. These claims are ambiguous enough to evade detection when it comes to their exertion by ordinary citizens, thus contributing to liberalism's proliferation and entrenchment as a social norm. Thinkers and activists with known liberal affinities, however, invite the full wrath of authority even when they are tenuously engaged in such activities. The progress brought about by hidden liberalism can therefore be frustratingly slow, irregular, dull. All the same, as this book will demonstrate in the case of Iran, it is *liberal* progress.

Indeed, the main motivation behind this book lies in the fact that the thought-practice of hidden liberalism has made observable inroads in advancing the cause of individual and group rights, toleration, accountable government and representative institutions, social and economic justice, and national independence that hitherto have largely gone unacknowledged as accomplishments of liberalism in a different key. To acknowledge this, however, is not to suspend critical judgment about the limits and shortcomings of liberalism as a political ideology. Since bodies of thought do not exist independently of human cognition and material conditions, they are, in one scholar's incisive formulation, "always *for* someone and *for* some purpose."[20] As such, problems internal to liberalism must also be accounted for in seeking out the reasons behind its

---

[19] The literature on democratic transitions is rife with such claims, especially as regards countries in the Middle East and North Africa. For example, see Fareed Zakaria, "The Rise of Illiberal Democracy," *Foreign Affairs*, Vol. 96, No. 6 (November–December 1997): 22–43, and Fareed Zakaria, "Islam, Democracy, and Constitutional Liberalism," *Political Science Quarterly*, Vol. 119, No. 1 (Spring 2004): 1–20. For a corrective to Zakaria's argument, see Christopher Hobson, "Liberal Democracy and Beyond: Extending the Sequencing Debate," *International Political Science Review*, Vol. 33, No. 4 (September 2012): 441–454.

[20] Robert W. Cox, "Social Forces, States, and World Orders: Beyond International Relations Theory," *Millennium: Journal of International Studies*, Vol. 10, No. 2 (June 1981): 129 (emphasis in the original).

Introduction 11

hidden practice in non-democratic societies. Who speaks for liberalism and on what authority? On whose behalf are liberal principles invoked, against whom, or what? Which ideologies or subset of non-liberal views can be considered fellow-travelers alongside liberalism? Which ideologies have been most antagonistic toward liberalism and on what basis? Are liberalism's challenges due to power imbalances or the result of deeper problems with the justification of liberal principles themselves? What specific objectives have engaged liberals' imagination over time in particular settings? How does the variation in the thought-practice of liberalism correspond to the course of social and political development in specific settings? Which modes of reasoning are more/less successful in spreading liberal values?

Answers to these questions are as varied as the experiences that occasion their asking in the first place, to be sure. *Hidden Liberalism* is but one reflection on a particular mode of reasoning, expression, and struggle that has been – and continues to be – evident in most subaltern or postcolonial societies. My main objective to explore these questions through a contextual consideration of liberalism in Iran, however, is to go beyond the existing terms of discourse within liberal political theory and intellectual histories of liberal thought that limit their contextual studies of liberalism to Western – and it must be said, predominantly English, French, and American – perspectives. I maintain that the latter trend has unwittingly privileged a particularly Western-centric discursive framework for discussions about liberalism that, when applied to non-Western contexts, simply overlooks the background conditions that produce demonstrably different liberal languages and practices. This oversight, in turn, has led to a fairly entrenched visibility bias against any domestication of liberal values that does not strictly adhere to the same patterns of development, modes of expression, and intellectual trajectories as those recorded in the canons of Western liberalism. In short, this book aims to expand the scope of comparative studies of liberalism beyond the modern West, and still further away from a universal model of liberal thought-practices that privileges the visibility and public expression of their underlying values.

Liberalism in the Iranian Context

Liberal ideas were but one ideological by-product of what Ali Gheissari has insightfully termed "Iran's dialectic of Enlightenment" (also sometimes referred to as Iran's "encounter" with modernity).[21] This process

---

[21] Ali Gheissari, "Iran's Dialectic of the Enlightenment: Constitutional Experience, Transregional Connections, and Conflicting Narratives of Modernity," in Ali Ansari,

12   Introduction

featured not merely the transmission of Enlightenment ideas from Europe into Iran, but also the interplay of "two distinct yet interrelated factors, namely, the tradition of reacting to domestic autocracy, a tendency with certain similarities to the teachings of eighteenth-century French Enlightenment as well as the example of the nineteenth century British parliamentary system, and the ideological consequences of Iran's semi-colonial situation, which was specific to Iran."[22] From roughly the second half of the nineteenth century to the onset of the Constitutional Revolution (Enqelab-e Mashruteh) in 1905, these factors – that is, achieving both a constitutional system of government and independence from foreign influence – structured the terms of social and political thinking about state-society relations in the political tracts and intellectual treatises of reformers. While some of these engagements were spurred by the propensity of elites to import and imitate Western ideas after their visits to, or education in, European cities, most were in fact mediated through political, commercial, and intellectual contacts with reform-minded and radical circles in the Ottoman Empire, the Russian Caucasus, and India.[23] The origins, multiple trajectories, and variable impacts of these protean intellectual encounters with aspects of modernity have been fertile grounds for inquiry within Iranian studies for some time,[24] especially as regards the genesis and implications of the Constitutional Revolution of 1906–1911.[25] The process that led to and

ed., *Iran's Constitutional Revolution of 1906: Narratives of the Enlightenment* (London: Gingko Library, 2016), pp. 15–47.

[22] Gheissari explains that "although Iran was never directly colonized, it was affected by imperial politics and economic incursions during the Qajar period (1785–1925)." Ibid., p. 17.

[23] Gheissari also notes the neglected but influential role of Shia pilgrimage destinations in Ottoman Iraq, collectively referred to as the *atabat* (sanctuaries). On the importance of these "transregional connections," see ibid., pp. 22–38. In his recent intellectual history of Iranian modernity, Afshin Matin-Asgari altogether "locate[s] the intellectual origins of Iranian constitutionalism in nineteenth-century encounters with 'the East,' i.e. the Ottoman and Russian empires, rather than 'the West' or Europe." Afshin Matin-Asgari, *Both Eastern and Western: An Intellectual History of Iranian Modernity* (Cambridge: Cambridge University Press, 2018), p. 8.

[24] For the most comprehensive English-language studies of these intellectual dialectics, see Mehrzad Boroujerdi, *Iranian Intellectuals and the West: The Tormented Triumph of Nativism* (Syracuse, NY: Syracuse University Press, 1996); Ali Gheissari, *Iranian Intellectuals in the 20th Century* (Austin, TX: University of Texas Press, 1998); Ali Mirsepassi, *Intellectual Discourse and the Politics of Modernization: Negotiating Modernity in Iran* (New York: Cambridge University Press, 2000); Farzin Vahdat, *God and Juggernaut: Iran's Intellectual Encounter with Modernity* (Syracuse, NY: Syracuse University Press, 2002); Negin Nabavi, *Intellectuals and the State in Iran: Politics, Discourse, and the Dilemma of Authenticity* (Gainesville, FL: University of Florida Press, 2003); and Matin-Asgari, *Both Eastern and Western.*

[25] For recent English-language accounts of the intellectual origins of the Constitutional Revolution, see Ali M. Ansari, ed., *Iran's Constitutional Revolution of 1906: Narratives of*

Introduction 13

followed after the advent of constitutionalism occupies a central place in the historiography of modern Iran because it exemplifies the complex array of ideas (Enlightenment and counter-Enlightenment narratives), personages (aristocratic elites, unaffiliated intellectuals, and religious thinkers), and material conditions (class divisions, economic concessions to foreign powers, and endemic corruption), whose mutual entanglements necessarily preclude singular description and neat characterization.

Indeed, the complex and multivalent nature of this process was representative of similar processes taking place in the West during the so-called "long nineteenth century" when industrialization and state-building resulted in the "great transformation" of politics, commerce, and culture in European societies.[26] Two significant and consequential differences in the historical unfolding of this dialectical process in Europe compared to Iran, however, were the former's imperial dominance of much of the globe in this period as well as the established presence of modern state institutions. Given this context, modern ideologies of progress such as liberalism (alongside socialism and nationalism)[27] not only developed in tandem with European methods of governance, but also helped to reinforce "a tripartite distinction between 'civilized humanity' (Europeans, white settlers and (some) Latin Americans), 'barbarous humanity' (the Ottoman and Persian empires, Central Asian states, China and Japan), and 'savage humanity'

---

the Enlightenment (London: Gingko Library, 2016); H. E. Chehabi and Vanessa Martin, eds., *Iran's Constitutional Revolution: Popular Politics, Cultural Transformations and Transnational Connections* (London: I.B. Tauris & Co. Ltd., 2010); and Janet Afary, *The Iranian Constitutional Revolution, 1906–1911: Grassroots Democracy, Social Democracy, and the Origins of Feminism* (New York: Columbia University Press, 1996). I cover the relevant Persian-language material on this period in Chapters 2 and 3.

[26] Prominent historical and analytical accounts of this period include Karl Polanyi, *The Great Transformation: The Political and Economic Origins of Our Time* (Boston, MA: Beacon Press, 1957); C. A. Bayly, *The Birth of The Modern World, 1780–1914* (Oxford: Blackwell Publishing, 2004); Immanuel Wallerstein, *Centrist Liberalism Triumphant, 1789–1914* (Berkeley, CA: University of California Press, 2011); and Jürgen Osterhammel, *The Transformation of the World* (Princeton, NJ: Princeton University Press, 2014). For a recent consideration of the impact of this period on international order, see Barry Buzan and George Lawson, *The Global Transformation: History, Modernity and the Making of International Relations* (Cambridge: Cambridge University Press, 2015).

[27] Buzan and Lawson also identify "scientific" racism as a separate ideology of progress; however, given the prevalence of racist views within the other dominant ideologies, it is clear that "scientific" racism was well-absorbed by the other ideologies in this period, rather than a separate ideological school of its own. For their explanation of the imprint of these ideas on international order, see ibid., pp. 97–126. For an excellent theoretical exploration of how developments in this period stigmatized non-Western societies as backward, underdeveloped, or undemocratic, see Ayşe Zarakol, *After Defeat: How the East Learned to Live with the West* (Cambridge: Cambridge University Press, 2011).

14   Introduction

(everyone else)."[28] I shall explore the historical weight of these distinctions on the substance and iterative practices of liberalism in Iran in Chapter 2; but it bears underlining here the vastly different geopolitical context in which Iran's "dialectics of Enlightenment" took place.

The early spread of the liberal strand of Enlightenment ideas in Iran was initially mostly facilitated through secret societies such as Malkum Khan's Faramoush-Khaneh. But as the movement for constitutionalism gathered pace, semisecret and even public national societies (*anjomanha-ye melli*) increasingly became instrumental in disseminating liberal ideas – such as individual, group, and minority rights – as well.[29] Although their membership was fairly exclusive in its elite and mostly courtier makeup in the late nineteenth century, over time religious, urban, and female luminaries either founded their own *anjoman*s or were granted entry into existing ones.[30] The principal function of these *anjoman*s was the contemplation and spread of knowledge about the virtues of modern reason – for example, individualism, liberty, political and economic rights, the rule of law, secularism – and, especially, about the corresponding transformations in society and political institutions necessary for propelling Iran into the modern era. Their proceedings often took the form of conversations and debates about shared readings, political events of the day in Iran or elsewhere, and various proposals for rethinking established beliefs, customs, and practices.[31] Far more significant than their respective records in actually approximating these ideals, however, was their cultivation of an institutional and discursive template for the safe airing of dissident and taboo ideas. Precisely because many modernist views directly challenged established traditions and sought checks on the arbitrary exercises of political power, they required protective spaces where they could be judiciously reframed and contextualized prior to being strategically deployed in public.

---

[28] Buzan and Lawson, *The Global Transformation*, p. 98. See also John M. Hobson, *The Eurocentric Conception of World Politics: Western International Theory, 1760–2010* (Cambridge: Cambridge University Press, 2012).

[29] On semi(secret) societies in the Qajar era and during the Constitutional Revolution, see Ann K. S. Lambton, "Secret Societies and the Persian Revolution of 1905–06," in *Qajar Persia: Eleven Studies* (London: I.B. Tauris & Co. Ltd., 1987), pp. 301–318.

[30] On the emergence and critical role of urban and women's *anjoman*s, see Afary, *The Iranian Constitutional Revolution*, pp. 63–88 and 177–208.

[31] For instance, on the eve of the Constitutional Revolution (on March 9, 1905), at a meeting of an influential small group calling itself Anjoman-e Makhfi (literally, the Secret Society), Malkum Khan's earlier call for the codification of the law was revisited and formulated into concrete and actionable political proposals. The proceedings of Anjoman-e Makhfi were recorded by one of its founding members, the liberal-minded Nazem al-Islam Kermani, in his *Tarikh-e Bidari-ye Iranian* [History of Iranians' Awakening] (Tehran: 1328/1910). See Lambton, *Qajar Persia*, pp. 312–313, nn. 35 and 44.

Introduction   15

The institutional and discursive practices born out of this prudent approach, however, were not without their drawbacks. As regards constitutionalism, for instance, although they succeeded in widening the base of support for such principles as the rule of law, representative government, and freedom from foreign control, they also diluted their liberal justifications that would have insisted on more robust and programmatic articulations of individualism, civil and political rights, and religious freedom. In their place, as Gheissari and others have pointed out, the struggle against arbitrary authority remained conceptually couched in the language of "individual justice out of grievance (*tazallom*), and resort[ed] to the normative paradigm of '*circles of justice*.'"[32] Once again, similar burdens also accompanied the development of modern liberalism in Western societies, but the crucial difference in the case of Iran was the additional burden of reconciling the progressive substance of liberal values with their political instrumentalization from without in the form of a "standard of civilization."[33] The challenge was not to merely deploy liberal principles against the state, but also to account for the myriad historical, geopolitical, and cultural factors that have conspired to keep state *and* society backward, inert, and disfigured.[34] In many respects, the Constitutional Revolution in Iran stands as *the* historical exemplification of this dual burden of responsibility on Iranian intellectuals.

The overlapping struggles to end arbitrary rule at home and mitigate the undue influence of foreign imperial powers on Iran's economy and politics culminated in the adoption of a written constitution in 1906 (amended by a set of supplementary laws in 1907), which significantly curtailed royal prerogatives, ushered in a representative assembly (*majles*),

---

[32] Gheissari, "Iran's Dialectic of the Enlightenment," p. 17. See also Nader Sohrabi, "Revolution and State Culture: The Circle of Justice and Constitutionalism in 19th-Century Iran," in George Steinmetz, ed., *State/Culture: State-Formation after the Cultural Turn* (Ithaca, NY: Cornell University Press, 1999), pp. 253–288.

[33] Indeed, this burden was felt most acutely across the (semi)colonial world. For the uneven imprint of the "standard of civilization" on influential intellectuals across Asia, see Pankaj Mishra, *From the Ruins of Empire: The Revolt against the West* (New York: Farrar, Straus and Giroux, 2012). In the case of India, see C. A. Bayly, *Recovering Liberties: Indian Thought in the Age of Liberalism and Empire* (Cambridge: Cambridge University Press, 2012); Maganlal A. Buch, *Rise and Growth of Indian Liberalism [from Ram Mohun to Gokhale]* (Baroda: Atmaram Printing Press, 1938); and Ravinder Kumar, "Liberalism and Reform in India," in Guy S. Méttaaux and François Crouzet, eds., *The New Asia* (New York: New American Library, 1965), pp. 177–202. On the standard of civilization, see Gerrit W. Gong, *The Standard of "Civilization" in International Society* (Oxford: Clarendon Press, 1984).

[34] These burdens are analytically laid bare in Homa Katouzian's description of state-society relations in the late Qajar period and in his "theory of arbitrary rule." See Homa Katouzian, *State and Society in Iran: The Eclipse of the Qajars and the Emergence of the Pahlavis* (London: I.B. Tauris & Co. Ltd., 2006), pp. 1–54.

16   Introduction

and enumerated basic rights and duties.[35] For reasons explained in Chapters 2 and 3, the constitutional experience was highly turbulent and eventually ended in the internecine confrontations between pro- and anti-constitutionalist fronts in 1911 (the latter, composed of royalists and conservative clergy, aided by imperial Russia). Nonetheless, the emergence of a pluralistic movement for constitutionalism in this period marked the formal commencement of liberal modernity's entanglement with Iranian cultural identity, Shi'ism, and state-building.[36] By virtue of its pluralistic composition and multiplicity of aims, it must be noted, constitutionalism did not denote the triumph of a single ideology, much less that of liberalism. Yet, even as its religious, nationalist, and socialist proponents went on to develop their own distinctive ideological programs and political agendas in the ensuing decades, the liberal intelligentsia struggled to chart a comparable ideological path of their own. Instead, the terms "liberal" and "liberalism," respectively, became prefixes and adjectives used to denote centrist, moderate, or reformist positions within non-liberal ideologies. Even during the more than half-century of Pahlavi rule (1925–1979), as aspects of economic and cultural liberalism were selectively adopted under the guise of social modernization and state-building programs, liberal reformers preferred to frame their efforts in nationalist or technocratic terms instead of concrete and political terms of their own. The period of relative parliamentary autonomy (1941–1953) – the interregnum between the forced abdication and exile of Reza Shah to the fall of the premier Mohammad Mosaddegh's government – certainly could have been the exception to these general trends. But even as liberal figures and parties became more assertive (as will be shown in Chapter 2), it is instructive that no singular, coherent, or programmatic liberal tradition of thought or political agenda emerged.[37]

Given this burdened context, it is impossible to attempt a taxonomy of liberal concepts and definitions in the case of Iran, and certainly foolhardy to identify a *sui generis* Iranian liberalism. As the previous section made clear, moreover, it is difficult enough to evince a singular definition of

---

[35] For the English translation of the written text of the adopted constitution, see "Appendix A: The Bases of the Persian Constitution," in Edward G. Browne, *The Persian Revolution of 1905–1909* (London: Frank Cass & Co. Ltd., 1966), pp. 351–400.

[36] As Abbas Amanat writes in his magisterial history of modern Iran, "Under the veneer of Western liberalism and constitutional order, the revolution tried to offer indigenous answers to a distinctly Perso-Shi'i problem of social justice that had long been present in the milieu of Iranian dissent." Abbas Amanat, *Iran: A Modern History* (New Haven, CT: Yale University Press, 2017), p. 317.

[37] As Fakhreddin Azimi has shown, these years were marked more palpably by a general "crisis" of representation and democracy than the emergence or triumph of a particular ideology. See Fakhreddin Azimi, *Iran, The Crisis of Democracy: From the Exile of Reza Shah to the Fall of Musaddiq* (London: I.B. Tauris & Co. Ltd., 1989).

Introduction 17

liberalism as a global ideology without the compounding burdens of domestic autocracy and global imperialism further obscuring the conditions around the reception and development of ideas. All the same, distinctively liberal traits may still be salvaged in the *political antipathies* and *prescriptions* of ambivalent, discerning, and taciturn intellectuals and political thinkers whose writings and actions advance liberal aims despite their non-affiliation with any coherent school of thought or political group.[38] In Chapter 2, I offer a broad overview of these antipathies (*antitraditionalism*, *anti-absolutism*, and *anti-imperialism*) and prescriptions (*liberal nationalism*, *constitutionalism*, and *pluralism*) as consistently present aspects of liberal political thinking in Iran. While neither of these traits is in itself sufficient for a political position to be regarded as liberal (especially since other ideologies such as Marxism, socialism, nationalism, and Islamism also share some of these concerns), each is typically a necessary component of a liberal intervention in political affairs. In contradistinction to the absence of a coherent liberal political tradition, these attributes are far from hidden in the political expressions and actions of dissidents, reformers, and lay practitioners. As such, their consistent deployment for progressive ends, however burdened or afflicted, is instructive in understanding the scope, depth, and limits of liberal endeavors in the course of Iran's development into a modern nation-state.

This book, then, is an interpretive account of an assorted set of internal intellectual dialogues, debates, and oppositions that reveal the contours of liberal thinking – mostly through objections to it – in the course of twentieth-century Iranian politics. The decision to limit the scope of inquiry to the end of the past century is deliberate. Twentieth-century Iranian politics is bookended by the advent and swift eclipse of two aspirational movements – that is, for constitutionalism and Islamic reformism – that were at once imbued with liberal ideas and wary of liberalism as the ideological gateway to Westernization. In the second half of the century, the latter concerns were of course compounded by the ascendance of a global discourse of liberalization, embedded and manifest in the hegemonic spread of an international architecture of political and economic institutions, legal-humanitarian regimes, and civil society alliances dominated by Western states, corporations, and nongovernmental organizations. These parallel developments at the global level were of course notable for their uneven impact and highly selective standards driven by variations in Western geopolitical interests. But they also draw attention to paradoxical

---

[38] As I explain in Chapter 2, I borrow and reconfigure this framing – of antipathies and prescriptions – from Ryan's work in *The Making of Modern Liberalism*, pp. 28–40.

18 Introduction

trends inside postcolonial societies that featured competing visions of liberation and self-government at odds with, if not directly opposed to, Western conceptions of liberal autonomy, equality, and reciprocity. In this context, the mutually inclusive emergence of liberationist ideologies based on nativist and Islamist thinking – conditioned, in no small measure, by the imperative of state-building – in opposition to overt expressions of liberalism in Iran is especially noteworthy. The public invisibility of political liberalism in Iran is largely a by-product of these antagonisms, which have carried on to the present moment.

Methodologically speaking, the same set of historical and hermeneutical approaches that are broadly used by historians of political thought and normative theorists also apply to the present study. These include, but are not limited to, examinations of primary source material, analyses of concepts and terms relative to their historical contexts, subjective interpretation of texts, speeches, oral and written histories, and other intellectual endeavors that fall within the general scope of inquiry, and the construction of new normative frameworks for understanding neglected phenomena. Added to these is of course the matter of language itself, and especially the subtle but notable changes in vocabularies over time, which render the interpretive challenge all the more fraught. To mitigate this, I have endeavored to provide the most accurate English translation of relevant primary and secondary source material, and, where available, I have relied on existing English translations by scholars of modern Iran. In cases where existing translations are insufficiently attentive to the context-specific usage of a term or concept, I have provided alternative translations of my own, with annotations attached.

The Structure of the Book

As a trained political theorist, I wish to be clear about my lack of credentials in intellectual history and my decidedly amateur status as an historian of modern Iran. Accordingly, the following is not a work in intellectual or political history; nor is it, for reasons explained in Chapter 5, an easy fit in the quite nascent but burgeoning genre of inquiry known as "comparative political theory." What it does hope to approximate by way of its form, scope, and mode of inquiry, however, is the methodological approach typical of inquiries in the "history of ideas" genre associated with the "Cambridge School" which feature the combination of aspects of the above-mentioned methodologies for a contextual understanding of the emergence and development of ideas in and over time. In the following, it is not my intention to provide a comprehensive history of liberal

Introduction 19

thought in modern Iran. My aim is more limited in scope: to account for its curious plight as an embattled yet influential political project in the course of Iran's development into a modern state. As such, my investigation is confined solely to the realm of political ideas, and to the extent that I draw on background material conditions (e.g. geopolitics, persistent class struggles, economies of patronage, etc.), I do so only as they relate directly to major shifts in established political orders and their corresponding intellectual justifications. Furthermore, given the general neglect of liberal thought-practices in most social, economic, political, cultural, and intellectual histories of modern Iran, the limited scope of this book allows for a more focused analytical dissection of liberalism's entanglements with, and appropriations by, its ideological rivals. This cross-ideological approach to liberalism's intellectual lineage and evolution within the Iranian context, in fact, permeates through the whole book since the factors behind liberalism's public invisibility are mostly traced back to the intellectual exchanges generated by these encounters.

In Chapter 2, I present a historical outline of six key aspects of liberal political thinking in Iran. Using a familiar schematic from mainstream histories of liberal thought, I group these into two broad categories of "liberal antipathies" (anti-traditionalism, anti-absolutism, and anti-imperialism) and "liberal prescriptions" (nationalism, constitutionalism, and pluralism). Together, I argue, these aspects combine to form the substantive core of much thinking and political action by Iranian liberals since the late nineteenth century. The common denominator linking these seemingly disparate elements into a coherent liberal project, the chapter shows, is an aversion to arbitrary exercises of power at the expense of individual liberty, the rule of law, and national sovereignty. Although by no means exhaustive, these aspects are introduced through the political thoughts and actions of Iranian reformers, intellectuals, politicians, journalists, and activists. While some of these figures (such as Malkum Khan) very much self-identified as liberals and wished to modernize Iranian society in accordance with Western templates, most were simply either unaware of or unconcerned by the liberal substance of their thought-practices. All the same, nearly all subscribed to the sort of prudential strategies described earlier that disguised the progressive essence of their beliefs from its would-be opponents. The implications of the inconsistencies produced by these strategies, as well as the general lack of coherence and coordination among these figures, is critically examined in the chapter.

After laying out the contours of liberal thinking in modern Iran, the rest of the book explores the reasons behind its invisibility in the century-long

20   Introduction

period since the Constitutional Revolution (a timespan also distinguished by the global diffusion of liberal values, institutions, processes, norms, and practices). Chapter 3 proposes that the thought-practice of hidden liberalism is chiefly necessitated by a set of binary grievances against "Westernism" – that is, reformist temptations brought on by Western modernity (e.g. materialism, secularism, individualism, capitalism, etc.), which many of its detractors regarded liberalism as being complicit in. In light of the troubling history of Western "liberal imperialism" in the domestic and regional politics of Iran, there is a long tradition of anti-liberal jeremiads that faults liberal thought as not sufficiently emancipatory in the face of imperial exploitation, or adequately protective of traditional values indigenous to Iranian society. This line of thought is espoused by a diverse array of rival ideologies to liberalism – ranging from leftist Marxist-Leninist views to political Islamism to nativist beliefs (or hybrid perspectives thereof) – which, while otherwise diametrically opposed to each other, often have made common cause in the persecution and purging of liberal thinkers and movements. This oppositional posture is especially evident in the works of nativist thinkers (secular and religious) whose dogmatic fealty to an imagined, purified set of cultural norms and values – often derived from a highly selective reading of Islamic and Iranian history – runs counter to the spirit of value-pluralism at the core of liberal and reformist tendencies even within their own ideological movements. This chapter surveys the range of opinions and schools of thought dubious of Westernism in parallel to the background political developments that either precipitated or were caused by such views. It concludes by examining the relationship between this persistent anti-liberalism and the advent of the Islamic Republic.

Chapter 4 examines the tentative and incoherent appropriation of liberal arguments by two distinct but overlapping varieties of Islamic pluralism in the aftermath of the 1979 revolution. The first variety, exemplified in the political thought-practice of Mehdi Bazargan and the Liberation Movement of Iran (Nehzat-e Azadi-ye Iran), championed civil rights and representative democracy based on a liberationist reading of Islamic doctrine and traditions. Although this perspective certainly stood in stark contrast to the monistic and hierarchical vision of Islamic authority favored by Khomeini and his supporters, as the chapter will explain, it did not offer a coherent political conception of how a pluralistic reading of Islam might translate into state ideology. The example of Bazargan and his supporters best illuminates the central tensions between a religious pluralist outlook and a political one. The second variety of Islamic pluralism examined in this chapter is represented in the works of perhaps the most influential intellectual figure behind the reform movement after the

Introduction

death of the founder of the Islamic Republic, Ayatollah Ruhollah Khomeini, Abdolkarim Soroush. The political and theological views of Soroush have been thoroughly surveyed and critically engaged with for some time within Iranian studies and beyond, and this chapter certainly builds on such insights. But it departs from conventional critiques of Soroush by specifically considering his reasoning behind the necessity of decoupling liberalism from democracy as the basis for his ideal of religious democratic government. In contradistinction to Bazargan's Islamic pluralism, Soroush's prescriptions are purposefully designed to guard against the deleterious effects of liberal ideology – for example, individualism leading to secularism – on the religious community and overall cultural cohesion of society. In the second half of the chapter, I demonstrate how this particular vision of Islamic pluralism, far from typifying an "Islamic liberalism," is in fact conceived in direct opposition to liberal political principles. Accordingly, this chapter departs from existing studies of Islam and liberalism that seek to either envision an "ideal ethical encounter" between the two, or fixate on their supposed (in)compatibility,[39] by instead reflecting on the impact of one (Islam) upon the other (liberalism) in the context of Iran's postrevolutionary politics. The invisibility of liberal thought-practices, as the chapter will show, is not due to the preponderance of traditionalist or Islamic views – as is sometimes falsely claimed by secular critics – to the contrary, and paradoxically, they remain so because of their repeated appropriation by religious modernists-cum-reformists who are engaged in a series of seemingly intractable struggles to reconcile monistic doctrines with pluralistic realities. Whether this will eventually result in the visibility of a confident, publicly avowed liberalism remains to be seen, but as the chapter endeavors to show, the predicament is far more complex than simple binaries that pit Islam against democracy, human rights, or liberalism.

The book concludes (with Chapter 5) by considering the implications of hidden liberalism for the study of liberal thought-practices in non-Western, postcolonial settings, and more generally of liberalism in the global context. In recent years, political theorists have begun to examine the complex relationship between liberalism and empire. These studies have ranged from meticulous genealogies of imperialist arguments in the works of Enlightenment-era thinkers, to dissections of liberal justifications and criticisms of empire during the eighteenth century, and still further to conceptualizations and classifications of liberal-imperialist

---

[39] See Andrew F. March, *Islam and Liberal Citizenship: The Search for an Overlapping Consensus* (New York: Oxford University Press, 2009); and Nader Hashemi, *Islam, Secularism, and Liberal Democracy: Toward a Democratic Theory in Muslim Societies* (New York: Oxford University Press, 2009).

22   Introduction

thought-practices in the long nineteenth century. Spanning the gamut from intellectual and political histories to conceptual and narrative analyses, these scholarly explorations have also been methodologically innovative in accounting for the contextual bases of normative thinking. Strikingly, however, the geographical scope of these inquiries – and the implications drawn from them – do not extend beyond the life and times of *Western* liberalism. Overlooked in nearly all of these studies are the implications of Western imperialism for the reception and development of indigenous liberal views and practices *inside* postcolonial societies. I offer a critical assessment of Western political theory's privileging of a contextually specific model of liberalism as a universal standard for understanding, appraising, and promoting liberal thought-practices across the globe. I argue that mainstream, critical, and comparative approaches in political thought unwittingly perpetuate this "visibility bias" as regards the study of liberalism in non-Western societies, and suggest ways of making these modes of inquiry more inclusive.

Together, these chapters are meant to probe – more than recover, recast, or uncover – the terms of political discourse in twentieth-century Iran for clues about the embattled, invisible, yet influential status of liberal thought-practices (especially relative to their ideological counterparts in the same period). As such, the book is necessarily diagnostic in both scope and substance. Liberalism's peculiar journey in formerly (semi-)colonized societies is fertile ground for inquiry and critical reflection in studies of political thought – a long-overdue charge that is only beginning to be taken up by scholars within area studies and in political theory.[40] My hope is that the present study, however imperfectly, stimulates discussion and further critical engagements with liberal thought-practices in Iran, with resonance in other non-Western contexts.

---

[40] For a representative survey of the relevant literature in this genre, see Chapter 5.

2 Aspects of Political Liberalism in Modern Iran

Whenever there is any talk of law or education in the country, without reading or knowing or understanding that these laws are only there to preserve the honor of the nation, and to strengthen the Sharia and respect the holy Qur'an, and not to imitate the foreigners, or God forbid, to implement traditions that are in opposition to the pure religion of Islam, they [the clergy] blow it out of all proportion. [1]

Is there such a thing as a liberal political tradition in Iran? More precisely, are there sustained patterns of thinking about politics, analogous to those in the modern West, which can be classified as "liberal" in both their substance and scope? Liberal political doctrines have not been alien to Iranian thinkers, nor have they been inconsequential to Iran's social and political development. From the advent of the "freethinking" intellectual tradition in the latter half of the nineteenth century,[2] to the introduction of constitutionalism at the dawn of the twentieth century, to the period of rapid modernization and state-building under Reza Shah, to the drive behind oil nationalization and parliamentary autonomy under the premiership of Mohammad Mosaddeq, and still to the intellectual debates about democracy and pluralism in contemporary political debates, liberal political ideas have been central to the advancement of representative politics and various rights-based social and political movements in modern Iran. A number of historical and analytical studies of Iranian political thought have reflected on the influence and development of certain liberal arguments – for instance, about social progress, representative government, civil and political rights, and the rule of law – in the political thought-practices of certain key figures from the late nineteenth to mid-

---

[1] Abdul-Rahim Talebof, *Safineh-ye Talebi ya Ketab-e Ahmad* [The Talebian Vessel or the Book of Ahmad] (Istanbul: 1311–1312/1893–1894), p. 99.

[2] The emergence of the freethinking tradition before the constitutional movement, and its evolution during and after the Constitutional Revolution, is capaciously explained in Gheissari, *Iranian Intellectuals and the 20th Century*, pp. 13–24. See also Ali Gheissari, "Iranian Intellectuals, Past and Present," interview by Ali Ahmadi Motlagh, *Muftah*, March 10, 2011 (http://muftah.org/?p=923, last accessed December 12, 2018).

24   Aspects of Political Liberalism in Modern Iran

twentieth centuries.[3] But these accounts remain fragmentary and, at any rate, make only fleeting references to liberalism as a public standpoint or contemplate its development as an organic political tradition. To date, the substance, scope, and impact of liberal ideas remain strikingly under-explored in studies of modern Iran.[4]

This oversight is not entirely coincidental. The reception and organic development of liberal principles in Iran have been intimately tied to the dual attempt to transform Iranian society in the image of its European counterparts while constructing an independent modern state immune from Western imperial interference in its domestic and foreign relations. This paradox has had two major implications for the study of liberalism in Iran. In the first case, scholarly examinations of liberal arguments and profiles have been subsumed under more capacious normative and empirical categories such as "modernity," "secularism," "constitutional-ism," or "nationalism," to name the most prominent. These classifica-tions are ultimately too conceptually broad and thematically sweeping to offer any methical account of the diverse array of oft-conflicting and multilayered ideological commitments, moral and philosophical doc-trines, and practical considerations that have engaged the liberal imagin-ation for nearly a century and a half in Iran. This does not render the use of such categories invalid or less valuable; but the general tendency to structure any account of political development in Iran only in reference to all-encompassing categories has in some instances produced more obscurities than illuminations and has further reified their usage.

---

[3] The entire works of Fereydoun Adamiyat are good examples of this, but especially his *Fekr-e Azadi va Moqaddame-ye Nehzat-e Mashrutiyat* [The Idea of Liberty and the Beginning of the Iranian Constitutional Movement] (Tehran: Payam, 1342/1961); *Andishe-ye Taraqi va Hokoumat-e Qanun: Asr-e Sepahsalar* [The Idea of Progress and the Rule of Law: The Age of Sepahsalar] (Tehran: Payam, 1351/1972); and *Ideoluzhi-ye Nehzat-eh Mashrute-ye Iran* [The Ideology of the Iranian Constitutional Movement] (Tehran: Payam, 1355/1976). Other influential accounts include Ervand Abrahamian, *Iran between Two Revolutions* (Princeton, NJ: Princeton University Press, 1982); Katouzian, *State and Society in Iran*; Nikki R. Keddie and Yann Richard, *Modern Iran: Roots and Results of Revolution* (New Haven, CT: Yale University Press, 2006); Gheissari, *Iranian Intellectuals in the 20th Century*.

[4] For examples of seminal scholarly contributions that make references to liberal thought-practices, but do not offer any systematic treatments, see Boroujerdi, *Iranian Intellectuals and the West*; Vahdat, *God and Juggernaut*; Gheissari, *Iranian Intellectuals in the 20th Century*; Matin-Asgari, *Both Eastern and Western*; and especially works by Ali Mirsepassi, *Intellectual Discourses and Politics of Modernization, Democracy in Modern Iran* (New York: New York University Press, 2010), *Political Islam, Iran, and Enlightenment: Philosophies of Hope and Despair* (New York: Cambridge University Press, 2011), *Transnationalism in Iranian Political Thought: The Life and Thought of Ahmad Fardid* (Cambridge: Cambridge University Press, 2017), and *Iran's Quiet Revolution: The Downfall of the Pahlavi State* (Cambridge: Cambridge University Press, 2019).

The second implication concerns the elusive and inconsistent representations of liberal thought-practices by Iranian liberals themselves. Strikingly, very few Iranian liberals have or continue to identify themselves or their efforts as devoted to the advancement of a liberal tradition. Unlike their Western counterparts, on the main they have been less concerned with constructing a self-consciously liberal political tradition than articulating pathways toward social progress and representative political institutions. The reasons for this pusillanimity are twofold. First, the preponderance of various arbitrary and avowedly anti-liberal political regimes in Iran, combined with the deep imprint of religio-cultural practices on Iranian society, have resulted in constricted social spaces in which liberals could freely espouse their beliefs, let alone publicly contest the legitimacy of reigning orders. The weaker the legitimacy of reformist forces – for instance, during the Constitutional Revolution, the brief period of parliamentary politics after Reza Shah's exile and following the advent of the reform movement in the late 1990s – the more confident and assertive public liberal expressions. Second, and most importantly, in light of the legacy of Western liberal imperial meddling in Iran's internal and foreign affairs, Iranian liberals have been selective and cautious about their espousal of liberal principles and their attendant vocabularies. Iranian liberalism, much like its counterparts in other semi- and postcolonial societies, has been marked by a heightened awareness of the susceptibility of liberal principles to exploitation by imperial/foreign interests – as explained in Chapter 1 – and its likely adverse implications for the course of progress in Iranian society.

Despite the absence of a self-conscious liberal school of thought or political movement, however, there is a discernibly consistent intellectual tradition of engagement with and appropriation of liberal principles among certain cohorts of Iranian intellectuals and political figures. This chapter is an examination of the substance, scope, and manifestations of this intellectual tradition, from roughly the latter part of the nineteenth to the dawn of the twenty-first centuries. The aim here is not to provide a linear or singular account of liberalism in Iran. Such an endeavor, as noted in the Introduction, would not yield a meaningful impression for the simple fact that, as with any ideology, there are multiple liberalisms, as divergent in scope and method as their exponents.[5] Rather, the purpose here is to attest to the existence of such a diverse family of viewpoints in

---

[5] The observation made about the development of "liberal languages" in the Western tradition by the political theorist Michael Freeden equally applies here: "[L]iberal thought is not only a narrative, but should be savoured as a *collective* narrative that is formed by conversations, reactions, and ripple-effects within large groups, allows the introduction of impermanence within constraining family resemblances, and concurrently enables the

26   Aspects of Political Liberalism in Modern Iran

the first place, and to then provide an overview of its essential and most consistently present attributes. The arguments explicated here, therefore, are limited only to an exploration of the *political* aspects of the liberal project in Iran. To be sure, social, economic, and cultural aspects of liberalism overlap with, and in many cases follow, its political openings; however, for purposes of cohesion and clarity, I have deferred their exploration to future study.

Moreover, it is important to note from the outset that my chief motivation in accounting for these viewpoints is not a partisan but a scholarly one. It is not my intention here to read liberalism into Iranian political thought, much less to recast any oppositional or embattled political idea as belonging to a liberal tradition. To this end, I am less interested in championing the cause of liberalism than merely bringing some coherence to its study as a consequential mode of political thought in the course of Iran's political development. Furthermore, the intellectuals and political reformers surveyed in the following are meant to stand as figures whose ideas or example illuminate aspects of liberal thinking; they are not, especially given the absence of a self-conscious liberal political tradition, to be regarded as standard-bearers of a liberal movement.

The following is organized in three parts. In the first section, I offer a conceptual framework for understanding liberalism in Iran and explain my methodology for applying it to a particular strand of political thought-practice among Iranian thinkers. The second and third sections cover the substance of liberal political thought in Iran through an exposition of key *liberal antipathies* – anti-traditionalism, anti-absolutism, and anti-imperialism – and *liberal prescriptions* – liberal nationalism, constitutionalism, and pluralism – that have respectively marked the contours of political development, however inconsistently or incompletely, in modern Iran. I conclude the chapter by considering the implications of this new framework for thinking about the variegated terrain of political thought in Iran.

Two Modes of Liberalism

As mentioned in the Introduction, I view liberalism as a vast and storied constellation of ideas, dispositions, institutions, and practices whose historical evolution is variable across time and space. In this chapter, I am more specifically concerned with a range of liberal *antipathies and prescriptions* shared among Iranian liberal political thinkers. I borrow this division from Alan Ryan's work, in which the liberal project is

idea of development, and of potential evolutionary improvement, to occupy the center stage." Freeden, *Liberal Languages*, p. 12.

Two Modes of Liberalism 27

intellectually divided among those who are concerned primarily with either the defense or the advancement of individual liberty, and hence the institutions and processes attendant to each. Although this division certainly shares some affinities with Isaiah Berlin's famous distinction between "negative" and "positive" liberty,[6] it ultimately encompasses a wider set of concerns than Berlin's somewhat abstract and constricted conceptions.[7] Liberal antipathies attest to a range of thought-practices that actively oppose the legitimacy of arbitrary systems of rule and dogmatic schemes that rely for their sustenance on the infringement of the personal and collective liberties of citizens. After all, as Ryan points out, "the history of liberalism is a history of opposition to assorted tyrannies."[8] The main liberal antipathies identified by Ryan – anti-absolutism, anti-theocracy, and anti-capitalism – although instructive in the Western European context (and even there they are not uncontroversial), do not easily fit the range of concerns covered by Iranian liberal positions that respond to vastly different historical and geopolitical circumstances. As such, in the following I present a modified set of antipathies, which in my view more accurately account for the historical antecedents and promptings that generated liberal thinking among Iranian thinkers. These are: *anti-traditionalism*, *anti-absolutism*, and *anti-imperialism*.

Liberal prescriptions are similarly conditioned by historical contexts from which they arise. But because they offer concrete visions of conditions that would replace non-liberal norms and institutions, they reveal the essence of liberalism as a *universal* moral and political doctrine more vividly than do expressions of liberal antipathies. Ryan classifies liberal prescriptions into three intersecting theories for the individual (the capacity for autonomous choice), society (the primacy of individual rights in collective decision-making), and the state (liberal-constitutional government), respectively.[9] These theories encompass a range of normative values – toleration, autonomy, reciprocity, equality, etc. – and political commitments – self-government, accountability, separation of powers, etc. – but given the uneven and variable admixture of these principles at

---

[6] Isaiah Berlin, "Two Concepts of Liberty," in *Four Essays on Liberty* (Oxford: Oxford University Press, 1969).

[7] For a constructive criticism of Berlin's celebrated essay, see Quentin Skinner, "A Third Concept of Liberty," *Proceedings of the British Academy*, Vol. 117 (2002), pp. 237–268.

[8] Ryan, *The Making of Modern Liberalism*, p. 28. L. T. Hobhouse's rather sweeping account of liberalism identifies opposition to authoritarianism as the beginning point for any liberal thought-practice: "The modern State [*sic*] starts from the basis of an authoritarian order, and the protest against that order, a protest religious, political, economic, social, and ethical, is the historic beginning of Liberalism." L. T. Hobhouse, *Liberalism* (Oxford: Oxford University Press, 1964), p. 19.

[9] Ryan, *The Making of Modern Liberalism*, pp. 35–40.

28   Aspects of Political Liberalism in Modern Iran

any particular historical juncture, classifying them in terms of the overall normative objectives they are meant to achieve seems particularly useful. In the absence of a self-consciously liberal school of thought in Iran, however, the scope and substance of liberal prescriptions argued for by Iranian intellectuals have been more practical and limited than their Western counterparts. As such, I have reconfigured the discussion of liberal prescriptions in Iran into categories that, as will be demonstrated below, best account for this difference: *liberal nationalism*, *constitutionalism*, and *pluralism*. These prescriptive views are premised on liberal theories for individuals, society, and state, to be sure; but they are also informed by reflective thinking about the effects of Western imperialism on Iranian political development.

A key methodological challenge facing the study of any political ideology – not to mention one as historically contingent and varied as liberalism – is to distinguish clearly between the substance of an ideology and the language used to communicate that substance. This distinction is significant since a particular political discourse may be co-opted by other ideologies and therefore either dilute or completely render meaningless the substance of the ideology from which it first sprang.[10] For instance, since the mid-nineteenth century, terms such as *azadi* (liberty), *qanun* (law), *'adalat* (justice), *mosavat* or *barabari* (equality), and *taraqqi* (progress) have been appropriated by thinkers of liberal, non-liberal, and avowedly anti-liberal persuasions for their respective purposes. Indeed, as Ervand Abrahamian has shown, the Iranian intelligentsia in general subscribed to these antipathies and prescriptions in reference to what held Iran back from joining modernity: "Western history persuaded them that human progress was not only possible and desirable but also easily attainable if they broke the three chains of royal despotism, clerical dogmatism, and foreign imperialism .... The intelligentsia thus considered constitutionalism, secularism, and nationalism to be the three vital means for attaining the establishment of a modern, strong, developed Iran."[11]

The *liberal* invocation of such terms, however, is attached to a specific political project, distinguished in substance and scope by a specified line of argument focused on individual autonomy, political equality, basic rights, and national self-determination, which are further elaborated on

---

[10] As Freeden notes, "The temporal and spatial attributes of ideologies become evident when they are explored as conceptual configurations, in which general concepts often courting universal appeal, and shared by the preponderant membership of an ideological family, are fleshed out by the adjacent and peripheral concepts whose main function is to construct a two-way link between the concrete and the abstract." Freeden, *Liberal Languages*, p. 241.

[11] Abrahamian, *Iran between Two Revolutions*, pp. 61–62.

Two Modes of Liberalism 29

below. In sketching out the contours of liberal thinking, therefore, I rely less on a particular parlance as a signifier of liberal ideals than a substantive set of principles espoused by political thinkers. This is not to suggest that discourse is never a useful metric for gauging the spread and influence of liberal ideas in any society. Indeed, that the movement for constitutionalism in Iran injected a great many liberal terms into Iranian political discourse is in some sense a testament to the discernible imprint the ideas behind such terms have left on Iranian public imagination. Rather, the point I am making here is that by "aspects" of Iranian political liberalism I primarily have in mind a specified and deeply contextual combination of antipathies and prescriptions that are *substantively* liberal, variations in parlance notwithstanding.

Liberal Antipathies

The second half of the nineteenth century saw the introduction of many modern ideas and projects in Iran. At the political level, the motivation behind modernization was the reassertion of state control in response to the growing influence of foreign – chiefly British and Russian – entities over Iran's internal economy and politics. The "defensive modernization" programs introduced by Naser al-Din Shah (masterminded by his able chief minister, Amir Kabir) were in essence state-building measures designed to reorganize executive and judicial prerogatives, and to establish the cultural and educational conditions for the emergence of a meritocratic elite capable of performing executive and administrative functions independently of foreign meddling and assistance. (As regards the latter, the establishment of Dar al-Fonoun [Abode of Learning] was a notable and constructive achievement, touted at the time as the crown jewel of social reforms) Although attempts at political reforms largely proved fruitless, and in fact exacerbated many of the Qajar state's internal contradictions, they were nonetheless remarkable in terms of the intellectual standards they ultimately failed to measure up against.

The intellectual imperative for modernization was spurred by a sense of cultural and political malaise with deep internal roots in the perceived backwardness of Iranian society itself. In the educated and peripatetic imagination of a new cohort of intellectuals, Iran's inferior position – in industry, military, and cultural affairs – relative to that of European powers stemmed chiefly from the superstitions, ineptitude, and general complacency of Iranians themselves.[12] Deliverance, then, could only

---

[12] See Homa Katouzian, "European Liberalisms and Modern Concepts of Liberty in Iran," *Journal of Iranian Research and Analysis*, Vol. 16, No. 2 (2000): 16–17.

30   Aspects of Political Liberalism in Modern Iran

come about in the form of a genuine upheaval in thought, an intellectual rupture with traditional ways of thinking about the relationship between self-knowledge and identity, empiricism and religious dogma, sovereign prerogatives and the basis for rule.[13] As Cyrus Masroori has shown, the yearning for such a rupture – born out of an acute sense of crisis – was soon "followed by attempts to re-interpret traditions in the light of liberal principles."[14] These liberal beginnings, moreover, were notable for their identification of myriad obstacles in the way of modern progress in Iranian society. In the Iranian liberal imagination, traditionalism, despotism, and imperialism not only held human potential back by restricting freedoms and rights, but also prevented the nation as a whole from advancing the best of its own traditions in science, industry, and the arts.

Anti-traditionalism

As with the emergence of liberal antipathies on the European continent, the dawn of liberal thought in Iran was singularly motivated by an intellectual opposition to traditionalism, understood as the unquestioning veneration of received traditions – best exemplified in, but not limited to, the seemingly permanent condition of stasis in religious thought and practice. The inaugural, and perhaps most vivid, expressions of this antipathy are to be found in the works of Mirza Fath'ali Akhundzadeh.[15] The life, times, and works of Akhundzadeh have been well-mined by scholars of political thought and intellectual history, and he is deservedly regarded as an important precursor to the intellectual movement behind the Constitutional Revolution.[16] The common thread running through Akhundzadeh's oeuvre is a criticism of

---

[13] In a series of lectures delivered at Columbia University in 1958, Hassan Taqizadeh, the founding editor of *Kaveh*, identified this intellectual awakening as the beginning of modernity in Iran. See Ali M. Ansari, "Taqizadeh and European Civilization," *Iran*, Vol. 54, No. 1 (2016): 47–58.

[14] Cyrus Masroori, "French Romanticism and Persian Liberalism in Nineteenth-Century Iran: Mirza Agha Khan Kirmani and Jacques-Henri Bernardine de Saint-Pierre," *History of Political Thought*, Vol. 28, No. 3 (2007): 543.

[15] According to Masroori, "Akhundzadeh is the most significant representative of the Iranian Enlightenment liberals." Ibid., p. 666. Although, it must be noted that Akhundzadeh's liberalism is more readily discernible in his antipathies than in any coherent vision or prescriptive political project. For instance, his readings of Voltaire's and Rousseau's thoughts yielded a more collectivist/etatist outlook than an individualist/liberal one. (I am grateful to Ali Gheissari for pointing this out.) See Maryam B. Sanjabi, "Rereading the Enlightenment: Akhundzada and His Voltaire," *Iranian Studies*, Vol. 28, Nos. 1–2 (2007): 39–60.

[16] Fereydoun Adamiyat, *Andishe-ye Mirza Fath'Ali Akhundzadeh* [The Ideas of Mirza Fath'ali Akhundzadeh] (Tehran: Khawrazmi Press, 1349/1970); Sanjabi, "Rereading the Enlightenment"; Hamid Algar, "Malkum Khan, Akhundzada and the Proposed Reform of the Arabic Alphabet," *Middle Eastern Studies*, Vol. 5, No. 2 (1969): 116–130; Mehrdad Kia, "Mirza Fath Ali Akhundzade and the Call for Modernization of the

Two Modes of Liberalism 31

unexamined traditionalist beliefs in "religion, language, and government which he condemned as root causes of Iran's decadence and defeat."[17]

Indeed, central to Akhundzadeh's thinking was the conviction that, as he relayed to his compatriots in his politically allusive tract, *Maktubat-e Kamal al-Dowleh* [Correspondences of Kamal al-Dowleh] (henceforth: *Maktubat*), ". . . knowledge could not be acquired unless through progress, and progress could not be achieved unless by being liberal, and being liberal is not possible without getting rid of [religious] beliefs."[18] Elsewhere, in his collection of essays, *Maqalat*, Akhundzadeh also repeatedly blamed Islamic dogma and especially the ulama – whom he routinely referred to as "charlatans" – as the enemies of knowledge and progress in Iran.[19] Yet, he was not naïve about the impossibility of cleansing Iranian cultural mores and institutions from Islamic influences entirely. He argued instead for the emergence of an "Islamic Protestantism" in Iran that would serve as an analogue to the Church of England's position in a constitutional political system based on the principle of the separation of church and state. It was in this particular context that Akhundzadeh (along with Mirza Malkum Khan) sought the reform of the Arabic alphabet in Iran, blaming "the high rate of illiteracy in Muslim countries to the deficiencies of the script."[20] Although this effort ultimately proved unfruitful – above all due to the opposition of other anti-traditionalist liberals such as Mirza Abdul-Rahim Talebof and Mirza Agha Khan Kermani[21] – it is nevertheless notable as a representative case of the near-obsessive preoccupation with stamping out traditional Arabic and Islamic influences in Iranian society and politics among those with otherwise liberal political fealties.

For Akhundzadeh, then, traditionalism was not merely a state of scientific and technological backwardness, but a particular consciousness beholden to superstition, dogma, and sophistry, as best exemplified by

---

Muslim World," *Middle Eastern Studies*, Vol. 31, No. 3 (1995): 422–448; Cyrus Masroori, "European Thoughts in Nineteenth-Century Iran: David Hume and Others," *Journal of the History of Ideas*, Vol. 61, No. 4 (2000): 657–674; and Mehran Mazinani, "Liberty in Akhundzadeh's and Kermani's Thoughts," *Middle Eastern Studies*, Vol. 51, No. 6 (2015): 883–900.

[17] Sanjabi, "Rereading the Enlightenment," p. 41.

[18] Although this work was written in 1860, Akhundzadeh kept revising it until 1863 and the manuscript was not published – along with his other works – by a major publishing house in Baku until 1905. Fath'ali Mirza Akhundzadeh, *Maktubat: Nameha-ye Kamal al-Dowleh be Shahzadeh Jamal al-Dowleh* [Correspondences of Kamal al-Dowleh to Prince Jamal al-Dowleh], ed. Bahram Chubineh (Frankfurt: Alborz, 2006), p. 56. Excerpt is also quoted in Masroori, "European Thought in Nineteenth-Century Iran," p. 666.

[19] Akhundzadeh, *Maktubat*, p. 56.   [20] Algar, "Malkum Khan," p. 117.

[21] Mehrdad Kia, "Persian Nationalism and Language Purification," *Middle Eastern Studies*, Vol. 34, No. 2 (1998): 12–16.

32   Aspects of Political Liberalism in Modern Iran

submission to Islamic norms and injunctions. As such, Islam was *an instance* of traditionalism.[22] Through the preaching of the ulama and the corrupt complacency of the Qajar court, Islam had become the chief purveyor of traditionalism. Under such conditions, the establishment of law alone would not emancipate the populace from their collective stupor; rather, traditionalist social practices must be eradicated so that individuals may begin to appreciate their inherent worth as civic-minded authors and subjects of the law in the first place.[23] This is an important aspect of Akhundzadeh's thinking that sets him apart from other liberal reformers and intellectuals of his time – figures such as Talebof, Kermani, Mirza Yusuf Khan Mostashar al-Dowleh, Malkum Khan, and even Jamal al-Din al-Afghani – who also held anti-traditionalist beliefs.[24] In their thinking, tradition and dogmatic belief systems could be tempered through either scientific advancement, the rule of law, or the reinterpretation of Islamic principles. In contrast, Akhundzadeh held that intellectual liberation from all manner of traditional thinking to be a precondition for the attainment of progress – traditionalism was the cause and not merely a symptom of backwardness.[25] More precisely – and this is what qualifies Akhundzadeh's formulation as a particularly "liberal" one – for him tradition was the ultimate enemy of individual liberty, which in Iran had been introduced through Islam and the influence of Arab culture. As he noted in a footnote in *Maktubat*, "The nations of the East, because of the advent of the Arabs' religion and their domination over Asia, have completely lost their freedoms, do not enjoy equality, and have been deprived of the gift of

---

[22] This is why Akhundzadeh did not advocate for the outright banning or eradication of Islam, but rather for reform of the ways (changing the alphabet) and means (through reason) by which Iranians engaged in social and political discourse with one another. Skepticism about Islam would set in once the ground for reasoned debate and thought was prepared. See Fath'ali Mirza Akhundzadeh, *Maqalat* [Essays], ed. Baqer Momeni, trans. Ahmad Taheri Araghi and Mohammad Ali Farzaneh (Tehran: Ava, 1351/1972), pp. 109–111.

[23] Ibid., p. 110. According to Adamiyat, Akhundzadeh's thinking here was premised on his understanding of the stages of social and political development in European societies: "First, the conditions necessary for an upheaval in thought and national growth must be made possible through the dissemination of knowledge. Once the people are able to stand on their own feet [through enlightenment], then they can overthrow the traditional order and replace it with a new regime. But without the necessary intellectual foundations, merely adopting and importing the expertise of others will not yield the desired result." Adamiyat, *Andishe-ye Mirza Fath'Ali Akhundzadeh*, pp. 166–167.

[24] Kia offers an excellent examination of the subtle differences between this cohort in considering their positions on nationalism and language purification. See his "Persian Nationalism and Language Purification."

[25] For comparisons with similar lines of thought among reformist contemporaries of Akhundzadeh in the Arab world, see Albert Hourani, *Arabic Thought in the Liberal Age, 1798–1939* (Cambridge: Cambridge University Press, 1983), especially chapters 2–5.

Two Modes of Liberalism

human rights."[26] Traditionalism was to be rejected because it infantilized those beholden to it, and in aggregate the nation as a whole.

To identify this aspect of Akhundzadeh's thought as a vivid example, and perhaps the dawn, of liberal anti-traditionalism, however, is not to overlook its import chiefly as a call for nationalism. Indeed, in modern Iranian historiography Akhundzadeh is often regarded as a "founding father" of Iranian nationalism.[27] As Homa Katouzian has pointed out, Akhundzadeh "was clearly a progressive man of his time but one who, like some of his intellectual descendants in Iran, Turkey, and elsewhere, combined an uncritical attitude toward what he knew of European social and cultural developments with a wholly rejectionist view of post-Islamic Iranian culture and civilization."[28] Akhundzadeh's romantic view of pre-Islamic Iranian national identity certainly cannot be excised from his espousals of liberal principles. All the same, his antipathy toward traditionalist thinking was not solely in the service of a romantic vision of nationhood. It is very clear from his published writings and letters to prominent ideological fellow-travelers that Akhundzadeh was chiefly interested in creating the conditions for a rationalist and individualist awakening, akin to the sociological preconditions prior to the advent of European liberalism. That nationalism offered an exit from a religio-cultural heritage – Islam – he perceived as responsible for instilling traditionalist thought-practices in Iranian society does not negate the fact that the source and substance of his antipathies were essentially liberal, *not* nativist.

This is evident in Akhundzadeh's liberal-humanist championing of "the art of critique" (*fann-e qiritika*), which in his view accounted for "order and progress" in European societies.[29] Although he manifestly

---

[26] Akhundzadeh, *Maktubat*, p. 56. A slightly different translation of the same passage appears in Masroori, "European Thought in Nineteenth-Century Iran," p. 666.

[27] Afshin Marashi encapsulates much writing on Akhundzadeh's thoughts by noting that they were mostly underwritten by "a romantic notion of a classical past and a racialized understanding of culture." Afshin Marashi, *Nationalizing Iran: Culture, Power, and the State, 1870–1940* (Seattle, WA: University of Washington Press, 2008), p. 69. According to Reza Zia-Ebrahimi, Akhundzadeh "played a crucial role in compiling disparate ideas about Iran's past and true national essence, amalgamating them with some of his own radical stances, and organizing this new corpus into a polemical discourse of nationalism, and ideology ready to be adopted by his followers." Reza Zia-Ebrahimi, *The Emergence of Iranian Nationalism: Race and Politics of Dislocation* (New York: Columbia University Press, 2016), p. 42. This predilection, Zia-Ebrahimi further explains by quoting Akhundzadeh himself, meant that "the 'liberal, progressive, and *civilisé*' objective of writing this treatise was to 'sow the seeds of zeal, honour, patriotism'." Ibid., p. 46. See also Ali M. Ansari, *The Politics of Nationalism in Modern Iran* (Cambridge: Cambridge University Press, 2012), pp. 30–31.

[28] Homa Katouzian, *Sadeq Hedayat: The Life and Legend of an Iranian Writer* (London: I.B. Tauris & Co. Ltd., 2002), p. 5.

[29] As he states in a letter to Mirza Yusuf Khan, "Today in all European countries there are satirical papers – that is, critique and satire – which every week write and publish the

34   Aspects of Political Liberalism in Modern Iran

failed to question the underlying Eurocentrism of his own ideas through the same critical approach,[30] the radical nature of his advocacy of rational critique in the context of his times cannot be overstated. His anti-traditionalism, after all, also necessitated a secular public sphere as well as a rights-based constitutional framework to accompany his vision of national reawakening. It is certainly the case that many of Akhundzadeh's intellectual descendants were chiefly inspired by his call for a "unity of thought and action" in achieving a "refashioned" national identity.[31] For some, like Akhundzadeh's disciple Kermani, this was done through even more jarring demonization of Arabs and fantastical depictions of a purposeful past.[32] But it is notable that in time – that is, the onset of constitutionalism and the advent of new, non-nativist methods of historiography – the liberal precepts behind anti-traditionalism out-survived the twin proclivities for reimagining the pre-Islamic past and what the historian Ahmad Kasravi called "Europeanism" (the tendency to imitate Westerners).

Akhundzadeh's anti-traditionalism, as mentioned earlier, is notable for being perhaps the fullest *inaugural* expression of a liberal antipathy of its kind in Iran. But since the late nineteenth century, liberal anti-traditionalism has been a constant accompaniment to secular-humanist, feminist, social-democratic, and even religious-reformist arguments for the priority of scientific knowledge and self-criticism over dogmatic beliefs. Variants of this liberal antipathy can be found, for instance, in the anticlerical screeds of pro-constitutionalist newspapers and journals such as *Qanun*, *Sur-e Israfil*, *Habl al-Matin*, *Mosavat*, and *Iran-e Now* prior, during, and after the Constitutional Revolution.[33] Anti-traditionalism was also

vulgar acts of their fellow countrymen. European nations have reached such order and progress by means of critique, not by counsel and sermon. The European peoples have reached this degree of wisdom and perfection by means of critique, not counsel and sermon." Fath'ali Mirza Akhunzadeh, "Akhundzadeh to Mirza Yusuf Khan," March 29, 1871, *Alifba*, repr. (Tabriz: 1357/1978), pp. 212–213. Cited in Sanjabi, "Rereading the Enlightenment," p. 48.

[30] As Kia rightly points out, "By refusing to apply to Europe the same critical approach which he had adopted in his critique of Islam, Akhundzadeh failed to transcend the simplistic dualism of the Occident versus the Orient." Kia, "Mirza Fath Ali Akhundzadeh," p. 444.

[31] For a rigorous exploration of this, see Mohamad Tavakoli-Tarqi, *Refashioning Iran: Orientalism, Occidentalism, and Historiography* (New York: Palgrave Macmillan, 2001), pp. 102–104.

[32] Zia-Ebrahimi, *The Emergence of Iranian Nationalism*, p. 56.

[33] Afary, *The Iranian Constitutional Revolution*, chapter 5. Ali Akbar Dehkhoda's irreverent writings in the constitutional period are especially exemplary in this regard as well. See Nahid Nosrat Mozaffari, "An Iranian Modernist Project: Ali Akbar Dehkhoda's Writings in the Constitutional Period," in H. E. Chehabi and Vanessa Martin, eds., *Iran's Constitutional Revolution: Popular Politics, Cultural Transformations, and Transnational Connections* (London: I.B. Tauris & Co. Ltd., 2012), pp. 193–212.

Two Modes of Liberalism   35

a central motivator behind the formation of women's *anjoman*s (councils) –
and long after that, extending to the present day, of feminist arguments
against discriminatory Islamic cultural norms and legal codes governing
women's bodies and their agency in Iranian society.[34] In this regard, it has
been most influential in its blunt interrogation and concrete shaming of the
obstacles in the way of scientific rationalism and individualism not merely
in the political domain, but in the all-important sociocultural milieus where
established thought-practices are constantly negotiated, subverted, or for-
cibly enforced.

Anti-absolutism

If anti-traditionalism has been a uniquely liberal antipathy espoused by
Iranian intellectuals, opposition to absolute power has sprung from
a variety of sources. The movements advocating for constitutional constraints on the arbitrary powers of various rulers, after all, have always also
featured Islamists, socialists, and assorted secular-nationalists not particularly beholden to liberal precepts such as individual autonomy or state
neutrality. But opposition to absolute *power* is not necessarily opposition
to absolut*ism*. The former merely touches on the modes, means, and the
capacity to coerce, whereas the latter is concerned with the rationale
behind not only the exercise of power but the source(s) of authority on
the ends which individuals may strive toward. As Ryan has argued, "What
makes liberal hostility to absolute rule liberal rather than merely constitutionalist is the liberal claim that absolute rule violates the personality or
the rights of those over whom it is exercised."[35] For liberals, absolutism is
the violation of personhood because it dictates to individuals the values
that they ought to live by. Absolutism, in other words, is the political
expression of monism, the notion that, as Berlin famously castigated, only
one set of values or principles are valid above all others.[36] In this regard,
liberal anti-absolutism entails unqualified opposition to any and all
systems of rule and belief that do not derive their political authority
from the consent of free and equal citizens.

---

[34] On women's *anjoman*s, see chapter 7 in Afary, *The Iranian Constitutional Revolution*. On
the use of liberal anti-traditionalist arguments by Iranian feminists during the Pahlavi era
and after the Islamic Revolution, see Haideh Moghissi, *Populism and Feminism in Iran:
Women's Struggle in a Male-Defined Revolutionary Movement* (New York: St. Martin's
Press Inc., 1996).

[35] Ryan, *The Making of Modern Liberalism*, p. 29.

[36] On monism contra pluralism, see Isaiah Berlin, "The First and the Last," *New York
Review of Books*, Vol. 45 (1998), pp. 52–60; see also Isaiah Berlin, "On the Pursuit of the
Ideal," *New York Review of Books*, Vol. 35, No. 4 (1998), pp. 11–18.

36   Aspects of Political Liberalism in Modern Iran

In Iran, liberal anti-absolutism has had many exponents among intellectuals since the late nineteenth century and has generally been expressed as opposition to both royal despotism and theocracy. Strong early expressions of liberal anti-absolutism can be found in the works of Akhundzadeh and Kermani, for whom the injury to personal liberty was as much inflicted by arbitrary monarchs as it was by clerical authority.[37] Kermani's *Sad Khatabeh* [A Hundred Lectures], which he wrote in his later years and never completed past the forty-second lecture, is the perfect distillation of such views.[38] In it, Kermani posited that the "natural prerogatives" of society were always in contention with the prerogatives of royal and religious despotism, which were arbitrarily claimed by kings and clerics for the advancement of their own interests above the natural rights of citizens.[39] Although these prerogatives were to be understood independent of legitimate government and religious belief, they nevertheless used the threat of arbitrary coercion and divine retribution, respectively, to instill fear in individuals in society.[40] As Kermani put it, "When religion and politics – through the arbitrary prerogatives of despots and religious fanatics – put pressure on and sap the hopes of society, they leave the public with no natural [i.e. free] breathing room and eventually bring about their end."[41] Anti-absolutism was the natural response of subjugated individuals to the unnatural circumstances imposed on them by these arbitrary forces.[42] In this vein, as Adamiyat and others have pointed out, Kermani was very much among the first Iranian intellectuals to argue for liberal precepts through the introduction of natural law philosophical arguments prevalent among European intellectuals.[43]

[37] See Mazinani, "Liberty in Akhundzadeh's and Kermani's Thoughts."
[38] Adamiyat considered the book to be a companion volume to Mirza Agha Khan Kermani, *Se Maktub* [Three Letters], ed. Bahram Chubineh (Frankfurt: Alborz, 2005), and in fact superior to it in both the range of subjects considered and the depth of his thoughts. For comprehensive considerations of the political thought of Kermani, see Fereydoun Adamiyat, *Andishehay-e Mirza Agha Khan Kermani* [The Ideas of Mirza Aqa Khan Kermani] (Tehran: Tahuri, 1346/1967); and Mangol Bayat Philipp, "The Concepts of Religion and Government in the Thought of Mirza Aqa Khan Kermani, a Nineteenth-Century Persian Revolutionary," *International Journal of Middle East Studies*, Vol. 5, No. 4 (1974): 381–400.
[39] See lectures 10–13 in Mirza Agha Khan Kermani, *Sad Khatabeh* [A Hundred Lectures], ed. Haroun Vohouman (Los Angeles, CA: Ketab Corp., 1386/2007).
[40] Ibid., lecture no. 13.   [41] Ibid.
[42] For an excellent, recent consideration of Kermani's anti-despotism, see Pejman Abdolmohammadi, "The Iranian Constitutional Revolution and the Influence of Mirza Āqā Khan Kermani's Political Thought," in Ali M. Ansari, ed., *Iran's Constitutional Revolution of 1906: Narratives of the Enlightenment* (London: Gingko Library, 2016), pp. 116–128.
[43] Adamiyat, *Andisheha-ye Mirza Agha Khan Kermani*, chapter 8 (part II). See also Bayat Philipp, "The Concepts of Religion and Government in the Thought of Mirza Agha

Two Modes of Liberalism 37

In the context of the Constitutional Revolution, liberal antipathy toward absolutism manifested itself in more tolerant and pragmatic positions vis-à-vis Islam, given the indispensability of reformist clerics to overcoming Qajar despotism. A central change in emphasis in this period was the adoption of the language of law and rights as the basis for claims against arbitrary rule. The person whose approach best exemplified this shift in emphasis was Malkum Khan.[44] A fixture of the pro-reform cohort of intellectuals close to the royal court, Malkum Khan was especially influenced by liberal European thinkers – most prominently, Auguste Comte and John Stuart Mill – whose ideas he, more than any other prominent Iranian intellectual of his time, sought to introduce to the ruling and religious elites in Iran. He did so through a series of translations – he translated Mill's essay *On Liberty* into Persian – published discourses on the imperative of reforms and modernization,[45] and through the founding of Faramoush-Khaneh (House of Oblivion), a secret society for freethinking aristocrats modeled after the European Freemason lodges of its time. Malkum Khan eventually grew impatient with the pace of reforms in the latter part of his career and came to increasingly view Qajar despotism as the main obstacle to social and political modernization. He communicated these grievances most viscerally through *Qanun*, which became a major outlet for propagating anti-absolutist and liberal-constitutionalist ideas, prudently composed to appeal to religious as well as secular intellectuals.[46] Among its frequent contributors were Kermani and Afghani, who often framed their advocacy for constitutionalism in terms familiar to religious intellectuals.[47] Its inaugural editorial, penned by Malkum Khan, served as a model for dexterous use of pious indignation for liberal purposes:

Khan Kermani"; Bayat Philipp, "Mirza Agha Khan Kermani: A Nineteenth-Century Persian Nationalist," *Middle Eastern Studies* 10 (1974): 36–59.

[44] See chapter 3 on Malkum Khan's life and intellectual corpus in Adamiyat, *Fekr-e Azadi*. For a critical treatment of his life and times, see Hamid Algar, *Mirza Malkum Khan: A Study in the History of Iranian Modernism* (Berkeley, CA: University of California Press, 1973).

[45] The most influential of these were *Ketabche-ye Gheybi* [The Booklet from the Hidden Realm], also known as *Daftar-e Tanzimat* [Book of Reforms], and *Rafiq va Vazir* [Friend and Minister]. These works are collected in his *Resaleha-ye Mirza Malkum Khan Nazem al-Dowleh*.

[46] Malkum Khan laid out his strategy for disguising liberal-constitutional principles in Islamic parlance and justificatory schemes in a public lecture in London; see Mirza Malkum Khan Nezam al-Dowleh, "Persian Civilization," *The Contemporary Review*, Vol. LIX (1891), pp. 238–244.

[47] Its inaugural editorial, penned by Malkum Khan, served as a model for dexterous use of pious indignation for liberal purposes. See Mirza Malkum Khan Nezam al-Dowleh, "God Has Blessed Iran," *Qanun*, Vol. 1, No. 2 (1890): 1–2.

38   Aspects of Political Liberalism in Modern Iran

God has blessed Iran. Unfortunately, His blessing has been negated by the lack of laws.

No one in Iran feels secure because no one in Iran is safeguarded by laws.

The appointment of governors is carried out without laws. The dismissal of officers is done without laws. The monopolies are sold without any laws. The state finances are squandered without laws. The stomachs of innocent citizens are cut open without laws. Even the servants of God are deported without laws.

Every one in India, Paris, Tiflis, Egypt, Istanbul, and even among the Turkman tribes, knows his rights and duties. But no one in Iran knows his rights and duties.

By what law was this mujtahed deported?

By what law was that officer cut into pieces?

By what law was this minister dismissed?

By what law was that idiot given a robe of honor?[48]

Part antipathetic (against absolutism), part prescriptive (for constitutionalism), *Qanun* embodied the liberal imagination in the interregnum between the demise of Qajar despotism and the dawn of constitutionalism in Iran. As such, it stood as a monument to the uneasy compromise that had to be forged between anticlerical and anti-autocratic interpretations of absolutism. If the rule of law were to be the starting point for meaningful reforms, Malkum Khan and his adherents surmised, then liberal opposition to clerical authority must be hidden from would-be supporters of constitutionalism among the ulama.

This strategy, however, always carried with it the risk of neither fully satisfying the ulama nor offering a robust liberal agenda.[49] Worse yet, the arbitrary nature of the state-society dialectic in Iran meant that if any faction on either side of this tenuous bargain found itself endangered by a new order, collusion with arbitrary rulers for the sake of survival (or the prospect of chaos and unrest) would be inevitable.[50] Indeed, it was precisely this factional dynamic that eventuated the demise of constitutionalism and the dawn of Pahlavi absolutism in Iran. Although the failure of constitutionalism tipped the balance briefly back toward more overtly anticlerical positions,[51] liberal opposition to absolutism henceforth

---

[48] Ibid. Translation used here is from Abrahamian, *Iran between Two Revolutions*, p. 68.

[49] As Ali Gheissari has perceptibly observed, "One serious drawback to this pragmatic, somewhat cavalier, approach to religion was that neither Malkam nor his fellow reformists were able to develop and sustain a coherent theory of national reform." Gheissari, *Iranian Intellectuals in the 20th Century*, p. 27.

[50] For under conditions of arbitrary rule, as Katouzian has convincingly shown, "unaccountable state and ungovernable society are two sides of the same coin." Katouzian, *State and Society in Iran*, p. 14.

[51] See, for instance, Ahmad Kasravi's defiantly anticlerical turn and biting critique of sophistry and superstition among the believers in his books *A'yin* [Guidelines] (Tehran: 1311–1312/1932–1933) and *Dar Piramun-e Islam* [About Islam] (Tehran: 1322/1943). Five years before his assassination Kasravi also founded the Society of

Two Modes of Liberalism 39

mostly sought to enfold and work with reform-minded clerics against both state and religious absolutism. Its main concerns became the nourishment of coalitions working toward the attainment of basic rights and representative government – not achieving political supremacy over its ideological counterparts.[52] This vision was in evidence early on from the founding of various liberal associations and secret societies during and after the Constitutional Revolution (e.g. the Society of Humanity, the Revolutionary Committee, Society for Women, etc.). Moreover, it certainly formed a major part of the Liberation Movement of Iran's political platform at the time of its founding by Mosaddeq and subsequently under the Second and Third National Fronts during the Pahlavi and the Islamic Republic regimes, respectively.

It may reasonably be argued that the earlier, more forthright iterations of liberal principles became regrettable casualties of this pragmatist approach. Certainly, the metamorphosis of the National Front into a more religious-minded coalition, and the eventual purging of the movement of liberal-secular thinkers, attest to the salience of this judgment.[53] But it is important to keep in mind that beyond domestic political considerations, the imperative of coalition-building was also impressed upon liberals by their steadfast opposition to Western imperialism. Liberal thinkers and political figures had to shoulder the dual burden of not only battling absolutism, but also being cognizant of, and accounting in their political strategies for, the manner in which the state's basic capacities were seriously hampered through decades of foreign interference and control.

Anti-imperialism

The relationship between empire and liberalism is a complex and storied one.[54] In the context of late nineteenth-century political thought, not only did some leading lights of liberal progress (such as Locke, Hume, and Mill) write favorably of colonialism, but many British and French

---

Free Men, which was almost completely dedicated to countering the public influence of Shia clergy in Iranian society. For more, see Ali Reza Manafzadeh, "Ahmad Kasravi," *Encyclopædia Iranica*, Vol. XVI, Fasc. 1, p. 97.

[52] Among the pragmatists in this period, the most exemplary were Ali Akbar Dehkhoda, Hassan Taqizadeh, Yahya Mirza Eskandari, Mohammad-Taqi Bahar, Ali Akbar Davar, Mohammad Ali Foroughi, and of course Mohammad Mosaddeq.

[53] For an acute analysis of the underlying considerations driving this process, see Houchang Chehabi, *Iranian Politics and Religious Modernism: The Liberation Movement of Iran under the Shah and Khomeini* (Ithaca, NY: Cornell University Press, 1990).

[54] For the most authoritative recent overview and dissection of this topic from a political thought perspective, see the essays in Bell, *Reordering the World*.

40 Aspects of Political Liberalism in Modern Iran

imperialists justified imperialism as a "civilizing mission" in the service of liberal ends.[55] It is also certainly the case that since the end of formal empire, attempts at disguising informal imperial practices as mere instruments of benevolent liberal internationalism have been routine.[56] Yet, for every such association, there are countless examples of liberal critiques of empire as well. Leaving aside many prominent anti-imperial Enlightenment figures (such as Diderot, Herder, Smith, Burke, Bentham, Kant, etc.), some of the leading critics of empire at the height of British and French imperial power were liberals – such as Benjamin Constant, J. A. Hobson, Herbert Spencer, Richard Cobden – for whom the greed, racism, and paternalism embodied in imperial ideology and practices were an affront to liberal values.[57] As Hobson pointed out in his classic study of imperialism, "We have taken upon ourselves in these little islands the responsibility of governing huge aggregations of lower races in all parts of the world by methods which are antithetic to the methods of government which we most value for ourselves."[58] In other words, the pursuit and administration of empire were not only immoral, but in fact contradicted cherished liberal values at home. Scarcely reflected upon but in fact more important (to imperial subjects, at least), moreover, were the deployment of similar arguments by non-Western liberal intellectuals.[59] For them, the substance of liberal anti-imperialism lay not so much in indictments of Western hypocrisy, but in the repudiation of the arbitrary control of their lands, resources, and sovereign prerogatives by foreign powers. Non-Western liberal anti-imperialism, then, was the result of liberalism "indigenized, adapted to local circumstances and traditions to provide a repertoire of arguments that could be utilized as part of an anti-imperial struggle."[60]

[55] See, for example, Uday Singh Mehta, *Liberalism and Empire: A Study in Nineteenth-Century British Liberal Thought* (Chicago, IL: University of Chicago Press, 1999); Jennifer Pitts, *A Turn to Empire: The Rise of Imperial Liberalism in Britain and France* (Princeton, NJ: Princeton University Press, 2006); Karuna Mantena, *Alibis of Empire: Henry Maine and the Ends of Liberal Imperialism* (Princeton, NJ: Princeton University Press, 2010); Sankar Muthu, ed., *Empire and Modern Political Thought* (Cambridge: Cambridge University Press, 2012). On the standard of civilization applied to such missions, see Gong, *The Standard of "Civilization" in International Society*.
[56] Sandra Halperin and Ronen Palan, eds., *Legacies of Empire: Imperial Roots of the Contemporary Global Order* (Cambridge: Cambridge University Press, 2015).
[57] For recent exploration of liberal anti-imperialism in these periods, see Sankar Muthu, *Enlightenment against Empire* (Princeton, NJ: Princeton University Press, 2003); and Pitts, *A Turn to Empire*.
[58] J. A. Hobson, *Imperialism: A Study* (Ann Arbor, MI: University of Michigan Press, 1965 [1902]), p. 123.
[59] Exceptions exist, such as the work by C. A. Bayly on liberal opposition to empire in in India. See Bayly, *Recovering Liberties*.
[60] Bell, *Reordering the World*, p. 111.

Two Modes of Liberalism   41

Indeed, such a "repertoire of arguments" has been prominent in the works and political activities of Iranian reformers from the second half of the nineteenth century to this day. They were less pronounced early in the writings of figures such as Akhundzadeh, Afghani, Talebof, Kermani, and Malkum Khan, to whom traditionalism and absolutism, as surveyed earlier, were of more urgent concern to Iran's path of progress than Western imperialism.[61] To the extent that crippling concessions to British and Russian interests were derided by the liberal intelligentsia in the latter half of the nineteenth century, they were seen as symptoms of arbitrary rule and cultural decadence induced by religious dogmatism. The advent of constitutionalism in Iran, albeit limited and short-lived, introduced the requisite public forums and legal processes for discussion and amelioration of these ailments (to liberals). However, as constitutionalism came to a halt and the country increasingly became a theater for imperial rivalry between Russia and Britain, Iranian liberals began to grapple more earnestly with the implications of undue foreign influence in their internal affairs. During the reign of Reza Shah (1925–1941), many prominent liberal-pragmatist figures such as Abdol-Hossein Teymourtash, Ali Akbar Davar, and Mohammad Ali Foroughi endorsed – the differences in their justifications notwithstanding[62] – the priority of state-building and constructing a coherent national identity over the constitutional-era imperatives of representative government and democratic rights.[63] In practice and effect, this was nothing short of a tacit endorsement of the autocratic shift under Reza Shah; even though none of these figures approved of the autocratic path on which the country would be placed under the Pahlavis.[64] The issue of Iran's neutrality in the

[61] This is not to suggest that other intellectuals viewed Iran's predicaments in the same manner. In fact, non-liberal dissidents such as Jamal al-Din al-Afghani very much viewed Western imperialism as the primary cause of Iran's backwardness. In this effort, he came to regard traditional Islam an important resource to wield against imperialism, unwittingly launching a Pan-Islamist movement that would inspire future political Islamists the world over. See Nikki R. Keddie, *Sayyid Jamal al-Din al-Afghani: A Political Biography* (Berkeley, CA: University of California Press, 1972); and Nikki R. Keddie, *An Islamic Response to Imperialism: Political and Religious Writings of Sayyid Jamal al-Din al-Afghani* (Berkeley, CA: University of California Press, 1983); for a recent reading of Afghani as the founding figure of transnational political Islam, see Mishra, *From the Ruins of Empire*, chapter 2.

[62] For instance, while Davar and Teymourtash were convinced that modern institutions and competent bureaucratic management would deliver Iranian society from decadence, Foroughi's justifications were grounded on cultural and educational approaches to national identity. I shall discuss Foroughi's contributions in this realm in the section "Liberal Nationalism."

[63] For a summary of Reza Shah's modernization programs, see Amanat, *Iran*, pp. 446–501.

[64] For an overview of the paradoxes and dilemmas of rapid modernization facing the technocratic elite in this period, see Mehrzad Boroujerdi, "Triumphs and Travails of Authoritarian Modernization in Iran," in Stephanie Cronin, ed., *The Making of Modern*

42   Aspects of Political Liberalism in Modern Iran

Central Powers' war against Germany had already galvanized a great deal of anti-Allied discussions in influential radical socialist periodicals such as *Kaveh* (which routinely praised Germany for its lack of imperial interests in Iran).[65] But whereas many of these public discussions were conducted in highly polemical and partisan tones, the advent of the rule of law afforded liberals with the opportunity to discuss imperialism in legalistic terms, as a violation of legally sanctioned sovereign prerogatives.

An instructive case in point here is Mohammad Mosaddeq's early legal work on the so-called capitulation agreements, through which the Qajars had ceded control of key national assets and industries to foreign powers without much legal recourse for the state in return. Under the terms of these nineteenth-century agreements, foreign merchants, traders, and diplomats were effectively exempt from prosecution, taxation, and conscription, on the grounds that, as Christians, they should not be subject to Islamic law. Mosaddeq correctly saw the roots of imperial meddling in Iran's internal affairs in the license provided to foreigners through these agreements. In a self-published manuscript entitled *Kapitulasion va Iran* [Capitulation Agreements and Iran], he argued that the extraterritorial privileges granted to foreigners in fact relegated Iranians to second-class citizenship before the law.[66] Using the example of the division between "private" and "public" law in European judicial systems, he was careful not to advocate for the total replacement of Sharia law, however. Sharia courts could still rule on private disputes, but public law should be redrafted so that it may not provide cover for foreign exploitation through religious exemptions.[67]

Ultimately, at issue for Mosaddeq was Iran's assertion of its sovereign rights. Indeed, to many liberal nationalists these were universal principles, which merely happened to have their fullest realization in Western countries. Incorporating them into Iran's circumstances was not tantamount to importing Western cultural traditions, less so ceding to imperialism. As Katouzian has explained, Mosaddeq's approach to this

---

Iran: State and Society under Riza Shah, 1921–1941 (New York: Routledge, 2003), pp. 152–160.

[65] Founded by Sayyid Hassan Taqizadeh, *Kaveh* was initially financed by the German government, and until the conclusion of World War I remained highly propagandistic and polemical against the Allies. In 1920, however, the paper became independently funded and was refashioned as a cultural periodical covering a deeper array of intellectual topics. See Iraj Afshar, "Kāva Newspaper," *Encyclopædia Iranica*, Vol. XVI, Fasc. 2 (May 31, 2013), pp. 132–135.

[66] Mohammad Mosaddeq, *Kapitulasion va Iran* [Capitulation and Iran] (Tehran: 1293/1914), chapter 1.

[67] For excellent exegeses of Mosaddeq's manuscript, see Iraj Afshar, ed., *Mosaddeq va Masa'il-e Hoquq va Siasat* [Mosaddeq and Issues in Law and Politics] (Tehran: Zamineh, 1358/1979); and Homa Katouzian, *Mosaddeq and the Struggle for Power in Iran* (London: I.B. Tauris Co. & Ltd., 2009), pp. 9–12.

Two Modes of Liberalism 43

problem, like his liberal forerunners, rested on "his belief in the creation of a synthesis between Iranian and European ideas, values and techniques … such that the country would neither remain backward nor lose what it had even if it achieved no lasting gain from pure aping and emulation."[68] Unlike any other liberal figure before or after him, however, he attained the political standing to put his beliefs into practice, first during his brief stint as governor of Azerbaijan province in 1921 (when he prosecuted a Soviet citizen under Iranian law), second as foreign minister in 1923 (when he compelled the premier to propose the reform of the penal code), and then as prime minister in 1951–1953 (when he led the domestic and international legal drive toward oil nationalization).[69] In each case, Mosaddeq's approach was to assert sovereign rights and duties through appeals to legal equality and self-determination, which unsurprisingly were also the pleadings of fellow liberal anti-imperialists in other postcolonial countries after the demise of formal European imperialism throughout the Third World.[70]

It is a commonplace in historical and contemporary studies of Iranian politics to classify Mosaddeq and Jebhe-ye Meli (the National Front) primarily as modernists-cum-nationalists. As we shall see below, nationalism certainly was an important prescriptive aspect of liberalism in Iran; however, it is often overlooked that in their struggles against Russian and British imperial interests liberal nationalists were primarily insistent on the sovereignty of law above arbitrary powers both at home and in international society. Indeed, this is a uniquely *liberal* disposition that differs considerably from other varieties of anti-imperialism and nationalism that harkened to more religious-centered or nativist principles. Therein lay Mosaddeq's – and the liberals' – seemingly perennial predicament: to assert liberal claims against both domestic forces suspicious of their Western origins and Western imperial interests partially liable for the semi-sovereign status of the state in international society. That this very much remains the plight of Iranian liberals to this day is a testament

---

[68] Katouzian, *Mosaddeq and the Struggle for Power in Iran*, p. 11.
[69] There are many excellent studies of the rise and fall of Mosaddeq that explore these episodes in greater depth. Prominent among these are ibid., chapters 2, 3, 7, 9–10; Mark J. Gasiorowski and Malcolm Byrne, eds., *Mohammad Mosaddeq and the 1953 Coup in Iran* (Syracuse, NY: University of Syracuse Press, 2004), chapters 1–2; Azimi, *Iran, The Crisis of Democracy*; Ervand Abrahamian, *The Coup: 1953, the CIA, and the Roots of Modern US-Iranian Relations* (New York: The New Press, 2013), chapters 1–2; Ali Rahnema, *Behind the 1953 Coup in Iran: Thug, Turncoats, Soldiers, and Spooks* (Cambridge: Cambridge University Press, 2014); and David R. Collier, *Democracy and the Nature of Influence in Iran, 1941–1979* (Syracuse, NY: University of Syracuse Press, 2017), chapters 1–5.
[70] For Indian variants of this approach, see Bayly, *Recovering Liberties*; for a global overview, see Jan C. Jansen and Jürgen Osterhammel, *Decolonization: A Short History* (Princeton, NJ: Princeton University Press, 2017), chapters 2 and 6.

44   Aspects of Political Liberalism in Modern Iran

to the resilience – and it must be said, resonance – of anti-liberal thought-practices that more often than not have co-opted liberal prescriptions to suit their agenda. It is to a consideration of these prescriptions that I turn to next.

Liberal Prescriptions

To mitigate the antipathies identified above, Iranian liberals have offered up a set of prescriptions similar to those proposed by their postcolonial counterparts in other parts of the world: liberal nationalism, constitutionalism, and pluralism. It is important to note, however, that much more than addressing any specific antipathy, these solutions are positive liberal projects in their own right. The common thread enjoining them are the twin principles of liberty and equal recognition, as enshrined in a written constitution at home and respected by foreign powers in international society. Where tradition and empire may have impeded progress domestically and denied the country the exercise of its sovereign prerogatives, liberals have prescribed an inclusive vision of a national "self" worthy of determination. In the same vein, constitutionalism was proposed not only as a means for establishing law and representative institutions but also as a bulwark of rights against arbitrary rulers. Of more recent vintage have been calls for the recognition of pluralism as both a sociological fact and a moral principle in political life; namely, the notion that the sources of the good life are not one but many. Together, these prescriptive views have shaped the course of Iranian political history for more than a century by defining the terms of debate and the substance of political grievances even among political parties and thinkers whose ideologies are in stark opposition to liberal values.

Liberal Nationalism

Since its emergence in the late nineteenth century in Iran, nationalism has been a two-dimensional ideological project intent on constructing a sense of collective identity (and hence interests) at home and asserting sovereign rights against imperial influences. Certainly, this inside/outside dichotomy is not peculiar to Iran. It is especially prevalent in postcolonial societies, where the organic impulse to "imagine" a political community is incessantly ceased upon by an equally powerful but synthetic compulsion to approximate a given "standard of civilization" or preexisting metric for progress.[71] The annals of postindependence nationalisms are filled with

---

[71] See, Benedict Anderson, *Imagined Communities: Reflections on the Origin and Spread of Nationalism* (New York: Verso, 1991), chapters 6–8; James Mayall, *Nationalism and*

Two Modes of Liberalism 45

examples of movements struggling – and mostly failing – to resolve this tension, wherein the ultimate burden is overcoming a sense of decadence or inferiority vis-à-vis the modern Western conceptions of statehood. In cases where the nativist imagination runs afoul of aspirations for representative and accountable government, the failure of effective independence may still reasonably be blamed on the putative imprint of imperial legacies on the minds and flawed institutions of the citizens and the state, respectively.[72] And yet, lamenting the excuse itself, too, has become a time-honored tradition in postcolonial literature.[73] This need not suggest, moreover, that liberal ideals – with their emphasis on individual autonomy and personal choice – are inherently opposed to the imperatives of nationalism such as kinship and patriotic loyalty. Indeed, to its proponents, liberal nationalism is the perfect blending of universal and particular commitments – albeit a balance that is best achieved through representative politics.[74]

The intersection of liberalism and nationalism in Iran is easier to temporize than to pinpoint. As mentioned earlier, anti-traditionalist liberals such as Akhundzadeh and Kermani are often singled out as the founding ideologues of Iranian nationalism. In his recent study of the subject, Zia-Ebrahimi identifies them as the foremost exponents of "dislocative nationalism," which denotes "a predominantly discursive and historicist ideology whose main objective was to soothe the pain of the traumatic encounter with Europe while making sense of Iran's backwardness."[75] Akhundzadeh's antipathy toward traditionalist thinking generated the raw intellectual material for a "systematic compilation of these ideas into ideological form," while Kermani's "further ... developed its racial component."[76] The resulting dislocation was "an

---

International Society (Cambridge: Cambridge University Press, 1990), chapters 7–8; and Eric J. Hobsbawm, *Nations and Nationalism since 1780*, 2nd ed. (Cambridge: Cambridge University Press, 2012).

[72] Some of the classics of the postcolonial cannon impart this message. See Franz Fanon, *Wretched of the Earth* (New York: Grove Press, 1963), chapter 3; Aime Césaire, *Discourse on Colonialism* (New York: Monthly Review Press, 2000); or Edward W. Said, *Culture and Imperialism* (New York: Vintage, 1993).

[73] The best example of this is V. S. Naipaul's masterpiece *A Bend in the River* (New York: Vintage, 1979), in which the contradictions of nationalist discourse are unsparingly examined through the realities of postindependence lived experience. In the case of Iran, Mahmoud Dowlatabadi's *The Colonel*, trans. Tom Patterdale (London: Haus Publishing Ltd., 2011) captures similar tensions and paradoxes.

[74] On the compatibility of nationalism and liberalism, see Isaiah Berlin, "The Bent Twig: A Note on Nationalism," *Foreign Affairs*, Vol. 51, No. 1 (1972): 11–30; Tamir, *Liberal Nationalism*. For a critique of the compatibility thesis, see Paul Kelly, "Liberalism and Nationalism," in Steven Wall, ed., *The Cambridge Companion to Liberalism* (Cambridge: Cambridge University Press, 2015), pp. 329–351.

[75] Zia-Ebrahimi, *The Emergence of Iranian Nationalism*, p. 71.   [76] Ibid., p. 9.

46   Aspects of Political Liberalism in Modern Iran

operation whereby the Iranian nation is dislodged from its empirical reality as a majority-Muslim society situated – broadly – in the 'East.' Iran is presented as an Aryan nation adrift, by accident, as it were, from the rest of its fellow Aryans (read: Europeans)."[77] The yearning for a reconstituted sense of self commensurate with the perceived standards of European modernity was of course a desire shared by many other intellectuals well after its emergence in the late nineteenth century.[78]

Even so, this constituted a minority view among liberals, whose antipathies, as the preceding section demonstrated, extended well beyond lamentations of cultural adulteration by Arabs or Islam. In fact, in the aftermath of the Constitutional Revolution, the chief drivers behind liberal nationalism were antipathies toward absolutism and imperialism. As a prescriptive project, liberal nationalism has been less about restoring a solid historical identity, and even less so of instilling a sense of belonging; rather, its chief ideological mission and import lay in, first, attempting to achieve unity through inclusion, and, second, to craft an autonomous, purpose-driven national profile. It is not accidental that the foremost programmatic articulations of this vision can be found in the pages of constitutional-era newspapers, whose encomiums to liberal-democratic principles were interlaced with calls for civic education and national unity. "Nationalism and pride in one's country," as Ali Ansari has argued about this period, "was part of a broader package of resurrection, and could not be understood as a means in itself."[79]

Among these, the newspaper *Iran-e Now* – an organ of the Democrat Party in the Second Majles and under the editorship of Mohammad-Amin Rasoulzadeh – was especially instrumental in charting a middle ground between nativist and Pan-Islamist conceptions of national identity. Through a series of poems and editorials by the likes of Mohammad-Taqi Bahar, Hassan Taqizadeh, Abol-Qasem Lahouti, Hossein Saba, and Rasoulzadeh himself, the paper's distinctly liberal outlook displayed an uncommon consistency in its heralding of constitutional principles and the requirements for national unity.[80] Not only did it insist on civic-centered, non-exclusionary representative principles, it also roundly criticized anti-Semitism (the first Persian-language paper to do so) and often offered a platform for dissident Azari and Armenian political voices.

---

[77] Ibid., p. 5.
[78] See Gheissari, *Iranian Intellectuals in the 20th Century*, chapters 3–5. On this theme and its myriad psychosocial configurations, see Arshin Adib-Moghaddam, *Psycho-nationalism: Global Thought, Iranian Imaginations* (Cambridge: Cambridge University Press, 2018).
[79] Ansari, *The Politics of Nationalism in Modern Iran*, p. 49.
[80] Nassereddin Parvin, "Irān-e Now," *Encyclopædia Iranica*, Vol. XIII, Fasc. 5 (December 15, 2006), pp. 498–500 (www.iranicaonline.org/articles/iran-e-now, last accessed September 15, 2019).

Two Modes of Liberalism

A representative article, entitled "We Are One Nation!," captures well the liberal spirit behind much of the paper's affectations:

> In the same manner that autocracy separated us from each other . . . liberty and the present constitutional rule . . . should inspire affection and unity among us . . . . Today our homeland, that suffering dear mother of all Iranians – be they Muslims, Jews, Armenians, Zoroastrians, Turks, or Persians – is calling upon all her children . . . to unite . . . . Iranians constitute a single nation, a nation that speaks in different dialects and worships God in different ways.[81]

Moreover, its trenchant criticisms of Anglo-Russian imperialisms were far ahead of its times in their advocacy of coalition-building among Eastern nations to assert their sovereign rights against foreign encroachments.[82] *Iran-e Now* was eventually forced to close down due to its opposition to the Russian occupation of the Azerbaijan region, but it played a pivotal role in the emergence of an alternative liberal discourse on nationalism that was to be improved on by later generations of liberals in the Pahlavi era and beyond.

A key aspect of the liberal project of weaving civic nationalism into the social fabric of Iranian society was the establishment of cultural and educational institutions as means of disseminating such ideals. Much like the founding of Dar al-Fonoun during the reign of Nasser al-Din Shah, the advancement of civic nationalist ideals through such institutions as the University of Tehran and Farhangestan under the direction of Pahlavi-era ministers served this purpose. The writer and three-time premier of Iran, Mohammad Ali Foroughi, was perhaps the most important proponent of the spread of liberal arts education and acculturation in this period.[83] For Foroughi, who also served as the founding director of Farhangestan, Iranian history and culture testified to the resilience of a diverse, inclusive, and even cosmopolitan heritage through the ages. Not only did Iranians not constitute a singular race (as the nativist imagination would have it), there also existed no such thing as a singular essence to Iranian national identity. Rather, what bound the nation together was a sense of shared history, whose coherent, unifying narratives could best be gleaned in the humanistic imagination of such

---

[81] *Iran-e Now* 1, 134 (February 16, 1910), p. 1.

[82] Afary, *The Iranian Constitutional Revolution*, pp. 282–283.

[83] For liberal underpinnings of Foroughi's thought, see Ali M. Ansari, "Mohammad Ali Foroughi and the Construction of Civic Nationalism in Early Twentieth-Century Iran," in H. E. Chehabi, Peyman Jafari, and Maral Jefroudi, eds., *Iran in the Middle East: Transnational Encounters and Social History* (London: I.B. Tauris & Co. Ltd., 2015), pp. 11–26; and Ansari, *The Politics of Nationalism in Modern Iran*, p. 100. For a great summation of Foroughi's views on nationalism, see ibid., pp. 100–109; Ramin Jahanbegloo, *Democracy in Iran* (New York: Palgrave Macmillan, 2013), pp. 14–15.

48   Aspects of Political Liberalism in Modern Iran

national treasures as the poets Hafez, Sa'di, Khayyam, and Ferdowsi.[84] Foroughi's non-essentialist views of national identity were echoed in the pages of intellectual journals of the time, most notably in *Ayandeh* and *Iranshahr*.[85]

These conceptions were of course concurrent with the advancement of state-building policies of Reza Shah whose investiture in nationalism was in no small measure driven by the imperatives of grounding his newly established monarchy in the founding myths and iconography of a monolithic civilizational identity (an effort replicated by his son Mohammad Reza Shah). For this reason, inclusive and non-essentialist conceptions of nationalism in this period cannot be considered in isolation from the cultural and political objectives of the Pahlavi regime that subsumed them. By the same token, the liberal substance behind such meticulous rearticulation of national myths cannot be dismissed so easily either.

Indeed, the import of this liberal conditioning became especially apparent in the period following the abdication of Reza Shah that ushered in a new era of parliamentary autonomy and increased tensions with Anglo-American interests in Iran. The populist movement for nationalization under Mosaddeq deftly mixed inclusive conceptions of national unity – as evidenced by the variegated ideological makeup of the National Front – with anti-imperialist sentiments to assert Iran's sovereign rights against financial and oil concessions arbitrarily signed by the Qajars. It is important to remember, however, that neither Mosaddeq nor his liberal fellow-travelers in this endeavor were of a fixed mind about Western interests in Iran. Mosaddeq was quite careful not to frame his confrontation with the Anglo-Iranian Oil Company (AIOC) as an eternal battle against an omnipotent British or Western imperialism. Rather, the struggle was in essence about Iran's rights as a sovereign country, and hence its implications for Iran's constitutional process. To this end, Mosaddeq and his coalition were keen on articulating and, indeed, dramatizing the literal

---

[84] Ansari attributes the contours of Foroughi's civic nationalism to his essentially "Whiggish" interpretation of history: "Change could only be constructively administered when a political culture was firmly and confidently anchored to its traditions: continuity begat change with a social contract (to paraphrase Edmund Burke) that looked to the past as well as the future. A lack of confidence in oneself and one's traditions obstructed a realistic diagnosis and hindered progress." Ansari, "Mohammad Ali Foroughi and the Construction of Civic Nationalism in Early Twentieth-Century Iran," p. 23.

[85] In the first volume of *Ayandeh* (edited by Mahmoud Afshar), Taqizadeh argued that "national unity" was foremost among "four pillars" – the other three were national security, reform of the bureaucracy by foreign experts, and reform of the general system by which government officials were elected – that would eventually secure the autonomy of the nation and set it upon a progressive path. *Ayandeh*, Vol. 1, No. 1 (1304/1925): 17–25.

legal substance and political spirit of self-government to their detractors through the dispute with the AIOC. The utility of a discourse of populist nationalism to this cause is lucidly explained by Ansari: "Nationalism and populism had its merits and uses, but the contest with Britain was a means to an end, not an end in itself ... it was important not to close any doors, not to be led by one's rhetoric, and not to be both confined and defined by a myth of anti-imperialism whose ultimate effect would be to emasculate not empower."[86]

Indeed, as noted in the previous section, Mosaddeq's legalistic approach to the problem of arbitrary agreements with foreign governments had its roots in his earlier legal dissection of Qajar-era "capitulation agreements" with Anglo-Russian interests. In each instance, the stated grievances were born out of the disregard for the legal rights of Iran and Iranian citizens, and as such were not merely the expression of reactionary nationalism. To the extent that reflexive nationalism had entered the political fray, it was a symptom and not a cause of Iran's woes. Mosaddeq's ultimate objective was to preserve the sanctity of the constitutional process inside Iran. The inequitable terms of agreement with the AIOC, after all, were significant for the manner in which they influenced Iran's domestic politics to the detriment of constitutionalist principles. By preserving the arbitrary privilege of a foreign entity over Iran's main natural asset and source of national income (i.e. oil), the status quo relationship with the AIOC would continue to privilege the role of arbitrary monarchs over that of Iranian citizens, thereby undercutting constitutional rights at home and prolonging its dependency on foreign powers.

As a prescriptive political project, this liberal nationalist vision must not be confused with other nativist or Third Worldist anti-imperial impulses evident at the time both inside Iran and in other parts of the world. Mosaddeq's struggles against the AIOC and the Shah served as a new metric for inclusive visions of nationalism to future generations of constitutionalist leaders and thinkers. This influence was most vividly evident in the political mission of the Liberation Movement of Iran whose founding members proudly proclaimed themselves as "Mosaddeqists" and espoused a similarly inclusive vision of nationalism. As Mehdi Bazargan noted in his declaration of the founding principles of the party, "Our love for Iran and our nationalism imply no racial fanaticism, and are on the contrary based on an acceptance of our own shortcomings and honoring

---

[86] Ansari, *The Politics of Nationalism in Modern Iran*, p. 135. Ansari quotes Mosaddeq imploring a crowd in 1951, "No, I will not have you say 'Death to Britain'; we want God to guide the British government to recognize our undoubted rights." Ibid.

50   Aspects of Political Liberalism in Modern Iran

of others' virtues and rights."[87] This conscious blending of loyalty to nation based on a fundamental commitment to the rights of all stands in stark contrast to nativist, Islamist (postrevolutionary), and communist visions of nationalism in the second half of the twentieth century. It exemplifies a major – if largely unacknowledged – shift in political consciousness about the priority of rights-based citizenship over imagined proclamations about Persian exceptionalism in discussions of national identity.

Constitutionalism

The Constitutional Revolution of 1906–1911 that sought to formally replace arbitrary rule with representative government was a complex, multidimensional historical phenomenon, and one whose ideological drivers continue to shape Iranian politics to this day. In the previous section I insinuated that for many liberals constitutionalism was regarded as a, if not *the*, cure for mitigating myriad maladies brought on by tradition, absolutism, and imperialism. Liberals such as Kermani and Malkum Khan took to heart Mill's assertion that the essence of constitutionalism was revealed in the "struggle between Liberty and Authority."[88] But far from confusing constitutionalism with liberalism, they viewed the former merely as an instrument for achieving a modern liberal society. Constitutionalism was a necessary but not sufficient ingredient for establishing representative government in Iran.[89] This recognition was reinforced by the multi-ideological character of the constitutional movement itself, which featured many political cohorts – the clergy, writers and artisans, liberal ministers, land-owning elites, and the merchant classes – who, despite their common calls for the rule of law and the establishment of a "house of justice," were in fact drawn to constitutionalism for different ends. Although these contradictions were soon exposed – most notably in the much-studied "mashruteh-versus-mashru'eh" constitutional struggles[90] – the liberal strategy to employ the neutral language of law remained consistent.

---

[87] Mehdi Bazargan, "Jaryan-e ta'sis-e nehzat-e Azadi-ye Iran," *Safahati az tarikh-e mo'aser-e Iran: Asnad-e nehzat-e Azadi-ye Iran* [A few pages from contemporary Iranian history: The documents of the Freedom Movement of Iran], Vol. 1, No. 1 (1982): 17.

[88] John Stuart Mill, *On Liberty and Other Writings*, ed. Stefan Collini (Cambridge: Cambridge University Press, 1989), p. 5.

[89] Adamiyat, *Ideoluzhi-ye Nehzat-e Mashrute-ye Iran*, pp. 205–206.

[90] For comprehensive overviews of this debates, see Mangol Bayat Philipp, *Iran's First Revolution: Shi'ism and the Constitutional Revolution of 1905–1909* (Oxford: Oxford University Press, 1991), chapter 8; and Afary, *The Iranian Constitutional Revolution*, chapter 4.

Two Modes of Liberalism 51

Strategic maneuverings notwithstanding, the essence of the liberal-constitutionalist project in Iran has long been the quest for basic rights and freedoms. In fact, what distinguishes liberal visions of constitutionalism most clearly from non-liberal prescriptions is the emphasis on the instrumental and intrinsic value of basic rights such as freedom of conscience, expression, assembly, and the rights to due process and property to the meaningful exercise of citizenship. In this regard, the liberal conception of constitutionalism in Iran, as Gheissari has noted, "was concerned not primarily with empowering the individual (in the sense inspired by the notion of liberty), but with placing limits on the arbitrary exercise of state authority and especially on the arbitrary application of law – thus demanding a unified legal system."[91] To this end, the liberal-constitutionalist project has been an iterative enterprise from the outset, based as it was on the failure of late nineteenth-century reformist attempts to modernize state administration and to place legal limits on the exercise of political authority.[92] For the purposes of intellectual genealogy, therefore, the Constitutional Revolution signifies neither the dawn nor the triumph of liberalism in Iran but a defining milestone in the form of a new political consciousness whose liberal underpinnings are perpetually in need of further elaboration.

Among the cohort of prominent liberals in this period, the political thought-practices of Malkum Khan and Mostashar al-Dowleh were especially notable. They both championed the rule of law as the basis for the establishment of representative government, even as each, in their respective ways, embodied an aristocratic liberalism premised on the guardianship of the learned and the well-connected. They were greatly influenced by the example of the French constitutionalist tradition as well as the practice of parliamentary politics in Britain, which in their estimation could only be replicated in Iran once a unified legal system and a modicum of civil and political rights were first realized. This was most clearly articulated in Mostashar al-Dowleh's work, *Yek Kalameh* [One Word],[93] which was a rumination on the 1789 Declaration of the Rights of Man and the 1791 French constitution.[94] In it he identified nineteen

---

[91] Ali Gheissari, "Constitutional Rights and the Development of Civil Law in Iran, 1907–41," in Chehabi and Martin, eds., *Iran's Constitutional Revolution*, p. 72.

[92] A lucid historical exegesis of this period is provided in Adamiyat, *Andishey-e Taraqi va Hokoumat-e Qanun*.

[93] For a recent translation in English, see A. A. Seyed-Gohrab and Sen McGlinn, eds., *One Word – Yek Kalameh: 19th Century Persian Treatise Introducing Western Codified Law* (Amsterdam: Leiden, 2010).

[94] Hadi Enayat echoes the judgment of most intellectual historians of Iran's constitutional movement when he refers to *Yek Kalameh* as "a foundational text in the discourse of liberal legality in Iran." Hadi Enayat, *Law, State, and Society in Modern Iran:*

52   Aspects of Political Liberalism in Modern Iran

principles that comprised the French constitutional tradition, and which, he argued, ought to guide Iranian liberal reformers in their mission to establish limited constitutional government. These included the universal (i.e. applicable to Muslims as well as non-Muslims) recognition of the aforementioned basic rights as well as general principles such as separation of powers, equality before the law, merit-based civil service, fiscal transparency, accountability through legal recourse, trial by jury, prohibition against cruel and unusual punishment, and universal primary education.[95]

Although the practice of constitutionalism proved short-lived, it achieved informal success by unfurling a new political consciousness and a vocabulary of struggle for rights, the rule of law, and representative government that continue to inform reformist and radical politics to this day. The liberal beginnings and substance of this political undercurrent cannot be denied, however much flawed, impressionable, or overly cautious its early proponents may have been.[96] This was a pragmatic liberalism that sought to assert liberal claims (e.g. justice, accountability, rights, legitimacy) against the state while being mindful of the myriad domestic- and foreign-induced factors that accounted for the disfigurement of the state in the first place (e.g. the prevalence of religious customs, invidious alliances between the crown and the clergy, widespread corruption, foreign meddling, etc.). Hence the early liberals' courting of the clerical establishment was intended to transform their role from that of obstacles to stakeholders in the cause of reform and progress.[97] This consideration meant that, as Gheissari has argued, the Constitutional Revolution "did not draw boundary lines between religion and politics," resulting in the inclusion of "religion in the emerging Iranian conception of democracy and national sovereignty."[98]

As a prescriptive model, the liberal vision of constitutionalism has accomplished more in the realm of political and legal thought than in practice. Its core and enduring achievements are the introduction of the very concept of "rule by consent" and the attendant set of civil and

---

Constitutionalism, Autocracy, and Legal Reform, 1906–1941 (New York: Palgrave Macmillan, 2013), p. 54.

[95] Mostashar al-Dowleh's nineteen points are best summarized in Adamaiyat, *Fekr-e Azadi*, pp. 189–193.

[96] As Bayat Philipp has noted, "the poet, the man of letters, the new breed of intellectual, as a result of the vital role played then and the national fame acquired, was able to ensure the triumph of his word over the mojtahed's, thus displacing the latter in public opinion." Bayat Philipp, *Iran's First Revolution*, p. 267.

[97] As Bayat Philipp notes further, "Politics demanded pragmatism and caution in breaking loose the ties with the religious culture." Ibid.

[98] Gheissari, "Constitutional Rights and the Development of Civil Law in Iran," p. 73.

Two Modes of Liberalism 53

political rights that are necessary for the meaningful discharge of that consent by the public. In the aftermath of the Constitutional Revolution, secular and religious attempts at conditioning popular consent on the divine rights of the ruler (i.e. the Shah and *vali-e faqih*, respectively) have necessarily found it difficult to reconcile those visions with a substantive set of liberal rights. Far from erasing these liberal precepts from political consideration, however, these autocratic models have unwittingly elevated liberal constitutionalism as the ideal yardstick against which advancements toward democratic government ought to be measured. This counterintuitive dynamic has in turn led to the further elaboration of liberal prescriptions around the concept of pluralism, which latter-day liberals have proposed as an ameliorative measure for achieving a more inclusive, explicitly rights-based political struggle against theocratic government in Iran.

Pluralism

Compared to the preceding antipathies and prescriptions, pluralism is of more recent vintage in liberal political thought generally, and particularly so in Iranian liberal thought. Its contemplation has primarily been instigated by the diffusion of liberal-democratic norms and values in the second half of the twentieth century, which at once facilitated inclusion and fostered new exclusionary forms. In standard accounts of modern liberalism, pluralism occupies a curious place given its unique status as both an empirical fact and an ethical value. As a fact, pluralism merely testifies to the varieties of human pursuits and beliefs. Society is made up of individuals and groups with different needs, desires, and belief systems, who may reasonably disagree about them and the ends they are meant to satisfy. In light of such "reasonable disagreements," liberal philosophical and political prescriptions have long been motivated by the imperative to, as the eminent liberal philosopher Charles Larmore has explained, "find principles of political association expressing certain fundamental moral values that, to as great an extent as possible, reasonable people may accept despite the different views about the good and about religious truth that divide them."[99]

As an ethical doctrine, pluralism is decidedly a more contentious matter, which political liberals such as Larmore and John Rawls find to be less of a complement to liberalism than a comprehensive doctrine with which one may reasonably disagree under a liberal political scheme. The

---

[99] Charles Larmore, *The Morals of Modernity* (Cambridge: Cambridge University Press, 1996), p. 154.

54   Aspects of Political Liberalism in Modern Iran

latter conception is closely associated with Berlin's reflections on the emergence of multiple objective views of the good against monistic notions – such as religious doctrine – which argued that ultimately the sources of the good life were one, not many. The ethical doctrine of pluralism, per Berlin's reading, attests to "a plurality of values, equally genuine, equally ultimate, above all equally objective; incapable, therefore, of being ordered in a timeless hierarchy, or judged in terms of some one absolute standard."[100] Far from advocating for the relativity of values, however, Berlin's point was that multiple objective (but not necessarily valid) views of a single good could well exist at the same time. The incommensurability of values that results from this multiplicity, therefore, behooves us to employ non-utopian accounts of human nature when proposing social and political institutions for achieving coexistence.

The distinction between pluralism as fact and as ethical doctrine is important to note because while the latter may be complimentary to liberalism, it is actually the former that necessitates the liberal principle of state neutrality in adjudicating between different values. This matters a great deal in the context of Iran because while a great many contemporary non-liberal thinkers – especially Islamic reformist intellectuals such as Abdolkarim Soroush, Alireza Alavi-Tabar, Hassan Youssefi-Eshkevari, and Mohammad Mojtahed Shabestari – endorse pluralism as an ethical doctrine, they do not ascribe to the state an impartial role when addressing reasonable disagreements.[101] What they seek, in brief, is the pluralistic *thought-practice of Islam* that allows for multiple interpretations of Islamic values and principles, but not a pluralistic *political system* in which Islam is merely one view among many competing for representation.[102] This cohort of thinkers is sometimes mistakenly referred to as "Islamic liberals," but the theological views espoused by them – as well as the reformist politics they have spawned – decidedly reject Islam's demotion to the level of other reasonable beliefs under a pluralistic political system. For this reason, this group can be more accurately described as "non-liberal Islamic democrats," whose toleration of disagreements in matters of governance goes only so far.

Notwithstanding this common confusion, although pluralism has been instrumental in the development of liberal thought in Iran since the dawn

---

[100] Isaiah Berlin, *The Crooked Timber of Humanity* (Princeton, NJ: Princeton University Press, 1998), p. 79.

[101] For a fuller discussion of this point, see Chapter 4.

[102] The two can certainly overlap and merge, as indeed it seemed they would during the first outburst of reformist ideas in the late 1990s. For an encapsulation of this moment, see Arshin Adib-Moghaddam, "The pluralistic Momentum in Iran and the Future of the Reform Movement," *Third World Quarterly*, Vol. 27, No. 4 (2006): 665–674.

Two Modes of Liberalism

of constitutionalism, it did not discernibly emerge as a prescriptive project until the 1990s.[103] Among Iranian intellectuals, Ramin Jahanbegloo is unique in his singular focus on the implications of pluralism as both fact and ethical doctrine inside Iran. In a series of written works, public talks, interviews, and conversations (most notably with Berlin himself) he has over the years not only chronicled and publicized the emerging currents of liberal thought in Iranian intellectual circles, but has himself been a central interlocutor between Western and Iranian liberal thought.[104] A major milestone in recent intellectual debates among Iranian political thinkers, according to Jahanbegloo, is the widespread recognition of pluralism as a means of overcoming staid monistic thought-practices that culminate in autocracy. As he puts it,

Unlike previous generations of Iranian intellectuals, the critical thinking of modernity has taught the new generation to adopt a general attitude of being at odds both with "fundamentalist politics" and with "utopian rationalities." This philosophical wariness is not joined to any kind of dream of totally rearranging Iranian society. The intervention here reflects not only the pluralistic mechanisms of politics but also the political self.[105]

The embrace of pluralism among contemporary intellectuals, Jahanbegloo believes, is born out of "two main philosophical attitudes: the extension of anti-utopian thinking on the one hand, and the urge for a non-imitative dialogical exchange with the modern West on the other."[106] These attitudes have helped to carve out an intellectual space for discussions of state neutrality, secularism, and religious belief in a manner that treats each as reasonable doctrines in need of reconciliation with its counterparts, and not merely perpetuating monistic adherence to one.[107]

---

[103] As demonstrated in Chapters 3 and 4, religious pluralism has a longer history and overlaps considerably with a secular conception of pluralism preferred by liberal thinkers. In any event, for reasons of clarity and cohesion, I shall only focus on the more contemporary usages of pluralism (ca. 1990s) since it is this period that pluralism as both an empirical and normative matter is taken up by Iranian intellectuals of both religious and secular persuasion.

[104] For representative works in English, see Ramin Jahanbegloo and Isaiah Berlin, *Recollections of a Historian of Ideas: Conversations with Isaiah Berlin* (New York: Charles Scriber's Sons, 1991); Ramin Jahanbegloo, ed., *Iran: Between Tradition and Modernity* (Lanham, MD: Lexington Books, 2004); Ramin Jahanbegloo, ed., *Civil Society and Democracy in Iran* (Lanham, MD: Lexington Books, 2012); and Jahanbegloo, *Democracy in Iran*.

[105] Ramin Jahanbegloo, "Two Concepts of Secularism," *Comparative Studies of South Asia, Africa, and the Middle East*, Vol. 31, No. 1 (2011): 18.

[106] Interview in Danny Postel, *Reading Legitimation Crisis in Tehran: Iran and the Future of Liberalism* (Chicago, IL: Prickly Paradigm Press, 2006), p. 88.

[107] This is certainly evident in the works of contemporary Iranian intellectuals Javad Tabatabai, Babak Ahmadi, Hamid Azodanloo, Moosa Ghaninejad, and Nasser

56   Aspects of Political Liberalism in Modern Iran

More than a chronicler of this shift, however, Jahanbegloo himself has been a key advocate of pluralism as a gateway to a more inclusive, just, and nonviolent politics.[108] In articulating this position, he has been especially adept at combining Berlin's insights on pluralism with Gandhian concerns for nonviolence into a coherent, nonutopian prescription for addressing political maladies in Iran. He notes, "To engage in nonviolent politics means the impossibility of finding perfect solutions; hence there will always be a price to pay. What remains essential here is a new culture of citizenship in Iran liberating itself from a monolithic and closed discourse that denies plural ways of discovering and building truth."[109] It is notable that for Jahanbegloo pluralism does not register merely as a fact that necessitates liberal solutions. Rather, he conceives of pluralism as a normative project that ought to be constantly urged and justified on account of its contributions to establishing a nonviolent public sphere in Iran. Moreover, Jahanbegloo's conception is representative of a characteristically non-Western liberalism that is not fixated on establishing hard and fast criteria for "rational discourse" or "reasonableness" in the absence of inclusive and accountable public institutions and norms.[110] As such, his own views embody a pluralism of values that take seriously the criticisms leveled at the Anglo-American liberal tradition by radical, agonistic, communitarian, and cosmopolitan liberals, for whom the lifeblood of democracy is a vibrant and resilient pluralistic public sphere.[111]

The emphasis on pluralism and a free public sphere can also be found in recent works by Ali Mirsepassi, whose reflections on the ongoing debates within and between secular-democratic, religious-democratic, and antidemocratic intellectuals inside Iran have culminated in the advocacy of a liberal-pragmatist pluralism especially inspired by the works of American pragmatists John Dewey and Richard Rorty. In contrast to

---

Fakouhi, whom Jahanbegloo identifies as exemplifying the philosophical predilections identified above.

[108] Ramin Jahanbegloo, *The Gandhian Moment* (Cambridge, MA: Harvard University Press, 2013).

[109] Jahanbegloo, *Democracy in Iran*, p. 96.

[110] For example, see Hashemi, *Islam, Secularism, and Liberal Democracy*; for an incisive reflection on the fluidity of liberal interpretations of these criteria in Iran, see Arshin Adib-Moghaddam, "Islamic Secularism and the Question of Freedom," in Faisal Devji and Zaheer Kazmi, eds., *Islam after Liberalism* (New York: Oxford University Press, 2017), pp. 189–202.

[111] See Chantal Mouffe, *The Democratic Paradox* (London: Verso, 2000); Pierre Rosanvallon, *Democracy Past and Present*, ed. Samuel Moyn (New York: Columbia University Press, 2006); Charles Taylor, *Multiculturalism: Examining the Politics of Recognition*, ed. Amy Gutmann (Princeton, NJ: Princeton University Press, 1994); and Seyla Benhabib, *The Claims of Culture: Equality and Diversity in the Global Era* (Princeton, NJ: Princeton University Press, 2002).

Two Modes of Liberalism 57

Jahanbegloo and most other Iranian intellectuals' focus on political or philosophical approaches to pluralism, Mirsepassi advocates for liberal-democratic politics from a largely sociological perspective. Pushing back against non-liberal Islamic-reformist perspectives, he argues: "To have a complete liberal-democratic system, one has to desacralize all spheres of politics .... [Since] if any element of government, leaders, ideologies, institutions, laws, and the like, is invested with the aura of the sacred, it cannot claim to have come from the will of the people."[112] Such a process, Mirsepassi specifies, requires the complete "desacralization of political discourse" and "desacralization of political institutions" so that a truly pluralistic public sphere may emerge. The emphasis on "desacralization" as *process* is especially notable because of the value it attaches to human agency – as opposed to structures and systems of thought – in bringing these changes about. Ultimately, the evolution of any political system depends upon the actions of citizens subjected to its ways and means, not political ideas about their melioration (of which there is often an ample supply).

Given the fact that both Mirsepassi and Jahanbegloo do not outright identify their positions as liberal ones ("cosmopolitanism" is their preferred moniker) and, indeed, only sparingly employ technical liberal terminology (e.g. "public reason," "overlapping consensus," "rational dialogue," "individualism," etc.), it may be asked whether their respective positions on pluralism can properly be identified as liberal. My classification of their interventions on pluralism as essentially liberal is based on the premise on which their cosmopolitan views rest, namely, the bedrock liberal principle of *equal respect for persons*. The moral principle of equal respect for persons reflects the Kantian rule that individuals must treat one another not merely as means toward a specified goal but as ends – "as persons in their own right."[113] Without the recognition of this principle, pluralism and an inclusive public sphere can neither be realized nor sustained. More importantly, "reasonable disagreement" as the basis of pluralism – that is, that individuals may disagree without wishing to eliminate one another from the public sphere – is only possible when the moral worth of individuals is recognized fully and equally. As Larmore makes clear, "Respect for persons must be considered as a norm binding on us independent of our will as citizens, enjoying a moral authority that we cannot fashion for ourselves. For only on its basis can we account for why we are moved to give our political existence the consensual shape it is

---

[112] Mirsepassi, *Democracy in Modern Iran*, p. 101.
[113] Charles Larmore, "Political Liberalism," *Political Theory*, Vol. 18, No. 3 (1990): 348.

58   Aspects of Political Liberalism in Modern Iran

meant to have."[114] Indeed, it is this assumption that underpins much philosophical and sociological prescriptive writings on pluralism among liberal Iranian thinkers today.

Conclusion

What I have endeavored to demonstrate in the preceding is an outline of the basic aspects of liberal political thought in Iran. I have done so by, following Ryan's schematic, classifying these aspects into what Iranian liberals have broadly rejected – traditionalism, absolutism, and imperialism – and the normative political projects they have proposed – liberal nationalism, constitutionalism, and pluralism – in order to redress the effects of a range of domestic and foreign maladies. In this regard, I have been interested less in forcing various political thinkers and actors into liberal straitjackets, and even much less so in identifying a liberal canon. Such an endeavor not only would obscure more than clarify about the tortuous path of liberalism in Iran, but it would also give the false impression of a self-conscious, programmatic, and sustained liberal project the likes of which has never actually existed in Iran. Rather, my aim in the foregoing exposition has been far limited in scope: to identify *aspects* of political thinking and action that attest to the imprint of liberal ideas on Iran's political development and intellectual discourse. Furthermore, I have been mainly interested in highlighting the inaugural or most impactful expressions of these aspects in written works by Iranian public figures. As such, with the exception of the section on pluralism, this has largely been an exercise in late nineteenth- and early twentieth-century intellectual analysis, given the origins and heavy circulation of these ideas in those periods.

More importantly, the preceding is strictly a consideration of the *political* aspects of liberalism in Iran; I deliberately eschew any discussion of economic, cultural, or social aspects of liberalism here. This is not due to the lack of historical evidence or intellectual debates in these areas – reflections on private property, the importance of trade and commerce, and state-market relations are as abundant as considerations of gender, sexual politics, education, and health in the thought-practices of liberal thinkers. It is my hope that the combination of the contextual and analytical approach used here to examine liberal political ideas has both utility and implications for similar investigations of aspects of liberal thought in those areas, which for the sake of analytical clarity I have not included here. Liberalism is a capacious and dynamic family of ideas, norms, and

---

[114] Charles Larmore, *The Autonomy of Morality* (Cambridge: Cambridge University Press, 2008), p. 150.

Conclusion

practices whose confidence and faith in the capacity of individuals for reasoning and self-examination have yielded a set of principles in various domains of human life. That the political aspects identified above have been subject to constant historical excavation, reexamination, and new articulation suggests a need for scholarly reference points that might better aid us in understanding their future reinventions.

3 The Specter of Westernism

The occidentotic hangs on the words and handouts of the West.[1]

We accept popular rule, and we accept freedom. But we do not accept liberal democracy.[2]

To achieve recognition is to rechart and then occupy the place in imperial cultural forms reserved for subordination, to occupy it self-consciously, fighting for it on the very same territory once ruled by a consciousness that assumed the subordination of a designated inferior Other.[3]

Introduction

The aspects of political liberalism surveyed in Chapter 2 have for the most part evolved from the encounter between Iranian intellectuals and varieties of Western modernity over the course of the last century and a half. To be sure, these engagements have spawned myriad organic iterations of principles and practices more attuned to the vicissitudes of internal Iranian concerns and aspirations. But the diffusion and development of liberal ideas in Iran have been primarily spurred by the dialectic with *Western* discourses and practices. Like any such encounters, the process of hybridization – ranging from blind imitation to genial dialogue to rigorous critique – is necessarily conditioned by the prevailing orders and customs that naturally assume an oppositional posture toward any ideas that would undermine their legitimacy or authority. In the postcolonial context, of course, such struggles are additionally burdened by the history of persistent Western imperial meddling in, and the subjugation of, local affairs. Native purveyors of modernist views and their interlocutors,

---

[1] Jalal Al-e Ahmad, *Occidentosis: A Plague from the West* (Berkeley, CA: Mizan Press, 1984), p. 97.

[2] Seyyed Ali Khamenei, "Remarks to the Members of the Basij in Kermanshah Province," October 14, 2011 (http://farsi.khamenei.ir/newspart-index?tid=1703#14379, last accessed June 6, 2018).

[3] Said, *Culture and Imperialism*, p. 210.

Introduction   61

therefore, have had to contend with charges of "Westernism" or, as in the
case of Iranian liberal intellectuals, *gharbzadegi* ("Westoxication" or
"Occidentosis") – an indictment, at once, of cultural backwardness,
intellectual inauthenticity, and political betrayal – when asserting their
claims against nativist and traditional viewpoints.[4]

The burden carried by Iranian liberals has been especially acute given
the instrumentalization of Western liberalism as a global "standard of
civilization," which in its various iterations since the nineteenth century
remained more of a normative disguise for naked imperial control of those
parts of the globe deemed strategically important to Western powers than
a principled facilitation of representative institutions and human rights
abroad.[5] Indeed, suspicion of the (un)intended consequences of liberal
reforms for Iran's independence and relations vis-à-vis the West is
a constant theme in works by liberal and non-liberal Iranian intellectuals
alike. As recounted in Chapter 2, the history of repeated Russian, British,
and American interference, sabotage, and even military occupation of
Iran is the sole reason behind the development of anti-imperialist and
nationalist strands of thought by Iranian liberals. But much more than the
constrictions imposed by the imperial context, the chief burden carried by
Iranian liberals has been the charge that their ideology constitutes the very
essence of what it means to be Western, and hence of Westernism.
Liberalism, these critics have alleged, is but a vessel for transplanting
unfettered individualism, secularism, materialism, and capitalism – the
very hallmarks of Western modernity – at the expense of Perso-Islamic
traditions and values. The immensely consequential imprint of this critical discourse on Iran's political development in the course of the twentieth century cannot be overstated. The charge of Westernism tilted the
axis of intellectual engagement toward defiantly anti-Western philosophies and commitments, whose ultimate triumph culminated in the

---

[4] Throughout this chapter, I will be using the term "Westernism" as a blanket concept
encompassing both the descriptive notion of a person engaged with/by Western ideas and
the more normative classification denoting the loss of authentic identity due to personal
infatuation with Western ideas and mannerisms (i.e. "Westoxication" or "Occidentosis").
I will only use the term "Westoxication" (*gharbzadegi*, in Persian) when specifically
referring to the conceptual framework advanced by the mid-twentieth-century cohort of
Iranian intellectuals who developed and popularized it as a term of abuse as well as
a disciplinary tool. I shall use the term "Westoxication" instead of "Westox*ification*"
since the former comes closer to attesting to a conceptual framework, a condition, and
a disciplinary tool – which in my estimation is a closer approximation of its function and
rhetorical intention – whereas the latter may infer an ongoing process of uncertain origins
or ends. The existing scholarly literature on the subject uses both spellings/terms.

[5] On this point, see Erez Manela, *The Wilsonian Moment: Self-determination and the
International Origins of Anticolonial Nationalism* (New York: Oxford University Press,
2007), chapters 7–10.

62   The Specter of Westernism

broad-based support for revolution in 1979 that birthed the Islamic Republic.

Yet curiously enough, although this sustained line of critique – the discourse of *gharbzadegi* – has been comprehensively studied in terms of its substance and intellectual trajectory (especially in relation to appropriations of Western Marxism and its fusion with Shia theology), its implications for liberal thought-practices remain glaringly underexplored.[6] The aim of this chapter is to remedy this oversight by recasting the critique of Westernism as not a broad rejection of Western modernity per se (since many of its adherents had appropriated conservative or radical Western ideologies in their arguments), but in fact as a particularly potent anti-liberal doctrine. Westoxication's allure to a diverse cohort of mid-twentieth -century Iranian intellectuals, I maintain, lay in its dismissal of a reading of Western progress that credited its milestones specifically to the unleashing of liberal rights, institutions, and ideals. Indeed, a shared antipathy toward liberalism was the definitive tie that bound Islamic and Marxist ideologies together, and which resulted in the marginalization of liberals and social democrats after the coup d'état that toppled Mohammad Mosaddeq's liberal-nationalist government in 1953. The campaign against liberalism was immensely aided by Mohammad Reza Shah's adoption of selective liberal social reforms – dubbed the White Revolution – as part of his hasty attempt to modernize Iran. But the implementation of these reforms in the absence of any meaningful political reforms only served to further cement the impression of liberalism, especially among the religious forces, as a companion to Western-backed autocracy.

This chapter will offer a critical examination of the origins and evolution of the opposition to liberalism as the ostensible ideology of Westoxication. This history will be traced back to the late nineteenth-century emergence of a binary between Westernism and Islamism in the political thought of Seyyed Jamal al-Din al-Afghani, and soon after in the political jeremiads of the anti-constitutionalist cleric Sheikh Fazlollah Nuri, whose rise and demise (by execution) have been mythologized to great effect by anti-liberal nativist and Islamist thinkers. In the second section, I provide a descriptive account of the state-directed modernization-cum-liberalization programs under the Pahlavi monarchy. This historical background sets the stage, in the third section, for an examination of the discourse of Westoxication and the anti-modern turn in post–World War II intellectual debates inside Iran. In particular, my aim is to

---

[6] One exception is the very recent work by Mirsepassi, *Transnationalism in Iranian Political Thought*. But even here, Mirsepassi's concerns are centered more on a critique of Westoxication as an inherently anti-modernist discourse than a specifically anti-liberal one, as is my focus here.

The Emergence of "Westernism" as a Binary Concern   63

reclassify the arguments of its foremost interlocutors – Seyyed Fakhroddin Shadman, Ahmad Fardid, Ali Shariati, and Jalal Al-e Ahmad – in a more analytically coherent fashion. The recasting of the terms of debate between these figures and their detractors, I hope, will make clear how the intellectual capture of oppositional politics by the discourse of Westoxication, more than any other factor, resulted in the marginalization of liberal lines of thought inside Iran. The concluding section will relate these arguments to the advent of the Islamic Republic and its concomitant ideology – "Khomeinism" – which for over four decades has positioned itself most defiantly against liberalism from within and without.

Afghani, Nuri, and the Emergence of "Westernism" as a Binary Concern

The first systematic preoccupation with "Westernism" as a potentially invidious politico-cultural influence in Iran appeared in the political thought of Jamal al-Din al-Afghani (1838–1898). The itinerant life of Afghani – born in Asadabad near Hamadan in Iran, educated and politically awakened in India, and thereafter an intermittent traveler-resident in Afghanistan, Iraq, Persia, Constantinople, Egypt, Britain, France, Russia, among other places – has been well-studied and reflected upon by scholars and cultural critics for some time.[7] Owing largely to his travels, Afghani was exposed from a young age to both the contingencies and the patterns that marked Muslim societies' encounters with modernist ideas flowing in from Western societies. His earlier reflections on these matters were indeed similar to those of other Iranian intellectuals, which consisted mostly of liberal antipathies against tradition, autocracy, and imperialism (as recounted in Chapter 2). He was especially convinced of the imperative of modernization in scientific, technological, and educational fields, and viewed Western progress in these areas as a model for Muslim societies. But as new liberal ideas increasingly captured the imagination of the ruling classes and the intelligentsia – who mostly wished to imitate or import them wholesale – Afghani gleaned a particularly insidious commensurability

---

[7] The most authoritative among these are Keddie, *Sayyid Jamal al-Din al-Afghani*; Keddie, *An Islamic Response to Imperialism*; and chapter 5 in Hourani, *Arabic Thought in the Liberal Age*. See also Eli Kedouri, *Afghani and 'Abduh: An Essay on Religious Unbelief and Political Activism in Modern Islam* (London: Frank Cass Co. Ltd., 1997); Rudi Matthee, "Jamal al-Din al-Afghani and the Egyptian National Debate," *International Journal of Middle East Studies*, Vol. 21, No. 2 (1989): 151–169. For a consideration of Afghani's thought in comparative political theory, see Roxanne L. Euben, *Enemy in the Mirror: Islamic Fundamentalism and the Limits of Modern Rationalism* (Princeton, NJ: Princeton University Press, 1999), pp. 96–105. For a recent reading of Afghani as the founding figure of transnational political Islam, see Mishra, *From the Ruins of Empire*, chapter 2.

64   The Specter of Westernism

between autocracy and imperialism. Blind imitation of Western ideas, to Afghani, was precisely the mode of exchange preferred by the British, French, and Russian imperialists, for it nourished a politics of dependency premised on native inadequacy and backwardness. Indeed, as Roxanne Euben has noted, these views testified to "the tension that defined his life: the repudiation of Western imperialism in all its forms and the conviction that Western rationalist methods and the technological and scientific expertise they produced were necessary for political strength and for the survival of the Islamic community."[8]

In his speeches and political writings, Afghani implored audiences to become aware of the fact that "the decay of the Muslim *umma* (community) and its manifest weakness in relation to European ascendance are inextricably tied to the neglect of science and philosophy."[9] To him, Western imperialism was a by-product of European advances in science and technology. As he noted in a famous lecture in Calcutta in 1882, "The Europeans have now put their hands on every part of the world. The English have reached Afghanistan; the French have seized Tunisia. In reality this usurpation, aggression, and conquest have not come from the French or the English. Rather it is science that everywhere manifests its greatness and power."[10] But unlike his anti-traditionalist counterpart Akhundzadeh, he did not regard the Arab roots and linguistic imprint on Islam to be the sources of the problem. To the contrary, he regarded the rationalist contributions of Muslim scientists and philosophers such as Ibn Bajja, Ibn Rushd (Averroes), Ibn Tufayl, and Ibn Sina (Avicenna) to be representative of the commensurability of rational thought and Islamic doctrine, as well as exemplars of indigenous capacities for scientific advancements independent of Western control.[11] The modernization of Islamic thought and practice, Afghani came to believe, was the last great hope for protecting the civilizational integrity and political autonomy of Muslim lands against Western imperial designs. In this effort, the instruments of Western modernity – science, philosophy, and technology – must be appropriated, not in order to replicate Western cultural and political institutions, but to aid the development of Islamic civilization. As Albert Hourani argued, the "novelty" of Afghani's views is in the "new emphasis" placed on Islam itself: "The center of attention

---

[8] Euben, *Enemy in the Mirror*, p. 97.   [9] Ibid.

[10] Sayyid Jamal al-Din al-Afghani, "Lecture on Teaching and Learning," in Keddie, *An Islamic Response to Imperialism*, p. 102.

[11] Ibid., pp. 101–108. See Afghani's response to Ernest Renan in Sayyid Jamal al-Din al-Afghani, "Answer of Jamal al-Din to Renan," in Keddie, *An Islamic Response to Imperialism*, pp. 181–187.

The Emergence of "Westernism" as a Binary Concern 65

is no longer Islam as a religion, it is rather Islam as a civilization."[12] Indeed, the resulting "Pan-Islamic" vision of unity against imperialism was to be Afghani's singular, and highly consequential, contribution to the course of political developments in all the lands he took residence in or sought to influence from afar.

Having observed firsthand the depredations of British imperialism in India (just prior to the "Mutiny" of 1957), and the enabling weakness and corruption of dynastic rulers from Herat to Istanbul, he had become keenly aware of the internal political limits of progress in Muslim societies. At the time, the transfer of scientific knowledge and technical expertise were premised on long-term guarantees of uneven profit for Western enterprises. Case in point was a string of lucrative concessions in Iran to British and Russian business interests, which effectively granted them immense economic and political sway over Iranian society.[13] Afghani viewed the willful profligacy and ignorance of the Qajar elite – especially that of the reigning monarch Naser al-Din Shah and his chief minister Amin al-Sultan – as the main reason behind foreign exploitation. Interestingly, he had on numerous occasions (both inside the country and abroad) been invited to share his reformist views with the Shah, but each time had disappointed the monarch by his grandiose views of Islamic unity and insistence on radical curtailment of royal powers. After falling to royal disfavor, Afghani's obstinacy in denouncing the Shah in fiery speeches and articles raised his profile as a dissident and led to his taking *bast* (sanctuary) at the shrine of Shah Abdol-Aziz in Tehran. In a provocative move, the Shah issued a royal decree to violate the sanctity of the shrine and have Afghani unceremoniously removed, whereupon he was escorted on horseback to the Turkish border.

While in exile, Afghani played an especially critical role in the tobacco protests of 1891–1892 that followed the ill-conceived decision by the Shah to grant a full monopoly over the cultivation, sale, and export of tobacco to the British-owned Tobacco Régie.[14] He took to encouraging

---

[12] Hourani, *Arabic Thought in the Liberal Age*, p. 114.

[13] Of these agreements, the most sweeping and exploitative was the Reuter concession signed in 1872 between the British banker Baron Julius de Reuter and Naser al-Din Shah. The concession granted Reuter exclusive rights to developing Iran's roads, telegraph, industrial capacities, public works projects, and the extraction of Iran's natural resources. The agreement generated mass opposition and was even met with resistance in the British government, and as such was cancelled by the Shah. A second Reuter concession, however, resulted in the establishment of the Imperial Bank of Persia, continuing, as the historian Abbas Amanat has noted, the "unreserved exploitation" of Iran by "large-scale Western capital." See Amanat, *Iran*, pp. 283–288. For an historical overview of concessions in Iran, see Mansoureh Ettehadieh [Nezam Mafi, pseud.], "Concessions (*Emtīāzāt*)," *Encyclopædia Iranica*, Vol. VI, Fasc. 2 (October 28, 2011), pp. 119–122.

[14] For a detailed historical account of the Tobacco Régie, see Lambton, *Qajar Persia*, chapter 8.

66   The Specter of Westernism

religious authorities to publicly denounce the Shah and issue fatwas calling for the boycott of tobacco inside Iran.[15] In a letter to the chief mujtahid, Mirza Hasan Shirazi, Afghani, as he was wont to do in nearly all his political pronouncements, raised the imperative of religious duty in boycotting the Régie: "... this criminal [the Shah] has offered the provinces of the Persian land to auction amongst the Powers [Britain and Russia], and is selling the realms of Islam and the abodes of Muhammad and his household ... to foreigners."[16] Shirazi obliged, and a fatwa forbidding the use of tobacco was summarily issued, likening it "to combatting the Imam of the Age, may God hasten his return."[17] The political effect of the edict was immediate as a nationwide boycott of tobacco products even extended into the Shah's harem. The galvanizing of religious duty proved to be the decisive blow, forcing the Shah to cancel the concession within a year.[18]

Concurrent with these developments, Afghani also sought to shape elite opinion abroad (especially in Britain) about the despotism of the Shah and his ministers. In an open letter published in Britain, suggestively titled "The Reign of Terror in Persia," Afghani offered a highly polemical catalog of economic and political mismanagement under Naser al-Din and made special note of the fact that "after each visit of the Shah to Europe he increased in tyranny."[19] He then cautioned the British elite on the implications of British hypocrisy in urging on the Shah to respect the rights of his subjects while also using him as a vessel for exploitation:

England does not know what a blow is being dealt to her prestige in the East .... You gaped at the Shah, he was amusing as a novelty. But the Persian people you exploit. Still it is not believable to them that England intends to do nothing, not so much as lift her voice – England, so ready to help Garibaldi – so willing to sacrifice untold wealth in order to put down the slave trade. Yet England refuses a word of remonstrance or advice when the firman [an earlier proclamation, which the Shah was effectively ordered by British ministers to issue, guaranteeing the security of

---

[15] For more on the intersection of religion and anti-imperial agitations in this episode, see Nikki R. Keddie, *Religion and Rebellion in Iran: The Tobacco Protest of 1891–92* (London: Frank Cass & Co. Ltd., 1966); and Mansoor Moaddel, "Shi'i Political Discourse and Class Mobilization in the Tobacco Movement of 1890–1892," *Sociological Forum*, Vol. 7, No. 3 (September 1992): 447–468.

[16] Sayyid Jamal al-Din al-Afghani, "Letter to the Chief Mujtahid [Mirza Hasan Shirazi], Written from Basra to Samara," in Browne, *The Persian Revolution of 1905–1909*, p. 19.

[17] Amanat, *Iran*, p. 309.

[18] Lambton's observation that "it was probably largely the call to rally to the defence of Islam which moved the people action" has indeed become the consensus view among historians of Iran. See Lambton, *Qajar Persia*, p. 275.

[19] Sayyid Jamal al-Din al-Afghani, "The Reign of Terror in Persia," *The Contemporary Review*, LXI (1892), p. 245.

The Emergence of "Westernism" as a Binary Concern   67

life and property of his subjects] to which she has been made a party through communication is torn to pieces before her eyes.[20]

Although the shape and content of Afghani's remarks on British hypocrisy can, in the parlance of our times, be read as little more than a rhetorical invitation to hasten "regime change" inside Iran,[21] they are in fact a judicious indictment of the consequences of British imperialism. Like many of his contemporaries, Afghani was especially adept at the art of political doublespeak to suit his purposes. His objective in this case was to bring into public view the concrete ways in which British support of the Shah was complicit in the daily humiliations visited upon Iranian subjects, but especially the denigration of religious authorities and dissidents whom the British press had done much to vilify in contrast to the many encomiums about the Shah. Indeed, this emphasis is what distinguished Afghani from other dissident exiles such as Malkum Khan in this period, whose doublespeak was aimed more at cajoling the religious establishment into endorsing secular constitutionalist principles. Although Afghani, too, was a prominent advocate of reform and constitutionalism, there is no mistaking his more religiously infused vision from those of secular-minded intellectuals such as Malkum Khan and Mostashar al-Dowleh.

For this reason, Afghani's role in the tobacco revolt did more than activate religious rhetoric. It carved out a new political role for the clergy as the omnipresent check against the excesses of the Shah. As Abbas Amanat has observed, in the religious jeremiads leading up to the cancellation of the Régie, Naser al-Din Shah was

held culpable for undermining the equally ancient, equally Persian, tradition of harmony between the twin pillars of sociopolitical stability – the state and the good faith. The shah was blamed by the 'ulama primarily for allowing foreign intrusion into the Guarded Domains, an incidence of neglect that in their eyes, as in the eyes of their traditional or tactical allies, was tantamount to a serious breach of the most important royal duty – the defense of the kingdom and the faith.[22]

Afghani's contributions in reasserting the oversight role of the clergy in this period cannot be overstated. His two-pronged strategy of recalibrating Islamic theology through appeals to modern reason and depicting Western-backed despotism as locked in a zero-sum struggle against

---

[20] Ibid., pp. 245–246 (emphasis in the original).
[21] He implores the British at the end of his remarks to endorse and help realize the protest chant "Change the Government, or Dethrone the Shah!" Ibid., p. 248.
[22] Abbas Amanat, *Pivot of the Universe: Naser al-Din Shah Qajar and the Iranian Monarchy, 1831–1896* (Berkeley, CA: University of California Press, 1997), p. 413.

68   The Specter of Westernism

Islamic identity created an autonomous political space for religious activism not only in Iran but across the Islamic world.[23]

More importantly, Afghani's would become the template for political action among the conservative and anti-liberal-constitutionalist ulama from the Constitutional Revolution onward. Once the role of the clergy as the true "Guardians of the Sacred Domains" had been established, the axis of political action would always turn on whose interpretation of Islam is more in keeping with the safe guardianship of the faith. Inevitably, this has meant the empowerment of reactionary and ultraconservative forces above pragmatic and reform-minded ones from the twilight years of the Qajar dynasty to this day. After Afghani's death, the pattern of lamenting the pursuit of European-inspired constitutionalism in Iran on grounds of its threat to Islam and its "sacred laws" first appeared in the political agitations of the anti-constitutionalist cleric Sheikh Fazlollah Nuri. Shortly after the introduction of parliamentary government, in the early months of the Constitutional Revolution (1906–1911), Nuri likened constitutionalism to "the inauguration of the customs and practices of the realms of infidelity," and declared it a religious duty to safeguard "the citadel of Islam against the deviations willed by the heretics and the apostates."[24] The latter group included secular intellectuals as well as the pro-constitutionalist ulama – led by Sayyed Abdollah Behbahani and Sayyed Mohammad Tabatabaie – whose support for constitutionalism was premised precisely on the protection of the faith from the inevitable corruptions of worldly powers and politics. To Nuri and his supporters, the constitutional guarantees for individual (male) liberty, for equal rights of ethnic and religious minorities, for freedom of the press and assembly, and above all the authority invested in a parliament and an independent judiciary untethered to religion – each and all amounted to the imposition of Western institutions and customs over Islamic ones.[25] As Nuri complained in his newsletter of the atmospherics surrounding the early

---

[23] According to Browne, Afghani "probably influenced the course of events in the Muhammadan East more than any other of his contemporaries." Browne, *The Persian Revolution of 1905–1909*, p. 12.

[24] Mohammad-Esmail Rezvani, "Ruznameh-ye Sheikh Fazlollah Nuri," *Tarikh I*, No. 2 (1977): 168–169. Translation used here appears in Said Amir Arjomand, "The 'Ulama's Traditionalist Opposition to Parliamentarianism: 1907–1909," *Middle Eastern Studies*, Vol. 17, No. 2 (1981): 180.

[25] For an in-depth analytical dissection of traditionalist clerics' opposition to constitutionalism, see Arjomand, "The 'Ulama's Traditionalist Opposition to Parliamentarianism"; Afary, *The Iranian Constitutional Revolution*, chapter 4; Bayat Philipp, *Iran's First Revolution*, chapters 8 and 9; Vanessa Martin, *Islam and Modernism: The Iranian Revolution of 1906* (London: I.B. Tauris & Co. Ltd., 1989); and Vanessa Martin, *Iran between Nationalism and Secularism: The Constitutional Revolution of 1906* (London: I.B. Tauris & Co. Ltd., 2013), chapter 2.

The Emergence of "Westernism" as a Binary Concern 69

drafting of the constitution, "Fireworks, receptions of the ambassadors, those foreign habits, the crying of hurrah, all those inscriptions of . . . Long Live [Liberty,] Equality, Fraternity. Why not write on them: Long Live the Sacred Law, Long Live the Qur'an, Long Live Islam?"[26] Indeed, upon portraying liberal constitutionalism as an affront to Islam, Nuri formally allied himself with the new Qajar monarch, Mohammad Ali Shah, who staged a coup (with assistance from Imperial Russia) against the parliament and restored arbitrary rule in 1907. In little over two years, however, constitutionalist forces recaptured the capital, deposed the Shah, and restored the constitution. Nuri was summarily arrested, charged, and found guilty of being involved in the murder of four constitutionalists four months earlier, and publicly hanged on July 31, 1909.[27]

There was a double advantage in highlighting the enthusiastic reception of European political and cultural traditions by Iranian secular intellectuals. First, by placing Islamic concerns at the center of political discourse, it enlarged the constituency of the clergy by delineating a clear message separate from those of the secular bureaucrats and liberal intellectuals. Second, it forced the pro-constitutionalist ulama to be more circumspect in their dealings with secularists, and to always justify their positions in relation to Islam and Islamic interests. As such, the complexity of drafting a balanced constitution was reduced to a binary between safekeeping or compromising Islamic values.[28] The insistence on this binary had a definite chilling effect on the contributions of pro-constitutionalist ulama to the process of drafting a new constitution. Thanks in large measure to Nuri's interventions, "the sympathetic *ulama*'s support was henceforth implicitly conditional, and they too insisted on the supervisory veto power of religious authority, the restriction of freedom of the press and the disavowal of any reforms entailing the secularization of the judiciary and education systems."[29] Put another way, the traditionalist framing of constitutionalism inexorably overshadowed the liberal antipathies toward tradition and absolutism which had been the initial triggers behind the movement for change. This was no small irony given Afghani's early championing of modernization and the rule of law; but, as Afary has noted, the "transitory" nature of any such

---

[26] Arjomand, "The 'Ulama's Traditionalist Opposition to Parliamentarianism," p. 180.
[27] Afary, *The Iranian Constitutional Revolution*, pp. 258–259.
[28] Nuri's formal refutation of constitutionalism was published in his *Ketab-e Tadhkirat-e al-Ghafil va-Irshad al-Jahil* [The Book of Admonition to the Misinformed and Guidance for the Ignorant] (Tehran: 1287/1908). For an introduction to and translation of this work, see Abdul-Hadi Hairi, "Shaykh Fazl Allah Nuri's Refutation of the Idea of Constitutionalism," *Middle Eastern Studies*, Vol. XXIII, No. 3 (1977): 327–339.
[29] Afary, *The Iranian Constitutional Revolution*, p. 259.

70   The Specter of Westernism

alliances was determined from the outset due to the fact that "Laws of the shari'at and the secular laws of the constitution were not reconcilable."[30]

The general historical context surrounding the emergence of political Islam in Iran and its subsequent entanglement with processes of Westernization bears recounting because of its specific implications for the expression of liberal-reformist dispositions in the ensuing century. As demonstrated in Chapter 2, liberal antipathies and prescriptions from this period forward had to retool and cloak their messages in a manner that appeared both unthreatening and unfamiliar to would-be opponents who could dismiss them on account of their promotion of Western imperial interests and values. To be clear: this was not due exclusively to the rise of political Islam, and nor was religious antipathy toward Western ideas uniformly shared by the ulama and their pious followers. Religious and lay political views have always spanned a spectrum, from very progressive to ultraconservative. Rather, the point here is that the trenchant framing of liberal political perspectives as, at best, permissive, but mostly Western and imperialistic, was to become a routine characterization with immense consequences for the pursuit of liberal aims in Iran. This trend was especially influential in shaping the formal conceptualization of *gharbzadegi* or Westoxication, which became the sole discursive source of antiliberal ideologies among both political Islamists and Leftists.

Modernization and Forced Liberalization under the Pahlavis

No sooner was the battlefield between modernity and tradition populated by champions and opponents of liberal constitutionalism than it was forced into abeyance by the descent of social chaos and political instability. With the irredeemably corrupt Qajar albatross foreclosing any possibilities for reform, the halting experiment with constitutionalism ended with the 1921 coup engineered by the Russian-trained Cossack Brigade (led by Reza Khan) of the Iranian army. On November 1, 1925, the Majlis formally abolished the Qajar dynasty, and shortly thereafter, on April 15, 1926, recognized the new Pahlavi monarchy with Reza Khan as the new Shahanshah (King of Kings).[31] The swift ascendance of a military commander from humble origins to a position of absolute power was necessitated as much by the imperative for competent, decisive, and centralized leadership as it was by the yearning for a modern state capable of warding

---

[30] Ibid., p. 71.

[31] The demise of the Qajars and rise of Reza Khan is chronicled minutely in Stephanie Cronin, *The Army and Creation of the Pahlavi State in Iran, 1921–1926* (London: I.B. Tauris & Co. Ltd., 1997).

Modernization and Forced Liberalization

off foreign influence.[32] Reza Shah delivered on both fronts as the parliament grew to be a mere rubberstamp of the royal court while top-down modernization programs developed Iran's infrastructure and reshaped its bureaucratic, administrative, scientific, and cultural institutions.[33] Moreover, the drive toward modernization under a strongman initially put an end to ongoing agitation between traditionalist ulama and secular intellectuals, each of whom found sufficient protection from the other in the new order.[34] Over time, however, the consolidation of royal power afforded Reza Shah the sufficient political clout to, in Abrahamian's words, "rebuild Iran in the image of the West" through the unbridled pursuit of "secularism, antitribalism, nationalism, educational development, and state capitalism."[35]

Naturally, these policies considerably marginalized the role of the clergy in state affairs while strengthening that of the secular intelligentsia. Nowhere was this alienation more apparent than in the judicial realm, where the Swiss-educated minister of justice, Ali-Akbar Davar (widely regarded as the "founder of the modern Persian judicial system"),[36] instituted significant reforms based on the French and Italian civil and penal codes.[37] Although he took special care not to completely stamp out the authority of Sharia legal codes – specifically in the domain of family law, thus preserving patriarchal privileges concerning marriage, divorce, inheritance, and child custody – his sweeping overhaul of bureaucratic, administrative, and court systems at all levels essentially amounted to what one eminent legal scholar called the

---

[32] For influential political histories of Reza Shah's twenty-year reign, see Hossein Makki, *Tarikh-e Bist Saleh-ye Iran* [Twenty-Year History of Iran], Vols. I & II (Tehran: Elmi, 1374/1995); and Mohammad-Taqi Malek al-Sho'ara Bahar, *Tarikh-e Mokhtasar-e Ahzab-e Siasi-ye Iran* [A Brief History of Political Parties in Iran], Vol. I (Tehran: 1323/1945). For a history of this period with a special emphasis on socioeconomic class determinants, see Abrahamian, *Iran between Two Revolutions*, pp. 118–165.

[33] For excellent scholarly consideration of various development projects under Reza Shah, see Stephanie Cronin, ed., *The Making of Modern Iran: State and Society under Riza Shah, 1921–1941* (London: Routledge, 2003); and Stephanie Cronin, *Soldiers, Shahs, and Subalterns in Iran: Opposition, Protest and Revolt, 1921–1941* (New York: Palgrave Macmillan, 2010).

[34] As Gheissari notes, "The intelligentsia regarded him as secular patriot capable of putting an end to political divisions and social chaos, isolating the forces of traditionalism, and limiting the power of the ulama. Many Shi'i leaders saw in him a strong patriot capable of suppressing the radical elements whose secularism and anti-clericalism had made the ulama both disillusioned and suspicious about the future course of Constitutionalism." Gheissari, *Iranian Intellectuals in the 20th Century*, p. 45.

[35] Abrahamian, *Iran between Two Revolutions*, p. 140.

[36] Baqer Aqeli, "Dāvar, 'Alī-Akbar," *Encyclopædia Iranica*, Vol. VIII, Fasc. 2 (November 18, 2011), pp. 133–135.

[37] For an excellent, detailed history and legal analysis of Davar's reforms, see Enayat, *Law, State, and Society in Modern Iran*, especially chapters 4 and 5.

72   The Specter of Westernism

"secularization of the shari'a."[38] Most importantly, the judiciary, under direct orders from Reza Shah, disregarded the customary practice of taking sanctuary (*bast*) inside holy shrines, long favored by politically active ulama, and outlawed the staging of religious passion plays and demonstrations on holidays. The ulama were by and large grudgingly resigned to these directives, however, for the government also succeeded in significantly curtailing foreign meddling, modernizing the army, and reasserting state control over national assets. Moreover, Reza Shah succeeded in ending the capitulation agreements with foreign companies, established the fully-autonomous National Bank of Iran (Bank-e Melli), and nationalized major industries such as telegraph, railways, and agriculture, albeit with the sole and notable exception of oil, where the lopsided control of the Anglo-Iranian Oil Company remained in place.[39] Additionally, a modern tax code was introduced to help fund construction projects and offset the imbalances in foreign trade. Together, these reforms, although not ideal in their ramifications for the place of religion in state affairs, reversed decades of Qajar neglect through a systematic construction of a modern, united national identity for Iranians.

The most significant social reforms followed suit after Reza Shah's visit to Turkey in 1934, where his modernizing counterpart, Mustafa Kemal Ataturk, had begun transforming the country in the image of European societies of the day.[40] The visit solidified in Reza Shah's mind the necessity of robust social engineering down to the level of standardized dress codes and forced unveiling of women.[41] The latter was indeed the starkest instance of a long-standing liberal-modernist conceit to force Iranian women to become "free" in the manner "imagined" by Iranian male travelers' observations of European women.[42] The cultural impact of Reza Shah's reforms was mostly felt in the liberalization of education

---

[38] Ali Shayegan quoted in ibid., p. 138.

[39] On Reza Shah's annulment of the capitulation agreements, see Michael Zirinsky, "Riza Shah's Abrogation of Capitulations," in Cronin, ed., *The Making of Modern Iran*, pp. 81–98.

[40] Afshin Marashi, "Performing the Nation: The Shah's Official State Visit to Kemalist Turkey, June to July 1934," in Cronin, ed., *The Making of Modern Iran*, pp. 99–120.

[41] For an examination of these policies as "nation-building" projects, see Houchang E. Chehabi, "Staging the Emperor's New Clothes: Dress Codes and Nation-Building under Reza Shah," *Iranian Studies*, Vol. 26, Nos. 3–4 (1993): 209–229.

[42] These are well and critically chronicled in Mohamad Tavakoli-Targhi, "Imagining Western Women: Occidentalism and Euro-eroticism," *Radical America*, Vol. 24, No. 3 (1990): 73–87. As Afsaneh Najmabadi has aptly noted, however, it is important "not to collapse all modernists into one particular trend." Such a perspective, she has warned, commits the error of "conflating modernists with those who sought disaffiliation from the Islamic past, rather than a reconfiguration of that past. It participates in writing out of modernity Iranians who were working for an Islamo-Iranian modern. The latter, who

Modernization and Forced Liberalization 73

and in the greater liberties experienced by middle- and upper-class women.[43] For the first time, a portion of tax revenues was directly invested in expanding public health and education infrastructure and improving access at all levels.[44] The notable result here was the founding of Iran's first modern institution of higher education, the University of Tehran, as well as the introduction of a modern school curriculum, "designed to uproot traditional customs and patterns in Iranian society, even if their effects did not always follow prescribed and anticipated scenarios."[45] Concurrent with these policies, new cultural institutes and centers – such as Farhangestan (Iranian Academy) and Kanoon-e Banovan (Ladies' Center) – were established, and their heads handpicked from among prominent members of the secular intelligentsia and the royal court,[46] in an effort to ensure unity of purpose and action between the formal and informal institutions of state and society, respectively.

To many liberal reformers, the modernization of the education sector and the civil service presented a crucial opening for cultivating and retaining the intellectual talent pool that in previous eras had either drained away to foreign capitals or festered at home in disillusionment. Moreover, a competent technocratic class would become the lifeblood of the kind of institutional progress that a quasi-sovereign nation like Iran desperately needed to develop into a fully independent modern state. This was representative of the thinking of leading liberal reformers such as the scholar-statesman Mohammad Ali Foroughi, who led the effort to standardize the Persian language as the founding director of Farhangestan and later served as prime minister in the early phase of

included important groups of women, did not advocate and at times opposed women's unveiling, although they fully supported women's education and social participation." Afsaneh Najmabadi, *Women with Mustaches and Men without Beards: Gender and Sexual Anxieties of Iranian Modernity* (Berkeley, CA: University of California Press, 2005), pp. 133–134.

[43] For a comprehensive consideration of the politics of culture and modernization under Reza Shah, see Biana Devos and Christoph Werner, eds., *Culture and Cultural Politics under Reza Shah: The Pahlavi State, the New Bourgeoisie and the Creation of a Modern Society in Iran* (New York: Routledge, 2014). On the impact of these policies on women, see Parvin Paidar, *Women and the Political Process in Twentieth-Century Iran* (Cambridge: Cambridge University Press, 1995), chapters 3–5.

[44] The impact of these educational reforms is discussed in Rudi Matthee, "Transforming Dangerous Nomads into Useful Artisans, Technicians, Agriculturalists: Education in the Reza Shah Period," *Iranian Studies*, Vol. 26, Nos. 3–4 (1993): 313–336.

[45] Ibid., p. 314. For the range of "unanticipated" consequences of these reforms, see David Menashri, *Education and the Making of Modern Iran* (Ithaca, NY: Cornell University Press, 1992).

[46] For instance, Reza Shah's daughter, Princess Shams, was made the honorary president and patron of the Ladies' Center of Iran while the scholar-statesman Mohammad Ali Foroughi became the founding director of Farhangestan.

74   The Specter of Westernism

Mohammad Reza Shah Pahlavi's reign.[47] Indeed, such state-led social engineering projects as compulsory education and increasing the public visibility of women had been advocated by leading liberal feminists and social democrats since the dawn of constitutionalism in Iran.[48] But as in the earlier periods, the imperative to reform in the same fashion as Western modernity was bedeviled by the resort to paternalism and elitist condescension. The robust commitment to modernization and the pushback against foreign interference under Reza Shah may have remedied the two liberal antipathies against traditionalism and imperialism, but the concomitant centralization of power and authority also resulted in the creation of a more formidable absolutist political order. The negative implications of this Faustian bargain, however tacitly forged, were most readily apparent in the case of the forced de-veiling of women. As Chehabi has noted, the policy of standardized dress codes, "while meant to unify the nation by eliminating visible class, status, and regional distinctions, in fact deepened another cleavage in Iranian society, i.e. that between westernizers, who welcomed the policies and took to European fashions willingly (and at times with a zeal that even Europeans themselves found astounding), and the rest of society, which resented the intrusion into their private lives."[49] Moreover, the brazen attempt at liberal paternalism not only made a mockery of respect for women's individual rights but also lent credence to the conservative clergy's reflexive, if simplistic, depiction of modernization as singularly akin to the imposition of Western cultural norms and values.

The forced abdication of Reza Shah after the Anglo-Soviet occupation of Iran in 1941 (due to the Shah's declaration of neutrality in World War II) momentarily ended the slide toward absolutism and ushered in a period of parliamentary politics, political revitalization, and intellectual pluralism. New political parties, periodicals, social organizations, and

---

[47] As Gheissari and Nasr have noted, "[Reza Khan] believed that a strong state would not only guarantee territorial integrity and aid progress, it would also promote liberty." Ali Gheissari and Vali Nasr, *Democracy in Iran: History and the Quest for Liberty* (New York: Oxford University Press, 2006), p. 37.

[48] See, for instance, the editorials of leading feminist Sediqeh Dowlatabadi in *Zaban-e Zanan* (1920–1944), who argued for the necessity of compulsory education and state-funded schools for women, and even defended the right of women to both wear and reject the veil. Similar lines of arguments were advanced – albeit in the fashion of the times, in more misogynistic terms – by progressive periodicals *Kaveh* and *Iranshahr*, both of which published widely on women's issues and featured correspondences by leading feminists. See Paidar, *Women and the Political Process in Twentieth-Century Iran*, pp. 90–101. For the inaugural political expression of such views, see Afary, *The Iranian Constitutional Revolution*, chapter 7.

[49] See Houchang E. Chehabi, "The Banning of the Veil and Its Consequences," in Cronin, ed., *The Making of Modern Iran*, p. 205.

Modernization and Forced Liberalization 75

cultural centers spanning the ideological spectrum were established. Having experienced the excesses of rapid modernization, the intelligentsia – many of them also veterans of the Constitutional Revolution and its aftermath – championed a return to constitutionalism, albeit while retaining the institution of monarchy. In order to achieve this, a great deal of effort was concentrated on the task of "depersonalizing" the state in the aftermath of Reza Shah's exile (in South Africa).[50] In many respects, the raucous parliamentary interregnum between 1941 and the coup d'état in 1953 that reestablished Pahlavi autocracy (this time under the Shah's son Mohammad Reza) was ultimately distinguished mainly by "the maximization of political gains and minimization of loss at the expense of other groups, as well as the arrangement of alliances in such a way as to undermine or destabilize the efforts of one group to gain the upper hand."[51] Precisely because Reza Shah's abdication did not result from a social revolution or any internal political upheaval, it was not akin to "regime change." In fact, nearly all members of the political and technocratic elites retained their positions, social and class hierarchies were hardly disturbed, and networks of influence and patronage remained intact. All the same, since so much of the identity of the state had been shaped around the person of the Shah, the very fact of his absence meant the opening of considerable political space for criticisms of established orders, for open contestation, and for calls to restore constitutionalism. As the historian Fakhreddin Azimi has observed, "In this period the hampered spirit of constitutionalism persevered in defiance of all obstacles, and the political culture of the country showed signs of enrichment, while the political consciousness of the urban population increased markedly."[52]

Thanks in large measure to Reza Shah's modernization programs, higher literacy rates more efficiently facilitated the dissemination of modern ideologies, creating opportunities for insurgent intellectual currents to supplant or more effectively compete with established ideas. Of these, two political parties in particular – Hezb-e Tudeh-ye Iran (The Party of the Masses) and Jebhe-ye Melli (National Front) – quickly emerged as formidable political organizations challenging the hegemony of the ruling establishment that dominated the cabinet and the Majlis. The Tudeh Party was an amalgam of socialist and Marxist groups with significant representation in the northern provinces of Iran (bordering Russia) and

---

[50] For an excellent survey of the intellectual climate and topography of this period, see Gheissari, *Iranian Intellectuals in the 20th Century*, chapter 4.
[51] Azimi, *Iran, The Crisis of Democracy*, p. 27.   [52] Ibid., p. 339.

76   The Specter of Westernism

among the industrial working class in central and southern provinces. The National Front was more diverse in its makeup, featuring nationalist, liberal, socialist, and even Islamic political groups enjoined to curb growing British political influence through the control of Iran's oil fields and industry. Although the party's profile would become indistinguishable with Mohammad Mosaddeq's personae and anti-imperial struggles after the latter's popularly elected government was overthrown through an Anglo-American-sponsored coup, in the historical imagination of the Iranian public it is remembered as perhaps the zenith of what Homa Katouzian has aptly termed "democratic patriotism."[53] In contrast to the Pahlavis' borrowed template of a Westernized "romantic nationalism," "democratic patriotism" represented "the social and psychological urge to defend one's home, culture, social existence, political sovereignty and economic independence from the aggressive designs of powerful states."[54]

It was against the backdrop of the foreign-induced defeat of this spirit that Mohammad Reza Shah resumed the autocratic Pahlavi order. Although he had been officially recognized as the head of state (at the tender age of twenty-two) upon the abdication of his father, he was but a ceremonial figure until the aftermath of the coup in 1953, when power was once again concentrated in the royal court. If Reza Shah's autocracy had been tolerated on account of his state-building and anti-imperial achievements, the young Shah was bedeviled from the outset in being viewed as an inauthentic and weak lackey of the West. Educated in Switzerland and socialized in jet-setting elite circles, the Shah's public personae had been conspicuous in its glamorousness, condescension, and self-regard. To boot, he had acquired the nickname "the suitcase Shah" for his proclivity to take a leave of absence from the country each time domestic upheavals threatened to reach the palace.[55] Nonetheless, after 1953 the Shah gradually grew into his position by continuing along the same modernizing script as his father, albeit now within the geopolitical

---

[53] Katouzian, *Musaddiq and the Struggle for Power in Iran*, p. 260.   [54] Ibid.

[55] For a comprehensive chronicle of Mohammad Reza Shah's political career, see Gholam Reza Afkhami, *The Life and Times of the Shah* (Berkeley, CA: University of California Press, 2009); Abbas Milani, *The Shah* (New York: Palgrave Macmillan, 2011); Amin Saikal, *The Rise and Fall of the Shah: Iran from Autocracy to Religious Rule* (Princeton, NJ: Princeton University Press, 1980), is more dated in its sourcing and analysis, but is especially instructive in its account of the geopolitical context surrounding the Shah's reign. An indispensable, if hagiographic (but even here, instructive), source are the diaries of the Shah's minister of court Asadollah Alam, *The Shah and I: The Confidential Diary of Iran's Royal Court, 1968–77*, ed. Alinaghi Alikhani (London: I.B. Tauris & Co. Ltd., 2008).

Modernization and Forced Liberalization 77

context of the Cold War and the dawn of the American-led liberal international order in which the normative framework of international law and human rights placed new strains, if not yet outright limitations, on autocratic rulers.[56] Furthermore, Iran's status as the world's second largest exporter of oil in this period blessed its treasury while cursing its politics by giving the Shah the mistaken impression of his indispensability to the stability of international order.[57] Thus the Shah adopted the same repressive approach toward the clergy and the leftist intelligentsia that his father had, and especially so toward the latter whose appeals for observance of basic human rights, political openness, and return to constitutionalism also both humiliated the Shah and exposed Western hypocrisy.

For all intents and purposes, the Majlis returned to being little more than a rubberstamp body made up of deputies handpicked by the royal court and kept in line by the Shah's secret police, the SAVAK (the Persian acronym for Sazman-e Ettala'at Va Amniyat-e Keshvar [Organization for National Intelligence and Security]).[58] Although the Shah went out of his way to create the illusion of a multiparty state, the two nominal governing parties "became known interchangeably as the 'yes' and the 'yes, sir' or 'yes, of course' parties."[59] Of course, this rigidly managed political system was ill-equipped to deal with the emerging crises of state. By 1960, a combination of economic stagnation, political repression, and corrupt parliamentary politics induced widespread public discontent that were especially acute in rural areas and among the urbanized working-class populations. Wary of the repeat of class-based revolutions in other parts of the Third World, the Kennedy administration urged the Shah to undertake reforms aimed at land redistribution and mitigation of socioeconomic inequality. The Shah followed suit by putting together a six-point (later

---

[56] On the Cold War context, see Roham Alvandi, *Nixon, Kissinger, and the Shah: The United States and Iran in the Cold War* (Oxford: Oxford University Press, 2016), chapter 1.

[57] Abrahamian, *Iran between Two Revolutions*, p. 420.

[58] SAVAK was established in 1957 with the aid of the Central Intelligence Agency and, in later years, Israel's secret intelligence agency, Mossad. For an overview of SAVAK's organizational history and its practices against dissidents, see Ervand Abrahamian, *Tortured Confessions: Prisons and Public Recantations in Modern Iran* (Berkeley, CA: University of California Press, 1999), pp. 88–120.

[59] Ervand Abrahamian, *A History of Modern Iran* (New York: Cambridge University Press, 2008), p. 130. All such pretenses were abandoned in 1975, when the Shah dissolved the multiparty system and announced the creation of the Rastakhiz Party, which only confirmed the conversion of the state into a dictatorship. For more on the Rastakhiz Party and the Shah's desperate attempt to refashion a united front against growing discontent, see Parvin Merat Amini, "A Single-Party State in Iran, 1975–78: The Rastakhiz Party – The Final Attempt by the Shah to Consolidate His Political Base," *Middle Eastern Studies*, Vol. 38, No. 1 (2002): 131–168.

78   The Specter of Westernism

expanded to nineteen) package of reforms, dubbed the "White Revolution" (in contrast to the bottom-up "Red Revolutions"), which, notably, abolished the existing quasi-feudal landholding schemes through government-assisted land redistribution, sought to redress class inequalities through new industrial profit-sharing and welfare assistance programs, extended the franchise to women, and significantly expanded education and health coverage through the establishment of literacy and health corps.[60] Although billed as a benevolent scheme to alleviate socioeconomic maladies, the chief purpose behind the reforms were of course political. As Ansari has explained,

> The Shah was anxious to be seen not only as a "democratic" monarch, progressive and benign, always with the welfare of his people in mind – a characterization he had pursued to variable effect in the post-Musaddiq period – but as a "revolutionary" monarch. In so doing, he would appropriate the myths of the Left and National Front as a champion of revolutionary nationalism which would assist in legitimizing himself and his dynasty. As the founder and guarantor of a new order for Iran, he would consolidate his dynasty's position within the political system, which he would argue was dependent upon the continuation and consolidation of his dynasty. "Modernism" and "Pahlavism" were to merge and become both synonymous and mutually dependent. Monarchy and modernism, perceived as contradictions by many, were thus rationalized into compatibility, even necessity, by the Shah, who saw no contradiction in drawing upon the traditional myths of past monarchs, likewise considered initiators of "just" order .... The "White Revolution" was therefore a strategy for legitimation, through the use of rationalization, universalization and eternalization. Socioeconomic benefits were emphasized in an effort to disguise the real political gains, though ... most commentators were aware of the "social reality" of the situation.[61]

The envisioned "political gains" were of course in the appropriation of progressive agendas without the trouble of holding any democratic discussions about them.[62] The hastily arranged public referendum on the reforms were widely dismissed by remnants of the National Front (by now mostly a mélange of Muslim nationalists) and other progressive

---

[60] For overviews of the Shah's White Revolution reforms and their aftermath, see Abrahamian, *A History of Modern Iran*, chapter 5; Keddie and Richard, *Modern Iran*, pp. 148–169; Amanat, *Iran*, chapters 10–11.

[61] Ali M. Ansari, "The Myth of the White Revolution: Mohammad Reza Shah, 'Modernization', and the Consolidation of Power," *Middle Eastern Studies*, Vol. 37, No. 3 (2001): 3.

[62] As Afshin Matin-Asgari has observed, "Without irony, the key planks of the 'White Revolution', soon to be called 'The Shah-People Revolution', were borrowed directly from Iran's socialist and communist movements." Afshin Matin-Asgari, "The Pahlavi Era: Iranian Modernity in Global Context," in Touraj Daryaee, ed., *The Oxford Handbook of Iranian History* (New York: Oxford University Press, 2012), p. 358.

Modernization and Forced Liberalization   79

groups.[63] For their part, the clergy, under the direction of Ayatollah Khomeini, found the very substance of the reforms – especially that of women's suffrage and political participation – inimical to Islamic teachings.[64] Comparing the Shah to the Sunni caliph Yezid, who martyred the much-revered Shia Imam Hussein, and arguing that the circle around the Shah was dominated by "sinister agents" of Israel, Khomeini took a page out of Nuri's playbook in urging on a zero-sum binary struggle: "We come to the conclusion that this regime also has a more basic aim: they are fundamentally opposed to Islam itself and the existence of the religious class. They do not wish this institution to exist; they do not with any of us to exist; the great and small alike."[65] Immediately following his speech, Khomeini was arrested and riots broke out across major cities, resulting in a violent crackdown by the regime. Thereafter, any meaningful opposition to the Shah was driven underground, effectively paving the road to the 1979 revolution. Once again, as in the case of opposition to his father's rule, the axis of resistance to the Shah turned on his antidemocratic means (to the secular-liberal intelligentsia) and the secular ends of his diktats (to the clergy and their supporters among the bazaar merchants).

In his rather eccentric account of the final days of the Shah, the Polish journalist and global nomad Ryszard Kapuściński captured an essential truth about moments of great national upheaval: "Several hundred languages are fighting for recognition and promotion; the language barriers are rising. Deafness and incomprehension are multiplying."[66] In many

---

[63] Soon after the 1953 coup, the National Front coalition was dismantled and its subsequent reincarnations – the National Resistance Movement (Nehzat-e Moqavemat-e Melli) followed by the Liberation Movement of Iran (Nehzat-e Azadi-ye Iran) – emphasized hybrid visions of "Islamic democracy" more than liberal constitutionalism. The Liberation Movement of Iran formed a significant faction of the coalition that brought down the Shah, and its rank and file formed the first transition government after the 1979 revolution. However, the LMI was soon sidelined and persecuted as the government clashed with Khomeini and his supporters over the takeover of the American embassy in Tehran and the ensuing hostage crisis. See Chehabi, *Iranian Politics and Religious Modernism.*

[64] Khomeini had earlier opposed a proposal that would have granted women the vote and allowed religious minorities to take the oath of office on their respective holy books. In protesting the proposed changes, he registered his displeasure in writing directly to the Shah: "As you know, national interests and spiritual comfort are both predicated on following Islamic laws. Please order all laws inimical to the sacred and official faith of the country to be eliminated from government policies." Quoted in Milani, *The Shah*, p. 291. The original source can be found in Javad Mansuri, ed., *Tarikh-e Qiyam-e Panzdah-e Khordad be Ravayat-e Asnad* [Documentary History of the June 5 Uprising] (Tehran: Markaz-e Asnad-e Enghelab-e Eslami, 1377/1998), pp. 252–253.

[65] Ayatollah Ruhollah Khomeini, "The Afternoon of 'Ashura'," sermon delivered at the Madrase Feyziye in Qom on June 3, 1963. Translated, annotated, and reprinted in Hamid Algar, *Islam and Revolution: Writings and Declarations of Imam Khomeini, 1941–1980* (North Haledon, NJ: Mizan Press, 1981), p. 177.

[66] Ryszard Kapuściński, *Shah of Shahs* (London: Penguin Books, 1985), pp. 10–11.

80   The Specter of Westernism

respects, the raison d'être of the Pahlavi monarchy, since its inception by Reza Shah, was to be the antidote to unruly competition between dissonant voices and ideologies – to be a bulwark against the seemingly endemic "deafness and incomprehension" that had become the hallmark of both late Qajar Persia and the raucous period of parliamentary politics under Mosaddeq. It undertook this mission through a controlled, top-down process of modernization that unevenly combined elements of Western secularity, materiality, and liberality with a pre-Islamic nativist imagination – all the while reducing constitutionalism to a hollow edifice. In retrospect, perhaps more than any other factor it was the Pahlavis' brazen dismantling of the constitutional process – in the name of liberation and progress – and suppression of liberal dissent that empowered the emergence of a decidedly anti-liberal opposition. As Kapuściński observed,

A dictatorship that destroys the intelligentsia and culture leaves behind itself an empty, sour field on which the tree of thought won't grow quickly. It is not always the best people who emerge from hiding, from the corners and cracks of that farmed-out field, but often those who have proven themselves strongest, not always those who will create new values but rather those whose thick skin and internal resilience have ensured their survival. In such circumstances history begins to turn in a tragic, vicious circle from which it can sometimes take a whole epoch to break free.[67]

Indeed, in the four decades since the collapse of the Pahlavi dynasty the "tragic, vicious cycle" of history in which the legacy of constitutionalism has been engulfed has yet to subside. Although the extent of the Pahlavis' own "deafness and incomprehension" would not become clear until after the advent of the Islamic Republic, as early as the 1940s there were signs of the collateral damage inflicted on liberal-modernist intellectuals whom, in the righteous lamentations of their anti-Western counterparts, were responsible for distancing Iranians from their authentic cultural traditions – for elevating "Europeanism" (*oroupagarayie*) to the status of a deity.[68] These *gharbzadeh* (West-stricken) peddlers of progressive change, the accusation went, were ultimately responsible for nurturing a culture of inferiority vis-à-vis the West.

Westoxication and the Liberal Other

Both the concept and discourse of Westoxication have been well examined by scholars of modern Iranian politics and intellectual history over

[67] Ibid., p. 58.
[68] The phrase was coined by the historian Ahmad Kasravi in his *Ma Cheh Mikhahim?* [What Do We Want?] (Tehran: Paydar, 1319/1940).

Westoxication and the Liberal Other 81

the past four decades.[69] Nearly all of these studies follow a similar analytical framework (i.e. the fraught "encounter" between modernity and mid-century Iranian identity), temporal span (from the end of the Constitutional Revolution to the advent of the Islamic Republic), cast of intellectuals (with variations, Seyyed Fakhr al-Din Shadman, Ahmad Fardid, Jalal Al-e Ahmad, Ehsan Naraqi, and Ali Shariati), and critical appraisal of the range of concerns involved (i.e. the poverty of nativism and the illusion of authenticity). Although these inquiries differ in their judgments of particular thinkers or works, there is clear consensus on the definitive imprint of this intellectual trend – that is, Westoxication as a genre of its own – on the 1979 revolution and the founding of the Islamic Republic.[70]

In this section, I wish to narrow the aperture further still by distinguishing between three strands of critique within the Westoxication genre: (i) a critique of pseudo-modernism (Shadman); (ii) a critique of Western modernity (Fardid and Shariati); and (iii) a critique of liberalism (Al-e Ahmad and Naraqi). To be sure, there are important areas of overlap between arguments and themes contained within each critique. For instance, all of these thinkers and even many advocates of modernization subscribed to (i), just as it was a foregone conclusion for those who endorsed (ii) to also enlist in the cause of (iii). But just as significant are divergences in the diagnoses and prescriptions advanced by each cohort that resulted in highly consequential reframing of particular ideologies, historical events, or sociocultural trends. The following is an examination of these differences between the critiques of Westernism in this period, with a special emphasis on the critique of Western liberal modernity, which to my mind has been especially overlooked in the scholarly literature on *gharbzadegi*.

---

[69] The most cited of these works in English are Abrahamian, *Iran between Two Revolutions*, chapter 9; Said Amir Arjomand, *The Turban for the Crown: The Islamic Revolution in Iran* (New York: Oxford University Press, 1988), chapters 2–4; Mohsen Milani, *The Making of Iran's Islamic Revolution: From Monarchy to Islamic Republic* (Boulder, CO: Westview Press, 1988), chapter 5; Hamid Dabashi, *Theology of Discontent: The Ideological Foundation of the Islamic Republic* (New Brunswick, NJ: Transaction Publishers, 1993), introduction and chapters 1–2; Boroujerdi, *Iranian Intellectuals and the West*, chapter 3; Negin Nabavi, *Intellectuals and the State in Iran: Politics, Discourse, and the Dilemma of Authenticity* (Gainesville, FL: University Press of Florida, 2003); Gheissari, *Iranian Intellectuals in the 20th Century*, chapter 5; Mirsepassi, *Intellectual Discourse and the Politics of Modernization*; Mirsepassi, *Political Islam, Iran, and the Enlightenment*, chapters 1–4; Mirsepassi, *Transnationalism in Iranian Political Thought*; Mirsepassi, *Iran's Quiet Revolution*, especially chapters 1, 2, and 8; and Matin-Asgari, *Both Eastern and Western*.

[70] For instance, in Matin-Asgari's view Mirsepassi "exaggerates" the impact of Ahmad Fardid's political thought, even as both agree on the overall impact of the discourse of *gharbzadegi*. Matin-Asgari, *Both Eastern and Western*, p. 4.

82   The Specter of Westernism

Westoxication as a Critique of Pseudo-Modernism

It is not surprising that the first wave of focused criticisms (ca. 1940s) concerning the appropriation of Western modernity should have been in the form of a trenchant attack on the utter superficiality and naivete of those Iranian elites and intellectuals who sought to merely imitate it. As state-sanctioned political and cultural modernization projects increasingly mimicked and yielded to Western models of progress, there emerged a real worry about the damage done to Iranian civilizational identity in the process. Impressionable elites and dogmatic traditionalists, according to this view, were either too shrill or dishonest to absorb the changes induced by modernity in a manner that would be conducive to the advancement of Persian civilization. The most succinct expression of this critique was put forward by Fakhr al-Din Shadman (1907–1967), a scholar-statesman in the mold of Foroughi, who certainly had the requisite personal, intellectual, and professional background to credibly advance this critique.[71] He did so in his book *Taskhir-e Tammadon-e Farangi* [The Capture of Western Civilization] (1948), which advanced a rather alarmist thesis about the internal threat posed by a pseudo-modernist archetype he called "*fokoli*."[72] Although the book is a lamentation against both the dogmatism of the clergy and the inauthenticity of the intellectuals,[73] the bulk of his criticism is aimed at "the great ailment" that is inflicted on "the great Iranian nation" by the "dirty enemy

---

[71] Born into a religious family, he was educated at Dar al-Fonoun and studied law at the College of Law (later the University of Tehran's School of Law) before obtaining two separate doctorates in law and history from the Sorbonne (1935) and the London School of Economics and Political Science (1939), respectively. Professionally, after his undergraduate studies he was invited into the Ministry of Justice by Ali-Akbar Davar and went on to serve as the deputy prosecutor in Tehran until the outbreak of World War II. Upon returning to Iran after a brief teaching career at the University of London, he became the director of Iran Insurance Company and went on to serve in the cabinet as the director of planning and budget organization, minister of finance, and minister of justice. He was an essayist, a novelist, and a translator of several historical books into Persian. For more on Shadman's background, see Abbas Milani, *Lost Wisdom: Rethinking Modernity in Iran* (Washington, DC: Mage Publishers, 2004), pp. 63–81; Abbas Milani, *Eminent Persians: The Men and Women Who Made Modern Iran, 1941–1979*, Vol. I (Syracuse, NY: Syracuse University Press, 2008), pp. 289–304; Boroujerdi, *Iranian Intellectuals and the West*, pp. 54–55; and Gheissari, *Iranian Intellectuals in the 20th Century*, p. 84. See also Ali Gheissari, "Shadman, Fakhr-al-Din," *Encyclopædia Iranica*, March 15, 2010 (www .iranicaonline.org/articles/shadman, last accessed June 15, 2018).

[72] After the French term *faux col*, which refers to a necktie or hat worn by men. The term had a clear derogatory connotation in Persian, and it was used by Shadman deliberately to single out those men who even before the introduction of European-style dress codes would don such attire.

[73] Shadman pillories both groups through two pejorative archetypes he calls "Sheikh Vahab Rouf'ay" and "Houshang Hanavid," respectively. Spelled backwards, the last names read Ya'four (traditional term for blockhead) and Divanah (deranged).

Westoxication and the Liberal Other 83

'*fokoli*'."[74] The latter, in Shadman's thinking, is represented across all social and class strata, and especially in government administration and the civil service – hence the scale of its menace compared to that of the clergy.

The core concern of Shadman is the proper method for absorbing Western modernity in Iran. Unlike later thinking in this genre, his was not reflexively anti-modern or anti-Western, but merely concerned with the *manner* in which ideas from the West were received and practiced in Iran. The important attribute in this dynamic for him was the mastery and attention to the indigenous development of the Persian language, which was necessary for the proper "capture of Western civilization" and thwarting the reverse. Yet, the "*fokoli*" was precisely that "dishonorable man who never complains of learning German, French, or English with their difficult syntax and pronunciation, but who eschews learning his mother tongue and prides himself for his ignorance of it."[75] The range of adjectives used by Shadman to describe the *fokoli* is quite revealing of his utter contempt for pseudo-modernism: he is at once "shameless," "ignorant," "superficial," "deceptive," "egotistic," "two-faced," "narcissistic," "pretentious," "lecherous," "narrow-minded," "untrustworthy," "treasonous," "dirty," and so forth. Indeed, the deliberate use of such pejoratives is meant to highlight that it is the deficiencies in character – and hence the institutions that nurture and instill them – that is the source of the problem. According to Shadman, these characteristics are responsible for the continued subjugation of Iran by Western powers, which may well one day wipe Iranian civilization from historical memory altogether: "As to why the *fokoli* is Iran's greatest enemy, we say that at a time when Iran is under civilizational assault from the West this domestic enemy is their accomplice . . . and since he wishes to hasten our capture by Western civilization, he does not shirk from betraying our great thoughts, language, customs and traditions."[76]

In Shadman's thinking, the Iranian civilization was one of the world's "greatest lights," which the *fokoli* – thanks to his ignorance of its linguistic foundations, literary traditions, and historical continuity – threatened to extinguish and surrender to darkness.[77] This was also true of the clergy, whose rejection of Westernism, as Shadman wrote in another tract,

---

[74] Fakhr al-Din Shadman, *Taskhir-e Tammadon-e Farangi* [The Capture of Western Civilization] (Tehran: 1326/1948), p. 13.
[75] Ibid.   [76] Ibid., pp. 22–23.
[77] Shadman employed the metaphor of light versus darkness with great frequency in his writings, and in fact *Tariki va Rowshana'i* [Darkness and Light] (Tehran: 1328/1950) is also the title of his most read novel that explores many of the critical themes covered in his nonfiction writings concerning the reception of Western modernity.

84   The Specter of Westernism

Teragedy-e Farang [The Tragedy of the West], had resulted in their veneration of Arabic texts and oral traditions to the detriment of the Persian language.[78] In contrast, he asserted, "Alive is the nation who preserves its virtues and sheds its vices freely, with the guidance of reason, and through its natural talents and interests ... and who treats its language as a treasury of its own accumulated knowledge and thoughts ... that would guide its views of the good, the bad, and the beautiful based on the wisdom contained in a book of its own writing."[79] For all the emphasis he placed on the importance of learning Persian, however, Shadman was not a dogmatic nationalist or a reactionary bent on the purification of the Persian language and cultural traditions. As Milani has shown, "He warned against futile attempts at linguistic social engineering .... The sharp edge of his criticism in this area was directed toward the kind of fokolis who had been – and continue to be even today – on a binge of coining neologisms."[80] For Shadman, the loss of an authentic, self-confident identity was merely symptomatic of the general nonchalance and even antipathy shown toward language by the *fokoli* and the religious reactionary alike. The solution to Iran's fraught encounter with modernity, therefore, was not a return to an imagined "pure" past, but in adjusting the methods by which new ideas may enrich established ways of life. This necessitates the use of "reason, prudence, and especially determination and willpower," if Iranians were to successfully capture the wisdom behind Western modernity and not let the latter conquer their imagination in Western terms.[81]

Remarkably, Shadman's diagnosis and prescription to the problem of pseudo-modernism is strikingly similar to those of his liberal predecessors and contemporaries, as surveyed in Chapter 2. His disdain for dogmatic traditionalism of the clergy is a restatement of liberalism's long-standing anti-traditionalism, which in his time is obviously less menacing to the cause of progress. But Shadman's contempt for the *fokoli*, too, is not dissimilar to the provisos about the dangers of blind imitation of Western ideas that accompanied early liberals' – for example, Akhundzadeh, Kermani, or Malkum Khan – advocacy of liberal-constitutionalist principles. Shadman's aforementioned formula for the "capture of Western civilization," for instance, is nearly the same as Malkum Kahn's blueprint

---

[78] Fakhr al-Din Shadman, *Teragedy-e Farang* [The Tragedy of the West] (Tehran: Tahuri, 1346/1967), pp. 86–87.

[79] Shadman, *Taskhir-e Tammadon-e Farangi*, p. 24.

[80] As such, his defense of the Persian language was far more didactic in nature than those of Zabih Behruz and Ahmad Kasravi, as Milani aptly observes. Milani, *Lost Wisdom*, p. 75.

[81] Shadman, *Taskhir-e Tammadon-e Farangi*, p. 79. These qualities are borne out by the central character (Mahmoud) in Shadman's novel *Darkness and Light*.

Westoxication and the Liberal Other 85

for "the reception of Western civilization without the dispossession of Iranians."[82] Indeed, his outright endorsement of key liberal tenets such as rationalism, liberty, rule of law, constitutionalism, while denouncing the *fokoli*'s half-baked ideas about them, render Shadman's perhaps the boldest critique of faux liberalism at the time. That his diatribe is mostly interpreted as the opening salvo in the discourse of *gharbzadegi*, moreover, is further proof, yet again, of the double burden of the liberal intellectuals to not only confront assorted tyrannies but to also account for one's own complicity in prolonging their implications.

Westoxication as a Critique of Western Modernity

The term "*gharbzadegi*," although popularized by the writer Jalal Al-e Ahmad in his political tract of the same title, was in fact first coined by the enigmatic and taciturn (in publishing terms)[83] philosopher Ahmad Fardid (1910–1994) in the 1950s.[84] Fardid's singular contribution to the development of political ideas in Iran was in the introduction of European counter-Enlightenment views to a new cohort of restive thinkers, activists, artists, and writers who were disaffected with the entrenchment of class hierarchies and foreign dependency after decades of top-down modernization. Through his lectures and salon-like gatherings (the so-called Fardid Circle), Fardid advanced a distinct anti-modern ideological line of critique among Iranian intellectuals.[85] Whereas earlier generations of critical intellectuals – such as Shadman and Kasravi – had questioned the uneven reception of modernity in Iran

---

[82] For a distillation of these principles – reason, liberty, the rule of law, education, etc. – in Malkum Khan's writings and correspondences, see Adamiyat, *Fekr-e Azadi*, pp. 113–149.

[83] The whole of his published works consisted of fragmentary translations and partial exegeses of works by Henry Corbin, Henri Bergson, John Dewey, and counter-Enlightenment trends from Kant to Heidegger (all published in the philosophical journal *Sokhan*). His only direct reflections on East-West encounters appeared in Ahmad Fardid, "Pasokh be Chand Porsesh Dar Bab-e Farhang-e Shargh" [Response to a Few Questions Regarding Eastern Culture], transcribed by Reza Davari, *Farhang va Zendegi*, Vol. 7 (January 1972): 32–39. Further reflections on this theme were published posthumously in Ahmad Fardid, *Didar-e Farrahi va Fotouhat-e Akhar al-Zaman* [Divine Encounter and Apocalyptic Revelations], 2nd ed. (Tehran: Nashr-e Nazar, 1378/2008). An unpublished manuscript entitled *Gharb va Gharbzadegi* [The West and Westoxication] is surveyed in Mirsepassi, *Transnationalism in Iranian Political Thought*.

[84] Given the dearth and intermittent nature of Fardid's thought in published works, it is impossible to pin down the precise date of his coinage of "*gharbzadegi*." The most comprehensive treatment of his life and times to date can be found in Mirsepassi, *Transnationalism in Iranian Political*, on which I rely most here.

[85] Some of the leading intellectuals of the day such as Daryush Ashuri, Javad Davari, Shahrokh Meskoob, and Daryush Shayegan were regular attendees, according to Boroujerdi, *Iranian Intellectuals and the West*, p. 63.

86   The Specter of Westernism

and bemoaned the inauthenticity of its purveyors, Fardid targeted the philosophical underpinnings of Western modernity altogether. In this endeavor, he borrowed rather heavily from, and in fact emerged as the chief exegete of, the German anti-modernist philosopher Martin Heidegger.[86]

In Fardid's view, the foundations and worldview (Weltanschauung) of Western modernity rested on a formal separation between the subjective reality/experience of the world and its objective truth. He traced this binary back to ancient Greek philosophers' invention of the rational, knowing subject who is capable of examining the world and objectively distilling its meaning. Such etymological acrobatics, however, came at the expense of "the totalizing, harmonious, and illuminative qualities of Oriental thought, [and] began a period of universal darkness that has since concealed the original unity and totality of Being."[87] For Fardid, therefore, the major intellectual challenge of the day was to resurrect the lost unity of thought in response to the onslaught of Western domination. At the epistemological level, this amounted to a spirited critique of the orientalist mode of knowledge production long before its systematic critical treatment by Edward Said and other postcolonial scholars decades later.[88] In Fardid's estimation, the "stereotypical" representations of Eastern societies diluted the "authenticity" of their cultures through the rationalist filter of Western secular humanism.[89] In contrast to the rationalist underpinning of these orientalist methods, however, Fardid champions the application of "intuitive thought," which draws on etymological (*esm-shenasi*) and genealogical methods of analysis. The latter would compel the observer to examine closely the "great distance between the true meaning of words and names" that a Westoxified understanding of the world – based on orientalist indoctrination – would simply take for granted.[90]

---

[86] Gheissari notes: "In the 1960s and 1970s, many of the chic among the intelligentsia, especially those with middle-class or upper-middle-class backgrounds, looked upon Fardid as a guru and were both fascinated and repelled by his flights of German metaphysics. Hence the passing infatuation with Heiddeger among a section of Iranian intellectuals who often gave an impression as if they were serving caviar to the masses." Gheissari, *Iranian Intellectuals in the 20th Century*, p. 179 (see note 101).

[87] Ibid., p. 89.

[88] Nearly all of Fardid's lectures, interviews, and short publications contain an affirmation of this anti-rationalist outlook, which indeed is what distinguishes him from later postcolonial critics of orientalism. In Said's corpus of critical works on Western production of knowledge about the East, for instance, it is imperialism's exploitative logic and not a surfeit of rationalism (as a mode of inquiry) that is held accountable for the propagation of the binary images, narratives, and relations between the Orient and the Occident. See Edward W. Said, *Orientalism* (New York: Vintage, 1979); and Said, *Culture and Imperialism*.

[89] Fardid, "Pasokh be Chand Porsesh Dar Bab-e Farhang-e Shargh," pp. 32–33.

[90] Ibid., p. 33.

Westoxication and the Liberal Other 87

For Fardid, therefore, Westoxication and its consequences could only be remedied through the study and reconstruction of language. "For me," he noted, "language has an authenticity that [ultimately] distinguishes communities from each other."[91] Indeed, language provided the means by which the "hidden essence" of the East could be revealed through a combination of the deconstruction of orientalist tropes and, à la Heidegger, the reconstruction of the "authentic" sources of being.[92] For Fardid, the authentic attribute most damaged by the advance of Western modernity was that of Islamic identity. The prophetic tradition within Islam that imbues political agency with mystical energy and ethical purpose, Fardid argued, was "concealed" by the Hellenistic tradition that prized individual initiative:

The concealment of the East was the beginning of Hellenism . . .. With the onset of Hellenism, thinking also required a new form. Divine books that were inherently Eastern, were interpreted based on metaphysical thinking. That is, with the arrival of metaphysics as a form of thinking, the gods are gone, and the God, for example, for Aristotle and even Plato becomes "cosmo-centric." Although during the medieval period, God, instead of the universe, became an important topic, interpretations of scriptures were more or less based on Greek thought.[93]

Acknowledging this sordid historical inheritance was of utmost importance for Fardid since it attested to the concurrent existence of two different versions of cultural traditions and beliefs in Eastern societies: the authentic version and the (Western) rationalized version. This was especially the case with Islam, which existed in both modern and spiritual/mystical forms. Fardid identified the latter as the only "authentic" form of Islamic thought-practice, which he then proceeded to prescribe as the only means of effectively countering Westoxication.

Indeed, as Mirsepassi has recently shown, at the core of Fardid's critique lay a rejection of "a humanist-inspired Western episteme" that regards traditions and cultural identity as perennially mutable constructions of human labor.[94] The subjugation of Eastern societies via a "standard of civilization" set by Western imperialism, it follows, reveal the very heights of this historical project, which may only be halted through a systematic "return" to the authentic language and practice of Islam. Of course, Fardid was far from alone in his eccentric reading of Western modernity's assault on "authenticity" in Iran; and his prescription in the form of a reimagined

---

[91] Ibid.
[92] For a meticulous consideration of Fardid's thinking on orientalism and his remedies, see Mirsepassi, *Transnationalism in Iranian Political Thought*, pp. 153–165.
[93] Fardid, "Pasokh be Chand Porsesh Dar Bab-e Farhang-e Shargh," p. 36. I rely on Mirsepassi's translation here in *Transnationalism in Iranian Political Thought*, p. 158.
[94] Mirsepassi, *Transnationalism in Iranian Political Thought*, p. 161.

88   The Specter of Westernism

Islamic episteme – an overdue "politics of spirituality," in Michel Foucault's exuberant phrasing – reflected the emerging zeitgeist of religion-led opposition to Western dominance in the Islamic world.[95]

Perhaps the most influential purveyor of this anti-modernist remedy – that is, the return to spiritual Islam – was Ali Shariati.[96] Widely regarded as the chief "ideologue" of Islamic revivalism in Iran,[97] Shariati's profile and intellectual imprint on the course of political developments in recent Iranian history has been thoroughly examined.[98] Yet despite the surplus of studies on Shariati, the contradictions in his political thought (i.e. the curiously incongruous melding of Marxism, Perso-Islamic mysticism, and orthodox Shia doctrine) and their culmination in the Islamic Republic leave ample room for debate about the coherence of the inherently monistic anti-modernism – however "mystical" or "universalist" – that underlaid it all. Shariati's call for a "return" to Islamic *agency* – not

[95] For a critical take on Foucault's fascination with the Shia liberation theology prior to the Iranian revolution, see Janet Afary and Kevin B. Anderson, *Foucault and the Iranian Revolution: Gender and the Seductions of Islamism* (Chicago, IL: The University of Chicago Press, 2005); for a sympathetic reading of Foucault's thought and involvement, see Behrooz Ghamari-Tabrizi, *Foucault in Iran: Islamic Revolution after the Enlightenment* (Minneapolis, MN: University of Minnesota Press, 2016).

[96] Hamid Enayat identified Shariati as "the most popular mentor of Islamic radicalism in modern Iran." He further noted, "As a teacher, orator and theorist, Sharī'atī has exercised an influence which is rarely matched by any other contemporary Muslim thinker anywhere in the Muslim world, not only in the development of the conceptual foundations of Islamic socialism as espoused by the educated youth, but also in the dissemination of the characteristics of militant Islam." Hamid Enayat, *Modern Islamic Political Thought: The Response of the Shi'i and Sunni Muslims to the Twentieth Century* (London: Bloomsbury Publishing, 2005), p. 226.

[97] According to Dabashi, "Shari'ati was an ideologue, first and foremost. One would be totally misled to treat him as a historian, a philosopher, a sociologist, an Islamicist .... Shari'ati wished to change, not interpret; lead, not argue; move, not convince; achieve, not rationalize." Dabashi, *Theology of Discontent*, p. 104.

[98] The most comprehensive treatment of Shariati's political biography in English is Ali Rahnema, *An Islamic Utopian: A Political Biography of Ali Shari'ati* (London: I.B. Tauris & Co. Ltd., 2014). Other exegetical treatments of Shariati's political career and thought in English include Ervand Abrahamian, *Radical Islam: The Iranian Mojahedin* (London: I.B. Tauris & Co. Ltd., 1989), chapter 4; Hamid Algar, *Roots of the Islamic Revolution in Iran* (Oneonta, NY: Islamic Publications International, 2001), chapter 3 (third lecture); Mangol Bayat Philipp, "Shi'ism in Contemporary Iranian Politics: The Case of Ali Shariati," in E. Kedourie and S. G. Haim, eds., *Towards a Modern Iran* (London: Frank Cass, 1980), pp. 155–168; Dabashi, *Theology of Discontent*, chapter 2; Boroujerdi, *Iranian Intellectuals and the West*, pp. 105–115; Gheissari, *Iranian Intellectuals in the 20th Century*, pp. 97–106; Mirsepassi, *Intellectual Discourse and the Politics of Modernization*, pp. 114–127; and Shahrough Akhavi, "'Ali Shari'ati," in John L. Esposito and Emad El-Din Shahin, eds., *The Oxford Handbook of Islam and Politics* (New York: Oxford University Press, 2013), pp. 169–179. For a reinterpretation of Shariati's thoughts in the postrevolutionary period, see Siavash Saffari, *Beyond Shariati: Modernity, Cosmopolitanism, and Islam in Iranian Political Thought* (Cambridge: Cambridge University Press, 2017).

Westoxication and the Liberal Other 89

merely identity[99] – as a means of confronting the cultural onslaught brought on by Western modernity was most acutely informed by the Third World liberationist movements of his time. His involvement in the Algerian anti-colonial struggles as well as in anti-Pahlavi dissident circles in Paris had convinced him of the need for a transcendental "authentic" ideology that avoided the trappings of Western modernity.[100] The latter, he maintained, used the illusion of material progress to alienate subalterns from their cultural heritage, thereby undermining their "commitment" and "responsibility" – what he identified as *ta 'asob* [zeal] – to their historical identity.[101] For Shariati, Islam was the binding element in this historical identity, but one whose revolutionary potential had for so long been tempered by the staid theological practices of the clergy and ingratiating impulses of Muslim modernizers.[102] These efforts had reinforced the false impression of faith as merely an aspect of social life, not a worldview (*jahan-bini*) in its own right. To counter these conceptions of Islam, Shariati proposed the Islamic principle of *towhid* (oneness of God and the universe), which in his view most accurately captured the essence of monotheism. In contrast to the prevalent practice of "social polytheism" that afforded "various groups and classes [to] compare the discrepancy in their social condition as well as their political-economic role with the discrepancy of human nature and their own racial roots," monotheism insisted on the unity of belief and action.[103]

Although Shariati drew heavily on varieties of Marxist and existentialist concepts to advance this revolutionary program, he was nonetheless avowedly hostile to the materialist conception of history that underpinned them. As he noted in his widely read tract, *Marxism and Other Western Fallacies*,

Islam and Marxism completely contradict each other in their ontologies and cosmologies. Briefly, Marxism is based on materialism and derives its sociology, anthropology, ethics, and philosophy of life from materialism. The Marxist

---

[99] Shariati's prescriptive remedy was first and foremost about authentic self-assertion (*bazgasht be khish* [return to oneself]) and the "revolutionary reconstruction of the self" (*khod-sazi-e enqelabi*), not the uncritical assumption of a purified Islamic identity. See Gheissari, *Iranian Intellectuals in the 20th Century*, pp. 104–107.

[100] Shariati translated both Franz Fanon's *Wretched of the Earth* and Che Guevara's *Guerilla Warfare* into Persian.

[101] Rahnema, *An Islamic Utopian*, p. 197.

[102] On this point, see Kamran Matin, "Decoding Political Islam: Uneven and Combined Development and Ali Shariati's Political Thought," in Robbie Shilliam, ed., *International Relations and Non-Western Thought: Imperialism, Colonialism, and Investigations of Global Modernity* (London: Routledge, 2010), pp. 124–140.

[103] Ali Shariati, *Islam and Man*, trans. Fatollah Marjani (Houston, TX: Free Islamic Lit. Inc., 1981), p. 21.

90   The Specter of Westernism

cosmos, i.e., the materialist cosmos, is, as Marx puts it, a "heartless and dispirited world" where man lacks a "real" destiny. By contrast, the cosmology of Islam rests upon faith in the unseen – the unseen [*ghayb*] being definable as the unknown actuality that exists beyond the material and natural phenomena that are accessible to the senses and to our intellectual, scientific, and empirical perception, and which constitutes a higher order of reality and the central focus of all the movements, laws, and phenomena of this world.[104]

A more vulgar form of this "economism" conditioned the credulous adherence to Western democracy and liberalism, which Shariati deigned too crude to merit any critical treatment:

> Democracy and Western liberalism – whatever sanctity may attach to them in the abstract – are in practice nothing but the free opportunity to display all the more strongly this spirit [i.e. economism] and to create all the more speedily and roughly an arena for the profit-hungry forces that have been assigned to transform man into an economic, consuming animal.[105]

For Shariati, "economism" belonged to a complex of "modern calamities that are leading to the deformation and decline of humanity."[106] To properly confront these forces, he argued, Muslims must resist the appropriation of their faith by modern concepts, and channel the disenchantment caused by modernity into recovering anti-modern progressive ideals. Shariati's alternative "world-vision" of Islamic renewal based on the principle of *towhid* captured the imagination of a rising generation of disaffected youth, for whom the blending of Marxism's radical egalitarian message with the unitarian repurposing of Shia doctrine cohered into a movable ideology of resistance.

That Shariati's revivalism of an Islamic worldview succeeded in enlisting vast segments of Iranian society into the revolutionary movement that eventually overthrew the Pahlavi monarchy raises the important question about the inability of liberal constitutionalists to do the same in this period. Why did an eclectic and curiously esoteric religious vision resonate more effectively than a worldly, secular program on

---

[104] Ali Shariati, *Marxism and Other Western Fallacies: An Islamic Critique*, trans. R. Campbell (Berkeley, CA: Mizan Press, 1980), pp. 65–66. It should be noted that although the authenticity of the English translation of this text has been disputed – it was first published as *Ensan, Eslam va Marxism* [Humankind, Islam, and Marxism] (Tehran: 1356/1977) – the passages quoted here are nevertheless representative of Shariati's thoughts on Western materialist philosophies. For a critical take on this, see Asef Bayat, "Shariati and Marx: A Critique of an 'Islamic' Critique of Marxism," *Alif: Journal of Comparative Poetics*, Vol. 9 (1990): 19–41.

[105] Ibid., p. 33.

[106] Ibid., p. 32. The other "intellectual systems" accompanying it were "historicism" (historical determinism), "biologism" (biological determinism), "sociologism" (sociological determinism), "materialism" (human life as "a material artifact"), and "naturalism" (viewing humans as animals). Ibid., pp. 34–35.

Westoxication and the Liberal Other

behalf of equal rights, the rule of law, separation of powers, and national independence? After all, it was not Shariati's philosophical anti-modernism that inspired his adherents – the conservative ulama's rejection of modernity had long occupied a vocal space on the ideological spectrum in Iranian politics. Nor was it the case that the substance of his thoughts was particularly coherent to his audience.[107] Moreover, Shariati's appropriation of modern concepts from a range of Western theories left ample room for different interpretations of his thought depending on the audience's background and interests.[108] Many scholars have cited Shariati's rhetorical talents and oratory in impressing upon the public the urgency of action and the need for political mobilization.[109] But this further begs the question as to why his powers of persuasion should have prevailed over those of others in the first place. The answer, I believe, lies in the *substantive* force of a concurrent line of critique especially aimed at liberals and Western-style liberalism, which resonated more concretely with embattled publics across the postcolonial world. The most important exponent of this critique in Iran was Jalal Al-e Ahmad, whose polemical essays did more to discredit and neutralize liberal-constitutionalist alternatives than anyone else's. The discourse of Westoxication as a critique of Western-inspired liberalism paved the way for Shariati's revival of Islamism as a return to an "authentic" selfhood.

Westoxication as a Critique of Western Liberalism

As mentioned earlier, although the term "*ghabzadegi*" was originally coined by Fardid in his lectures in the 1950s, it was Jalal Al-e Ahmad's 1961 booklet, *Gharbzadegi*, that helped to catapult the concept into the mainstream of Iranian cultural and political discourse.[110] But whereas Fardid's philosophical critique centered on modernity's alienating consequences (what Shariati called "modern calamities"), Al-e Ahmad's highly polemical tract focused exclusively on the cultural and political influences of Western ideas on Iranian society, which he likened to the spreading of

---

[107] As Dabashi rightly points out, "the minutiae of Shi'i scholastic debates were as strange and irrelevant as the concocted and hesitant language of the Marxist and Nationalist ideologies." Dabashi, *Theology of Discontent*, p. 113.

[108] For contextual receptions and reinterpretations of Shariati's thought especially in the postrevolutionary period, see Saffari, *Beyond Shariati*, chapters 1 and 3.

[109] Ibid. Shariati's gifted oratory was especially evident in his lectures at the Hosseiniyeh Ershad in Tehran, where most of his philosophical and political ideas were communicated to students, seminarians, religious intellectuals, and lay members of the public. See Rahnema, *An Islamic Utopian*, chapter 16.

[110] The English translation of the book drawn from here is entitled *Occidentosis*.

92   The Specter of Westernism

a disease (called "*gharbzadegi*").[111] Although he had been brought up in
a clerical family, Al-e Ahmad forewent training to become a clergyman
and instead attended night classes at Dar al-Fonoun, and from there went
on to study Persian literature at Tehran Teachers College and the
University of Tehran.[112] Prior to the 1953 coup, he was an active member
of a range of leftist political parties: he first joined the communist Tudeh
Party, but in the aftermath of a bitter internal split over its leadership he
left to cofound the Toilers' Party of Iran (Hezb-e Zahmatkeshan-e Iran)
and later the Third Force (Nirou-ye Sevvom), before turning to a life of
writing as a literary figure, translator, and political essayist.[113]

Echoing much of the anti-colonial literature of the time (especially
Fanon's *The Wretched of the Earth* and Aimé Césaire's *Discours sur le
colonialism*), Al-e Ahmad's account was structured around a vague polarity between the plentiful, yet avaricious, West, and the impoverished,
wronged East: "The West comprises the sated nations and the East, the
hungry nations ... on the one hand, a world with its forward momentum
grown terrifying and, on the other, a world that has yet to find a channel to
guide its scattered motive forces, which run to waste."[114] This polarity,
which since Afghani's time had been part and parcel of the critique of
Westernism in Iran, found its most strident expression in Al-e Ahmad's
blunt prose style, and more importantly in the narrowing of his target on
advocates of Westernization in Iran. For Al-e Ahmad, the technological
prowess of the West had not only enabled it to dominate the means of
material production but those of cultural production as well. The condition of being struck by the West was in essence the inability to escape the
depredations brought on by this "machine":

[111] Al-e Ahmad starts off the book with this analogy: "I speak of 'occidentosis' as of
tuberculosis. But perhaps it more closely resembles an infestation of weevils. Have you
seen how they attack wheat? From the inside. The bran remains intact, but it is just
a shell, like a cocoon left behind on a tree. At any rate, I am speaking of a disease: an
accident from without, spreading in an environment rendered susceptible to it." Al-e
Ahmad, *Occidentosis*, p. 27.

[112] As many intellectual biographers of Al-e Ahmad have noted, his decision to not become
a cleric was significantly influenced by his exposure to the anticlerical views of the
historian and reformist Ahmad Kasravi. Kasravi, as noted earlier, was among the first
intellectuals in the Reza Shah period to question the "blind imitation" of Western
societies in Iran, while also remaining unsparing in his criticism of the clergy's dogmatism and complicity in Iran's social backwardness. For an excellent description of
Kasravi's influence on Al-e Ahmad, see Dabashi, *Theology of Discontent*, pp. 45–46.

[113] Boroujerdi's description of Al-e Ahmad as a "bohemian belletrist" is especially apt.
Boroujerdi, *Iranian Intellectuals and the West*, pp. 65–76. For other overviews of Al-e
Ahmad's life and works, see Dabashi, *Theology of Discontent*, chapter 1; Hamid Algar's
introduction to *Occidentosis*, pp. 9–21; Mirsepassi, *Intellectual Discourse and the Politics of
Modernization*, pp. 97–114; Gheissari, *Iranian Intellectuals in the 20th Century*, pp. 88–92;
and Matin-Asgari, *Both Eastern and Western*, pp. 175–188.

[114] Al-e Ahmad, *Occidentosis*, pp. 28–29.

Westoxication and the Liberal Other

We have been unable to preserve our own historicocultural character in the face of the machine and its fateful onslaught. Rather we have been routed. We have been unable to take a considered stand in the face of this contemporary monster . . . . So long as we remain consumers, so long as we have not built the machine, we remain occidentotic. Our dilemma is that once we have built the machine, we will have become mechanotic, just like the West, crying out at the way technology and the machine have stampeded out of control.[115]

The mixture of righteous indignation and agonistic quandary conveyed in this passage can be found on nearly every page in *Gharbzadegi*. Al-e Ahmad is agonistic toward the general condition of society and its relation to the West; but he is positively combative and even prosecutorial toward the class of "occidentotic" intellectuals and ideas that have made these conditions possible. He traced the origins of *gharbzadegi* to the "first infections" of liberal reformers and intellectuals at the time of the Constitutional Revolution. Tellingly, the death of Nuri – or, rather, the circumstances surrounding his rise and demise during the Constitutional Revolution – looms large over the proposition behind *Gharbzadegi*. Al-e Ahmad argued that Nuri had been executed because he was

an advocate of rule by Islamic law (and as an advocate for Shi'i solidarity) . . . [which occurred] in an age when the leaders among our occidentotic intellectuals were the Christian Malkum Khan and the Caucasian Social Democrat Talibov! Now the brand of occidentosis was imprinted on our foreheads. I look on that great man's body on the gallows as a flag raised over our nation proclaiming the triumph of occidentosis after two hundred years of struggle. Under this flag we are like strangers to ourselves, in our food and dress, our homes, our manners, our publications, and, most dangerous, our culture. We try to educate ourselves in the European style and strive to solve every problem as Europeans would.[116]

The triumph of this cohort of Westernized intellectuals in the movement for constitutionalism, Al-e Ahmad emphasized, marked the surrender of Iranian culture to and under the terms of the Western machine. Specifically, the denigration of Islam and tradition – as reflected in the drive to modernize the Persian language and cultural customs – created a false binary between religion and constitutionalism in the public imagination, and prepared the ground for the alienation of successive generations of Iranian intellectuals. As he lamented about the latter: "So far as I can see, all these homegrown Montesquieus of ours fell off the same side of the roof . . . they all had an instinctive feeling that our ancient society and tradition could not withstand the onslaught of Western technology. They all went astray in opting for 'adoption of European civilization

---

[115] Ibid., p. 31.   [116] Ibid., pp. 56–57.

94   The Specter of Westernism

without Iranian adaptation.'"[117] This "infestation" of the constitutional process by the liberals' reflexive anti-traditionalism, Al-e Ahmad concluded, effectively transformed constitutionalism into "the vanguard of the machine."[118]

In a subsequent collection of ten essays entitled *Dar Khedmat va Khiyanat-e Rowshanfekran* [On the Service and Betrayal of Intellectuals],[119] Al-e Ahmad expanded beyond his narrower jeremiad in *Gharbzadegi* by reflecting more broadly on the role and responsibilities of intellectuals in Iran.[120] Although he did not abandon the binary East-West framework in delineating between those whom he viewed as working "in the service" (i.e. authentic resisters) of their country and those who "betrayed" it (i.e. Westoxicated collaborators), the volume on the whole displayed more concretely those qualities of the mind, cultural dispositions, and political loyalties Al-e Ahmad believed to be characteristic of the intellectual's responsibility to "the public good."[121] Strikingly, however, many of these attributes run counter to the nativist tenor and mode of intellectual reflection that Al-e Ahmad himself provides in writing on the subject. Consider, for instance, his description of the intellectual as someone who "climbs out from the pitfalls of their own self, home, city, land, language and religion to see the world via the expanse of a singular humanity, encompassing diverse peoples, languages customs, cultures, and religions."[122] His lamentations about the loss of tradition, culture, language, and an "uncontaminated" sense of self among West-stricken Iranian intellectuals seem to betray the attributes he venerates in the intellectual-as-public-servant. Curiously, even as he denies that those with religious dispositions could ever possess the independence of mind essential for intellectual pursuits (given their "obedience" (*ta'abod*) to divine entities), he nonetheless repeatedly refers to Islam and traditional culture as indispensable intellectual resources for countering Western imperialism.[123]

Further puzzling is Al-e Ahmad's fulminations against modern institutions of higher learning in Iran, which he holds responsible for instilling

---

[117] Ibid., p. 58. The phrase quoted by Al-e Ahmad was a famous line by Malkum Khan.

[118] Ibid., p. 59.

[119] The collection's title was a nod to the French philosopher Julien Benda's 1927 book *La Trahison des Clercs*, and sought to provide a similar critical commentary on the responsibilities of intellectuals. Jalal Al-e Ahmad, *Dar Khedmat va Khiyanat-e Rowshanfekran* [On the Service and Betrayal of Intellectuals] (Tehran: Ravaq Publishers, 1356/1977).

[120] For an excellent, recent appraisal of *Dar Khedmat va Khiyanat-e Rowshanfekran*, see Matin-Asgari, *Both Eastern and Western*, pp. 183–188.

[121] Ibid., p. 27.

[122] Ibid. I borrow Matin-Asgari's precise translation of this short excerpt in ibid., p. 183.

[123] Al-e Ahmad, *Dar Khedmat va Khiyanat-e Rowshanfekran*, p. 33.

Westoxication and the Liberal Other   95

a fondness for Western ideas and models of progress at the expense of indigenous ones. For instance, he emphatically declares that technical colleges such as Dar al-Fonoun were detrimental to the traditional institutions of learning in Iranian society, fully neglecting the reasons that necessitates their founding in the first place (i.e. outdated curricula, dogmatic instruction, insular learning environments, etc.).[124] Yet, he rather credulously overlooks the crucial role modern institutions of higher learning played in cultivating the methods of scientific skepticism and critical reasoning skills among the generation of dissident intellectuals and even reformist politicians advocating for liberty of conscience, political equality, impartial legal institutions, national independence, and accountability in the period before and after the Constitutional Revolution. Indeed, those salutary intellectual qualities Al-e Ahmad identifies as beneficial to the interests of Iranian society were amply present in the works by the cohort of constitutionalist liberals he abjures in both *Gharbzadegi* and *On Service and Betrayal of Intellectuals* for turning "the machine" against the clergy and indigenous traditions.[125]

These contradictions in Al-e Ahmad's thoughts arise from his rather crude criteria for what constitutes "service" and "betrayal" in intellectual discourse. For him, resistance to Western-inspired ideas, practices, and institutions – that is, "the machine" – was a mark of intellectual "service," while any intellectual enthusiasm for the substance of Western ideas and models of progress amounted to a "betrayal" of tradition and country. This is due to "a fundamental difference" between Iranian intellectuals and their Western counterparts, which Al-e Ahmad indignantly describes in the following manner:

The Western intellectual in the *metropole* (the capital), who has open access to all the institutions of learning and research as well as museums – which all have been enriched through colonial plundering – is endowed with the power to replace ancient religious metaphysics with a new quest based on a scientific worldview that serves as a monument to freethinking. In contrast, the Iranian intellectual exists in a neocolonial setting devoid of access to any of the institutions that have plundered his society, and without the luxury of living in a society in which opinions and votes are freely exchanged (due to the illiteracy of a majority of his

---

[124] As Gheissari correctly points out, Al-e Ahmad (along with Shadman who also lamented the transformation of traditional schools) "failed to note the underlying dangers of rigidity inherent in such settings." Gheissari, *Iranian Intellectuals in the 20th Century*, p. 91.

[125] Fereydoun Adamiyat's intellectual biographies of the leading thinkers of the constitutional movement attest to precisely such rooted but also cosmopolitan attributes. See *Fekr-e Azadi, Andisheha-ye Mirza Fath'Ali Akhundzadeh, Andisheha-ye Mirza Agha Khan Kermani,* and *Andisheha-ye Talebof Tabrizi* [Talebof Tabrizi's Thoughts], 2nd ed. (Tehran: Damavand, 1363/1984).

96   The Specter of Westernism

compatriots, etc.) is in the first place confronted with the daily assaults brought on by colonialism, which in addition to [Western] technology and products also imports its voices, opinions, and customs . . .. This colonial assault which plunders the colonies' natural and human resources (in the form of a brain drain), is also meant to destroy their language, music, customs, morals, and religious traditions. And is it appropriate for any Iranian intellectual to enjoin this all-out colonial assault instead of resisting it?[126]

Al-e Ahmad's fixation with, and contempt for, the liberal proponents of constitutionalism in Iran – the likes of Akhundzadeh, Kermani, Talebof Tabrizi, Mostashar al-Dowleh, and Malkum Khan, whose documented "liberal antipathies" were reviewed in Chapter 2 – was precisely that they represented the prototypical "peripheral" intellectual class who neglected the wider colonial setting in which they operated. "Unless the Iranian intellectual understand that in a colonial context his first priority should be to train against colonialism," Al-e Ahmad inveighed, "then there shall never be any trace of his existence."[127] This is why liberal constitutionalists and their successors remained distant from "the people" in both thought and action – their ideas and solutions remained "non-native" and "inauthentic" to the end and only served to empower secular autocracy.[128] Under the terms of Western imperialism, Al-e Ahmad argued, liberal ideals such as liberty, equality, impartiality, and the rule of law were little more than borrowed hypocrisies of a colonial age in which the powers of interpretation, distribution, and profit lay squarely in the metropolitan imaginations of colonial elites and their interests.[129] In the case of Iran, this was most evident in Western support for the Pahlavi regime.[130]

Al-e Ahmad's inflection of the *gharbzadegi* discourse, then, was qualitatively different from the critiques of pseudo-modernism and Western modernity that exercised his predecessors and contemporaries, respectively. By singling out the perversions of liberal constitutionalism and dramatizing their consequences in relation to the execution of Nuri and the rise of Pahlavi autocracy (backed by Western democracies), he instilled in the popular imagination a secular impression of liberalism as the insidious ideology of Western imperialism. Yet, much of the weight of his criticisms rest on the power of his prose as opposed to any coherent

---

[126] Al-e Ahmad, *Dar Khedmat va Khiyanat-e Rowshanfekran*, pp. 51–52 (emphasis in the original).

[127] Ibid., p. 407.   [128] Ibid., pp. 407–408.

[129] This is a major theme of the penultimate chapter of the volume. Ibid., pp. 402–432.

[130] As Boroujerdi notes, "Al-e Ahmad's disillusionment with liberalism was caused by the fact that despite its vow to safeguard democracy all that the West provided for Iran was (neo)colonialism and support for autocratic rulers." Boroujerdi, *Iranian Intellectuals and the West*, p. 75.

Conclusion: *Gharbzadegi* contra Westernism 97

engagement with the substance of liberal thought and practice in Iran. His constant references to the ethno-religious backgrounds of notable liberals ("the Armenian-Christian Malkum Khan," "the Georgian Akhundzadeh," etc.), and innuendos about Bahai-run "intellectual hangouts" and Freemason lodges as centers of liberal insurrectionary ideas, do more to stoke xenophobic fears than remotely address the deficiencies of liberal ideology.[131] In this regard, he was more of a chronicler of what he took to be the adulterating "misdeeds" of (non-native) intellectuals than a rigorous interlocutor of their thoughts.[132] All the same, the near-liturgical status of his particular interpretation of *gharbzadegi* in both Persian- and English-language discussions of Iran's intellectual development speak to the purchase his polemics had on the generation of revolutionaries that vowed to be and yearn for "Neither Eastern nor Western, but the Islamic Republic!"[133]

Conclusion: *Gharbzadegi* contra Westernism

The discourse of *gharbzadegi* was both a symptom and a cause of changes in the socioeconomic, political, and cultural structures that shaped the concerns of Iranian intellectuals in the second half of the twentieth century. The beginnings of these changes can in turn be dated back to the period of the Constitutional Revolution in Iran (1906–1911), which, as Chapter 2 chronicled, itself resulted from the confrontation between Western-inspired liberal-reformist ideas and the forces of traditionalism, absolutism, and imperialism. In essence, *gharbzadegi* was a rejection of the spirit of Western liberal modernity behind the movement for constitutionalism, which it blamed for having "infested" the course of cultural and political development in Iran. As I hope the preceding has made clear, there is very little by way of substantive critique of these liberal-reformist ideas in the writings and rhetorical statements of the leading intellectual exponents of *gharbzadegi*, except for their rather perfunctory dismissal as the ideological toolkit of Western colonial/imperial interests. Despite this purely polemical line of attack, however, *gharbzadegi* offered a simple but powerful diagnostic that questioned the utility of modern

---

[131] See ibid., pp. 409–423.

[132] As Gheissari has aptly observed, "He did not engage in any systematic evaluation of traditional institutions, knowledge, or value judgments, and his analysis barely went beyond the level of introducing historical arguments into a political controversy." Gheissari, *Iranian Intellectuals in the 20th Century*, p. 92.

[133] In the aftermath of the Iranian revolution and the subsequent advent of the Islamic Republic (through a national referendum), this became a signature slogan of the regime to signal its independence from both the West and the Soviet Union in the global Cold War.

98   The Specter of Westernism

liberal-reformist ideas to achieving authentic cultural and political independence. In their place, it offered a prescriptive model that, characteristic of other Third-Worldist movements, blended elements of Marxist revolutionary thought with Islamic ideology in order to seek out a new constituency that was at once recognizably aggrieved by the political, socioeconomic, and cultural "assault" of Western interests and their domestic collaborators.

By the mid-1970s, the discourse of *gharbzadegi* had been successfully transformed into a plan of action for a range of opposition groups such as the People's Mojahedin, the Freedom Movement of Iran, the Islamic Association of Students, the Confederation of Iranian Students in Exile, and even the moderate secular National Front.[134] Perhaps most significantly, given its popular resonance, it forced the dissident clergy such as Khomeini – and clerical organizations such as the Combatant Clergy Association and the Coalition of Islamic Societies – to reframe their political ideals in Third-Worldist binaries and terminologies that connected them to popular grievances. Hence Khomeini's noticeable appropriation of secular-leftist concepts and terms in communicating his theories of state and society.[135] In retrospect, it is not surprising that Khomeini should have become the avatar and spiritual leader of the revolutionary movement that most dramatically registered *gharbzadegi*'s prescriptive program by toppling the Shah and repudiating the Western-led international order – nor that his vision of an Islamic Republic became, in reality, a monument to the contradictions, rigidities, and nativist tendencies inherent in *gharbzadegi*'s insistence on political and cultural authenticity. Prior to the outbreak of the revolution, many

---

[134] In fact, the discourse of *gharbzadegi* had become so powerful in this period that in the last two years of the Pahlavi regime, the state-sponsored journal *Bonyad Monthly* published a series of articles which sought to invert and appropriate *gharbzadegi*'s underlying themes of dispossession, anti-imperialism, and calls for authenticity in order to neutralize its wide appeal. For a recent dissection of this attempt, see Ali Mirsepassi and Mehdi Faraji, "De-politicizing Westoxification: The Case of *Bonyad Monthly*," *British Journal of Middle East Studies*, Vol. 45, No. 3 (2018): 355–375.

[135] He repositioned the ulama's role as defenders of "national consciousness" against the Western secularism, capitalism, and imperialism, and borrowed heavily from a Marxist-inspired vocabulary that, as Abrahamian has shown, "depicted society as sharply divided into two warring classes (*tabaqat*): the *mostazafin* (oppressed) against the *mostakberin* (oppressors); the *foqara* (poor) against the *sarvatmandaran* (rich); the *mellat-e mostazaf* (oppressed nation) against the *hokoumat-e shaytan* (Satan's government); the *zagheneshinha* (slum dwellers) against the *kakh-neshinha* (palace dwellers); the *tabaqeh-ye payin* (lower class) against the *tabaqe-ye bala* (upper class); and *tabaqeh-ye mostamadan* (needy class) against the *tabaqeh-ye a'yan* (aristocratic class)." Ervand Abrahamian, *Khomeinism: Essays on the Islamic Republic* (Berkeley, CA: University of California Press, 1993), p. 26. For an examination of the shift in Khomeini's framing of his political agenda, see ibid., pp. 17–32.

Conclusion: *Gharbzadegi* contra Westernism 99

opposition groups with disparate ideologies and political agendas were compelled by Khomeini's unflinching airing of their grievances against the Shah, the global capitalist system, and Western hypocrisy on democracy and human rights. In his speeches, interviews, and written correspondence, many evinced a reactivated liberation theology in solidarity with lay aspirations to national independence and cultural dignity, not the dawn of religious fundamentalism. As Abrahamian has persuasively argued, "Khomeinism" was from the start less about fundamentalist adherence to Islamic doctrine than "pragmatic – even opportunistic – populism."[136] The 1979 revolution and the advent of the Islamic Republic, moreover, enabled Khomeini to both restore Shiism's status as the authentic source of politico-cultural life and to undertake "a far-reaching transformation of the Shi'ite tradition that can best be characterized as a revolution *in* Shi'ism."[137] The latter was reflected in Khomeini's theory of *velayat-e faqih* (guardianship of the jurist), which argued for the political rule of Islamic jurists (*foqaha*) over the people, and which became the basis for the constitution of the Islamic Republic.

In light of this history, the morphing of *gharbzadegi* into "Khomeinism" was less the case of a misappropriation of political ideology by clerical opportunism than merely the logical unfolding of events according to a grievance-based telos. For if Islamic identity as a resource for authenticity ought to have become the measure of meaningful political agency – as Shariati and Al-e Ahmad argued it should – then who more legitimate than those ordained by God to, per scripture, "enjoin what is right and forbid what is wrong" (*amr-e be ma'roof va nahy az monkar*)? Khomeinism's exalted new status as a standard for political participation in the Islamic Republic, however, predictably exposed the limitations of this discourse as a governing ideology. As erstwhile leftist allies and secular boosters were either marginalized, brutally suppressed, or exiled, the inherent characteristic of Khomeinism as a *monistic* political vision became abundantly clear.[138] This was further consolidated through Khomeinism's cultivation of a "paranoid style" in Iranian politics – which saw "satanic plots," "Zionist machination," and "behind-the-scenes" imperial scheming – that

---

[136] Ibid., p. 4. Abrahamian notes, "'populism' is a more apt term for describing Khomeini, his ideas, and his movement because this term is associated with ideological flexibility, with political protests against the established order, and with socioeconomic issues that fuel mass opposition to the status quo." Ibid., p. 2.

[137] Amir Arjomand, *The Turban for the Crown*, p. 177. See the entirety of chapter 9 in this volume, pp. 177–188.

[138] For a granular history of one particularly segment of this coalition, see Abrahamian, *Radical Islam*.

100   The Specter of Westernism

could be used as a pretext for the elimination of dissident groups.[139] Indeed, Khomeinism's "paranoid style" was merely the continuation of the discourse of *gharbzadegi*, which provided it with the vocabulary of a grievance-based politics of authenticity that reduced the complexities of life in a pluralistic society to simple, self-affirming binaries. "Thus," Abrahamian notes of the early years of the Islamic Republic, "political activists tended to equate competition with treason, liberalism with weakmindedness, honest differences of opinion with divisive alien conspiracies, and political toleration with permissiveness toward the enemy within."[140] Of course, the paranoid style was also exacerbated by the geopolitical context surrounding the first decade of the Islamic Republic, as Iran was isolated by Western powers and much of the international community, shunned by Sunni and secular Muslim-majority countries, and engulfed in a costly eight-year war with Saddam Hussein's Iraq (one of the longest conventional interstate conflicts of the twentieth century). But even with this broader context in mind, Khomeinism's utility was chiefly to preserve and consolidate the ideological aims of the Islamic Republic as a political regime.

The emergence of a reform movement in the late 1990s was in large measure the beginnings of a reckoning with the tragic consequences of Khomeinism. It was in this period that scholars, intellectuals, and political activists began to critically reassess the binary terminology, distorted histories, and selective enmities that informed the ideological foundations of the Islamic Republic.[141] As part of these renewed engagements, a discerning, albeit ambivalent, discourse of "pluralism" began to emerge that sought to at once reject the reflexive anti-Westernism of reigning revolutionary discourses and refocus the terms of political debate around concepts such as "Islamic democracy" and constitutionalism. That open

---

[139] See Abrahamian's chapter on "The Paranoid Style in Iranian Politics" in his *Khomeinism*, pp. 111–131. The mass executions of members of the opposition group, the Mojahedin-e Khalq, in 1981–1982 and in 1988 were the starkest examples of this tactic. As Abrahamian notes of the 1981–1982 executions, "In six short weeks, the Islamic Republic shot over one thousand prisoners. The victims included not only members of the Mojahedin but also royalists, Bahais, Jews, Kurds, Baluchis, Arabs, Qashqayis, Turkomans, National Frontists, Maoists, anti-Stalinist Marxists, and even apolitical teenage girls who happened to be in the wrong street at the wrong time. Never before in Iran had firing squads executed so many in so short a time over so flimsy an accusation. Real fears had merged with unreal ones. The paranoid style had produced tragedy as well as comedy." Ibid., p. 131.

[140] Ibid., p. 130.

[141] See Mehran Kamrava, *Iran's Intellectual Revolution* (Cambridge: Cambridge University Press, 2008); and more recently, Eskandar Sadeghi-Boroujerdi, *Revolution and Its Discontents: Political Thought and Reform in Iran* (Cambridge: Cambridge University Press, 2019).

intellectual debates about the merits of the latter are once again in vogue is as much a testament to the currency of liberal-constitutional antipathies toward the monistic, repressive, and exploitative maladies imperiling Iranian politics from within and without, as it is a test of its prescriptions to meet the challenges ahead.

4   Liberation without Liberalism

Not the "Republic of Iran," nor the "Democratic Republic of Iran," nor the "Democratic Islamic Republic of Iran," just the "Islamic Republic of Iran."[1]

The tradition of all the dead generations weighs like a nightmare on the brain of the living. And just when men seem engaged in revolutionizing themselves and things, in creating something that has never yet existed, precisely in such periods of revolutionary crisis they anxiously conjure up the spirits of the past to their service and borrow from them names, battle cries and costumes in order to present the new scene in this time-honored disguise and this borrowed language.[2]

If the Iranian revolution in 1979 was a political triumph for the discourses critical of Westernism in Iranian society, it was equally, if not more so, a crisis of political representation. No sooner had the revolutionary movement succeeded in toppling the Western-backed Pahlavi autocracy than it was beset by intense factionalism and discord over the future shape of government. Once again, at the heart of these disputes lay questions about the proper constitutional order – for example, of membership, representation, rights, the balance between religious and secular legal principles, justice, etc. – for a restive public that sought to resolutely move beyond absolutist systems of rule. As the de facto leader of the revolution (although by no means representative of its heterogeneity), Ayatollah Ruhollah Khomeini enjoyed a unique advantage in promoting his own particular vision of government, which represented a curious admixture of Platonic ideas and Islamic principles as a prescriptive model for governing the state.[3] The principle of *velayat-e faqih* (guardianship of

---

[1] Ayatollah Ruhollah Khomeini quoted in Amir Arjomand, *The Turban for the Crown*, p. 137.
[2] Karl Marx, "The Eighteenth Brumaire of Louis Bonaparte," in *Selected Works* (Moscow: Progress Publishers, 1958), p. 247.
[3] Khomeini's political views were first published in *Kashf al-Asrar* [The Unveiling of Secrets] (Tehran: 1322/1943), which was a refutation of reformist critiques of traditional Islam by a former seminarian, Ali Akbar Hakimzadeh. His thoughts on Islamic government, and specifically his concept of *velayat-e faqih* (guardianship of the jurist) were collected in *Hokoumat-e Eslami* [Islamic Government] (Tehran: 1357/1978). For a comprehensive scholarly treatment of Khomeini's constitutional vision, see Vanessa Martin, *Creating an Islamic State: Khomeini and the Making of a New Iran*

Liberation without Liberalism 103

the jurist) formed the cornerstone of this vision, and soon after Khomeini's ascendance to power became the basis for the Constitution of the Islamic Republic of Iran.[4] As the preamble to the newly adopted constitution noted, the enumerated laws, representative institutions, and rights of citizens were designed to promote Islamic values: "The Constitution of the Islamic Republic of Iran advances the cultural, social, political, and economic institutions of Iranian society based on Islamic principles and norms, which represent an honest aspiration of the Islamic Ummah."[5]

Khomeini's conception of Islamic government was in contrast to more liberalconstitutionalist views espoused by the cohort of religious modernists in the Liberation Movement of Iran (LMI) (Nehzat-e Azadi-e Iran), led by the interim premier Mehdi Bazargan. Indeed, the LMI's preference was for a modified version of the 1907 Supplementary Fundamental Laws of the Iranian Constitution. The latter recognized Twelver Shiism as the official religion of the state while making a clear distinction between the judicial authority of the ulama in matters pertaining to Sharia codes and those of lay jurists concerning civil law (*'urf*).[6] In the course of deliberations about the draft constitution, however, the Khomeinist faction, led by Ayatollah Hossein-Ali Montazeri, argued that any distinctions between religious and civil laws diluted the Islamic character of the revolution and would eventually lead once again to the marginalization of the clergy in social and political realms.[7] "If we want to follow Islamic law," Montazeri noted, "we must say that the enactments of the Majles are not legal and enforceable without the approval of the jurists of the Council of Guardians."[8] With the balance of forces favoring the Khomeinists in the Assembly of Experts, the final draft of the constitution was significantly altered in favor of clerical authorities. The new

---

(London: I.B. Tauris & Co. Ltd., 2010); and Sadeghi-Boroujerdi, *Revolution and Its Discontents*, pp. 93–135.

[4] Algar, *Islam and Revolution*, pp. 27–166.

[5] "The Constitution of the Islamic Republic of Iran, Preamble" (Tehran: adopted 1979; amended 1989). For a wide-ranging exegesis of the constitution, see Said Amir Arjomand, "Constitution of the Islamic Republic," *Encyclopædia Iranica*, Vol. VI, Fasc. 2 (1992), pp. 150–158.

[6] Moreover, the religious authorities had to still be approved by parliament once they had been nominated by a *marja'-e taqlid* (a source of emulation or supreme religious authority). See "The Supplementary Fundamental Laws of October 7, 1907," in Browne, *The Persian Revolution of 1905–1909*, appendix A.

[7] Montazeri presented the religious justifications for this view at the fortieth session of the Assembly of Experts on October 9, 1979; see the minutes in S. J. Madani, *Hoquq-e Asasi dar Jomhouri-ye Eslami-e Iran* [Constitutional Laws of the Islamic Republic of Iran], Vol. II (Tehran: Soroush, 1365/1986), pp. 177–178.

[8] Ibid., p. 178, n. 23. Translation from citation in Amir Arjomand, "Constitution of the Islamic Republic," p. 152.

104   Liberation without Liberalism

document was put to a national referendum and ratified on December 2–3, 1979, as the Constitution of the Islamic Republic of Iran.

Conventional accounts of the Iranian revolution have characterized the defeat of religious modernists in the aforementioned debate as both a power grab by a long-ignored clerical establishment and a rejection of "Islamic liberalism" as represented by Bazargan and his allies.[9] Certainly, the supporters of the LMI and later reformists have viewed this historical juncture much the same way. Yet, in a significant sense, the historical juxtapositions of Khomeinist Islam against the "Islamic liberalism" of religious modernists overlook a crucial factor in the crisis of representation embedded in their respective conceptions of constitutionalism. The source of this persistent crisis – unresolved since the Iranian revolution – is the difficulty of reconciling an essentially *monistic* vision of governance (i.e. political Islam, in both its fundamentalist and reformist varieties) with the *pluralistic* demands of democratic politics. In the four decades since the revolution, the prevailing Khomeinist conception has been unequivocal in its rejection of the possibility of an equitable reconciliation (Khomeini's remark at the top of this chapter is a good rhetorical representation of this). For their part, religious reformists have denied that a monistic vision of constitutionalism is the core issue. Instead, they have pointed to arbitrary structural designs that, in the name of Islam, concentrate power in select institutions of government. The antidemocratic or arbitrary aspects of the Islamic Republic, influential reformist thinkers such as Abdolkarim Soroush and Hassan Yousefi Eshkevari (among others) have noted, can be remedied by restoring the division of religious and civil legal codes, and by removing the clerical oversight (i.e. the guardianship of the Islamic jurist) of the legislature and the judiciary.[10]

The quite limited confines of this intra-Islamic political debate have left little room for any considerations of alternative democratic-constitutional

---

[9] Among influential accounts, see Shaul Bakhash, *The Reign of the Ayatollahs: Iran and the Islamic Revolution* (New York: Basic Books, 1984); Amir Arjomand, *The Turban for the Crown*; Milani, *The Making of Iran's Islamic Republic*; and Charles Kurzman, *The Unthinkable Revolution in Iran* (Cambridge, MA: Harvard University Press, 2004).

[10] Abdolkarim Soroush, *Reason, Freedom, and Democracy in Islam*, trans. Mahmoud Sadri and Ahmad Sadri (Oxford: Oxford University Press, 2000); Hassan Yousefi Eshkevari, *Remembering the Days: Political Approaches of the Reformist Movement in Iran* (Tehran: Gam-eh No, 2000). Representative arguments by other leading reformists include Saeed Hajjarian, "Velayat-e Motlaqeh-ye Faqih va Qanun-e Asasi" [The Absolute Rule of the Jurist and Constitutionalism], *Asr-e Ma*, No. 61 (February 7, 1997); Mohsen Kadivar, *Hokumat-e Vela'iy: Andishe-ye Siasi Dar Eslam* [Government by the Guardian: An Exercise in Islamic Political Thought] (Tehran: Nashr-e Ney, 1377/1998); and Mohammad Mojtahed Shabestari, "Demokrasi va din-dari" [Democracy and Religious Piety], in *Naqdi bar Qara'at-e Rasmi az Din: Bohran-ha, Chalesh-ha, Rah-e Hal-ha* [A Critique of Literal Interpretations of Religion: Crises, Debates, and Solutions] (Tehran: Tarh-e Now, 1379/2000).

Liberation without Liberalism

schemes inside Iran. But it is a striking demonstration of the enduring purchase of revolutionary ideals even among reformist intellectuals that liberal antecedents of core democratic values such as individual autonomy, political equality, and reciprocity have either remained unacknowledged, appropriated without attribution, or dismissed as inauthentic (i.e. un-Islamic) altogether. In pointing out this peculiar dynamic, I do not wish to construct a binary relationship between Islam and liberalism. Rather, my aim here is to navigate the postrevolutionary political and intellectual landscape in search of reasons behind liberalism's continuing invisibility as a public standpoint despite its subliminal presence in nearly every major discussion about the imperative of reforms, the future of Islamic government, and the possibility of non-liberal democracy in Iran.

There are two sets of reasons – historical and philosophical – for the persistence of this paradox. As a historical matter, the reasons for the marginalization of liberal and other secular viewpoints simply boil down to the balance and structure of power in the Islamic Republic. As with the Pahlavi period, the monopoly over the means and exercise of power are concentrated in institutions whose prerogatives are ultimately arbitrary and, by design, immune from popular recourse. Under such circumstances, any ideology that would seek an alternative power arrangement may easily be outlawed and repressed, as has been the case with secular viewpoints since 1979. In philosophical terms, moreover, the substantive differences between religious and secular views of constitutionalism (in any tradition) clearly entail that any overlap between inherently monistic (political Islam) and pluralistic (liberalism) ideologies will be tenuous. Again, this is not to suggest a zero-sum dynamic between Islamic doctrine and liberal beliefs; but rather to underscore the unavoidable clash of conflicting interpretations of each ideology in the nonideal world, where political actors – that is, political Islamists in power since 1979 – may view their status in binary terms vis-à-vis their opponents.

My aim in this chapter, however, is not to rehearse these reasons, which have been examined thoroughly in the literature on political Islam and Islamic reformism within Iranian studies.[11] Nor do I intend to reproduce arguments on the relationship between Islam and liberal democracy that became a cottage industry of sorts in the post–Cold War period (largely in

---

[11] Notable accounts in English include Ali M. Ansari, *Iran, Islam, and Democracy: The Politics of Managing Change* (London: Royal Institute of International Affairs, 2000; reissued with Gingko Library in 2019); Daniel Brumberg, *Reinventing Khomeini: The Struggle for Reform in Iran* (Chicago, IL: The University of Chicago Press, 2001); Farhang Rajaee, *Islamism and Modernism: The Changing Discourse in Iran* (Austin, TX: University of Texas Press, 2007); Kamrava, *Iran's Intellectual Revolution*; Mirsepassi, *Political Islam, Iran, and the Enlightenment*; and Laura Secor, *Children of Paradise: The Struggle for the Soul of Iran* (New York: Riverhead Books, 2016).

106   Liberation without Liberalism

response to hegemonic proclamations of "the end of history" and an impending "clash of civilizations" between the West and Islam).[12] The subject matter of this chapter is much narrower in scope. In keeping with my larger inquiry about the fate of liberalism in Iran, I am merely interested in exploring the implications stemming from the advent of the Islamic Republic for liberal thought-practices inside Iran. Specifically, I am keen to clarify the differences between liberal objections to all varieties of religious governance and Islamic modernist-cum-reformist efforts to reconcile monistic doctrines with pluralistic realities. The latter cohort's appropriation of some aspects of liberal thinking – by the LMI in 1970–1980 and by religious reformists after the election of Mohammad Khatami in 1997 – has obscured significant substantive differences between these visions, allowing for incoherent labels such as "Islamic liberalism."[13] Efforts to make the Islamic Republic more democratic or to advance a pluralistic vision of political Islam, however much progressive in the context of their times and political possibilities, nonetheless are substantively different in depth and scope from liberal-constitutional principles and visions of progress championed by advocates of political liberalism around the globe and inside Iran. Curiously, these differences have largely been downplayed, if not altogether overlooked, in political studies of postrevolutionary Islamic modernism and reformist thought. This oversight is due to two distinct but overlapping factors: (1) the limited, selective, and ahistorical appropriation of liberal concepts by religious advocates of political reforms inside Iran; and (2) post–Cold War liberal anxieties (and conceits) about the imperative for facilitating an "Islamic reformation" (akin to the Protestant Reformation) as a means toward the eventual liberalization of culture and politics. In the following, I examine each of these issues in turn and offer an explanation for their

---

[12] See Abdullahi Ahmed An-Na'im, *Toward an Islamic Reformation: Civil Liberties, Human Rights, and International Law* (Syracuse, NY: Syracuse University Press, 1996); John L. Esposito and John O. Voll, *Islam and Democracy* (New York: Oxford University Press, 1996); Khaled Abou El Fadl, *Islam and the Challenge of Democracy* (Princeton, NJ: Princeton University Press, 2004); Asef Bayat, *Making Islam Democratic: Social Movements and the Post-Islamist Turn* (Stanford, CA: Stanford University Press, 2007); and Jocelyn Cesari, *When Islam and Democracy Meet: Muslims in Europe and in the United States* (London: Palgrave Macmillan, 2006); and Hashemi, *Islam, Secularism, and Liberal Democracy*, to name just a few. Almost all of these works were in response to the provocative theses contained in Francis Fukuyama, *The End of History and the Last Man* (New York: Simon & Schuster, 1992); and Samuel P. Huntington, *The Clash of Civilizations and the Remaking of World Order* (New York: Simon & Schuster, 1998).

[13] See Houchang E. Chehabi, "Society and State in Islamic Liberalism," *State, Culture, and Society*, Vol. 3, No. 1 (Spring 1985): 85–101; and Ahmad Ashraf and Ali Banuazizi, "Iran's Tortuous Path Toward 'Islamic Liberalism'," *International Journal of Politics, Culture, and Society*, Vol. 15, No. 2 (Winter 2001): 237–256.

Monism and the Islamic Republic

combined impact on liberal political thought in contemporary Iranian intellectual discourses.

Monism and the Islamic Republic

The Islamic Republic of Iran was quite literally born out of a binary choice. On March 30–31, 1979, a national referendum was put to Iranians over the age of sixteen as follows: "To change the old [Pahlavi] regime to the Islamic Republic, the constitution for which shall be subject to approval by the public: Yes or No." In the deliberations preceding the vote many secular and nationalist political factions objected to the label "the Islamic Republic," the substance behind which ominously hinted at a theocratic form of government.[14] The issue was not merely about semantics, however, since there were palpable signs everywhere of clerical assertiveness in political affairs immediately in the days and weeks following Khomeini's return from exile. Not only had Khomeini taken it upon himself to appoint a provisional civilian government (led by Bazargan), he also had set up a "Revolutionary Council," which from the outset acted as a parallel and more consequential governmental authority. The latter was predominantly led by clerics, most of whose names and associations were at the time not disclosed to the public or to the provisional government. In the public imagination, however, these portentous developments were largely overshadowed by more immediate transitional worries about increasing domestic instability[15] or the prospect of a foreign-induced coup (à la 1953) – not to mention Khomeini's considerable popularity at the time.[16] Together, these factors combined to ensure the overwhelming passage – with 98.2 percent voting in the affirmative – of the referendum. The following day (April 1, 1979), Khomeini marked the occasion by proclaiming it "the first day of God's government."[17]

---

[14] Secular leftist groups preferred the labels "Democratic Republic of Iran" or "People's Republic of Iran," the Liberation Movement of Iran proposed the label "Democratic Islamic Republic of Iran," and secular nationalists suggested the more succinct "Republic of Iran" as an alternate moniker. Leading clerical figures rejected the term "democratic" outright, which Khomeini derided as too "Western" and antithetical to Islam. See Amir Arjomand, *The Turban for the Crown*, p. 137.

[15] Kurdish and Turkman separatism was a serious threat, as armed rebellions had flared up in March 1979.

[16] For more on the circumstances surrounding the vote, see Martin, *Creating an Islamic State*, pp. 147–159.

[17] Upon passage of the referendum Khomeini declared, "This day of Farvardin 12 [1358], the first days of God's government, is to be one of our foremost religious and national festivals; the people must celebrate this day and keep its remembrance alive, for it is the day on which the battlements of the twenty-five hundred-year old fortress of tyrannical government crumbled, a satanic power departed forever, and the government of the

108   Liberation without Liberalism

At the direction of Khomeini, the nascent clerical establishment moved swiftly to capitalize on the results of the referendum by "purifying" state ministries and public institutions (such as universities, broadcasting units, and even mosques) on the basis of sufficient fealty to Islamic principles and strictures as propagated by Khomeini. As a matter of political strategy, the ominous goal of such actions was to draw a clear distinction between those with proven allegiance to the Khomeinist vision of the Islamic Republic (*Nezam-e jomhouri-ye eslami*) and those who objected to the new clerics-led order.[18] To further clarify this objective, Khomeini used the occasion of the June 1963 (15 Khordad) uprising against the Shah – the key turning point at which political Islam was reawakened in Iran – to issue a stern warning to "the intellectuals" about the grave consequences of opposing Islamic government under clerical leadership. He implored:

Now is the time for Islam to be implemented. If we do not implement Islam and its ordinances with this Revolution, with this movement, when will we ever implement it? ... Those who say it is impossible to implement them now should tell us when it will be possible; if they are honest, they will say, "we will never want Islam." ... How much you talk about the West, claiming that we must measure Islam in accordance with Western criteria! What an error! In gratitude for the bounty of liberty you have received, you should be loyal to Islam; that is my advice to you .... Do not oppose the religious scholars, for they are also of benefit to you .... They understand what human rights are all about better than we do! ... I advise them [the intellectuals] not to make their course follow a path that diverges from Islam and the religious scholars. The power afforded the nation by the religious scholars is a God-given power; do not lose it. If you do, you will become nothing .... Intellectuals, do not be Western-style intellectuals, imported intellectuals; do your share to preserve the mosques. Jurists, start going to the mosques and help to preserve their role ...[19]

Although framed in reference to "Western-style" intellectuals, Khomeini's address was clearly aimed at both secular- and religious-minded critics who opposed his clerics-led theocratic vision. The speech also highlights the imperative of claiming the mantle of anti-imperialism from leftist and secular-nationalist movements that were once a crucial part of the coalition against the Shah, but whose recalcitrance now threatened to marginalize the clergy's newfound political opportunities. To Khomeini and his

---

oppressed – which is the government of God – was established in its place." Algar, *Islam and Revolution*, p. 266.

[18] A significant political-social binary was thus devised between *khodi-ha* (one of us) and *gheyr-e khodi-ha* (not one of us), respectively, as a tool of political policing.

[19] Khomeini's speech was printed in full in most daily newspapers the following day. For consistency in translations, I refer to Algar's translation of it here. Algar, *Islam and Revolution*, pp. 271–274.

Monism and the Islamic Republic 109

supporters, the insistence of the latter cohort – made up of the Islamist-Marxist Fadai'yun, the Mojahedin-e Islam, the Communist Tudeh Party, and the religious-nationalist LMI – for a more democratic political process, would simply dilute the Islamic essence of the revolution and over time lead to the relegation of the clergy to the seminaries, as had been the case in previous transitional periods. By portraying any such criticisms as enabling or collaborating with Western imperial interests, Khomeini intended to bolster the role of the clergy as the true guardians not only of Islam but also of authentic political, socioeconomic, and cultural development in Iran.[20]

The programmatic vision underlying much of Khomeini's political posturing in the months after his return from exile were first spelled out in a treatise entitled *Hokumat-e Eslami* [Islamic Government].[21] The book represents his ideas for how the sovereign divinity of Islam should be preserved in the absence or occultation of the Twelfth Imam, the Messiah (Mahdi), who in the Twelver Shia tradition of Islam is the rightful successor to the Prophet Muhammad. Rejecting the "quietist" tradition in Shiism, Khomeini argued that the function of the clergy and religious jurists is not merely to act as "guides" (*marja '*) to the faithful, but that they are in fact to be entrusted with the preservation of divine sovereignty until such time that the Mahdi emerges from hiding. Far from abstaining from political life, therefore, the clergy had a duty to act as the political guardians of divine sovereignty in Muslim societies. What this meant in practical terms is summed up by Hamid Algar in his introduction to Khomeini's treatise: (1) "the need for subordinating political power to Islamic goals, precepts, and criteria"; (2) "the duty of religious scholars (the *fuqaha*) to bring about an Islamic state, and to assume legislative, executive, and judicial positions within it – in short, the doctrine of "the governance of the *faqih*" (*velayat-e faqih*); and (3) "a program of action for the establishment of an Islamic state, including various measures for self-reform by the religious establishment."[22] Taken together, these overlapping injunctions secured the foundations of divine

---

[20] As Abrahamian points out, "Khomeini reminded his audience [that] clerics had risen to the occasion in times of crisis to protect Islam and Iran from imperialism and royal despotism … [that] the clergy as a whole had kept alive 'national consciousness' and stood firm as the 'fortress of independence' against imperialism, secularism and other 'isms' imported from the West." Abrahamian, *Khomeinism*, pp. 25–26.

[21] This treatise arose out of a series of lectures that Khomeini gave in Najaf, Iraq, between January 21 and February 8, 1970, to a group of seminary students. The lectures were first transcribed by a student, and subsequently revised by various publishers and translators. In English, the most reliable version of the tract is found in Algar, *Islam and Revolution*, pp. 25–166.

[22] Ibid., p. 25.

110   Liberation without Liberalism

sovereignty (*hakemiyat-e elahi*) through the guardianship of religious authorities.

In its insistence on the mutual constitution of religious leadership and politics, Khomeini's vision stood in stark contrast with centuries-old Shia jurisprudential perspectives that favored a more compartmentalized role for religious jurists within the state. The most developed versions of the latter conceptions were advanced by pro-constitutionalist ulama such as Mohammad Kazem "Akhound" Khorasani and his pupil Mirza Mohammad Hussein Na'ini at the outset of the twentieth century. In their estimation, the clergy's vital role was in shaping societal norms and the cultural mores of the faithful, which would ensure the overall welfare of the *umma* (the Muslim community). This perspective was laid out in detail by Na'ini in a treatise published in 1909, entitled *Tanbih al-umma wa tanzih al-milla, hokumat az nazar-e eslam* [On the Admonition and Refinement of the Nation: Or, Government from the Perspective of Islam].[23] Na'ini argued that in the absence of a truly just leader, and until such time that the Messiah returns, the most optimal form of government from an Islamic perspective would be a constitutional system that checked the power of the executive and honored the basic civil liberties of the people. "These two principles and their corollaries," Na'ini emphasized, "were constituted by the founder of the religion. So long as they were protected, and Islamic government did not degenerate from [constitutional to tyrannical] form, the pace of the expansion of Islam was mind-boggling."[24] Na'ini further noted that after the martyrdom of Hussein – the third Shia Imam – Muslim communities succumbed to tyranny and fell behind their Christian counterparts precisely because Muʿawiya and his successors established absolute rule.[25] The key implication of Na'ini's reflections on government and Islam was clear enough: the gravest danger to any society, especially the Muslim community, is absolute power in the name either of expedience or Islam. Na'ini believed that constitutionalism, as such, served as both a check against the accumulation of power and a guarantor of the sanctity of divine sovereignty within the Muslim community. This meant that the locus of *political* sovereignty ultimately rests with the people, who are subject to the contingencies of time, and therefore have to decide for themselves whether a given order/government is just or not. For these

---

[23] Mohammad Hussein Na'ini, *Tanbih al-umma wa tanzih al-milla, hokumat az nazar-e eslam* [On the Admonition and Refinement of the Nation: Or, Government from the Perspective of Islam], 6th ed. (Tehran: Sherkat-e Sahami-e Enteshar, 1339/1960).

[24] The translation is by Mahmoud Sadri in Charles Kurzman, ed., *Modernist Islam, 1840–1904: A Sourcebook* (New York: Oxford University Press, 2002), pp. 120–121.

[25] Ibid., p. 121.

Monism and the Islamic Republic 111

reasons, Na'ini held that Muslim citizens are better left to engage in the practice of *ijtihad* (independent interpretation of the Qur'an and the Sunna) or refer to the judgment of a *mujtahid* (someone who interpreted religious laws independently).[26]

Khomeini's views, however, were more aligned with those of the anti-constitutionalist cleric Sheikh Fazlollah Nuri, for whom popular sovereignty was wholly antithetical to Islam, and a deliberate ruse to undermine the mission and function of the Imamate (i.e. God's representatives in the *umma*). As surveyed in Chapter 3, Nuri was particularly incensed about the provision of equal rights to individuals – especially to Zoroastrians, Armenians, and Jews – as well as the notion that a simple parliamentary majority could produce new laws and strictures. In his sermon denouncing constitutionalism, Nuri protested that Islam was fundamentally about creating hierarchies of actions and individuals based on degrees of religiosity.[27] As such, he wondered, "How can Islam, which thus distinguishes among provisions of different matters, tolerate [the idea of] equality?"[28] By failing to appreciate the "just" hierarchies adumbrated in Islamic law, constitutionalism served only to weaken the divine sovereignty of God through its deputies. As Nuri explained in a tract attributed to him, *Ketab-e Tadhkirat-e al-Ghafil va-Irshad al-Jahil* [The Book of Admonition to the Misinformed and Guidance for the Ignorant], "Participation in the affairs of the community by anyone other than the Imam[ate] amounts to denigrating the authority of the Prophet and the Imam. ... If anyone else sits in his [the Imam's] place it is obligatory to oppose it."[29] This belief reflected Nuri's interpretation of Islamic history wherein the periods of relative strength and justice coincided with the reign of the Prophet and his disciples, and weakness and injustice ensued only when the polity did not follow their lead. As such, Nuri concluded, "it has become evident that, if justice is to spread, it is necessary to strengthen ... those who know [Islamic] provisions and those who possess power among Muslims. This is the way for earning the correct and useful justice."[30] For these reasons, during the Constitutional Revolution Nuri branded the Majlis "the house of infidelity" (*khaneh-ye kofr*) and was among the first to support its bombardment by Mohammad Ali Shah in 1908.[31]

[26] Ibid., pp. 122–125.
[27] Hairi, "Shaykh Fazl Allah Nuri's Refutation of the Idea of Constitutionalism."
[28] Ibid., p. 334.
[29] Mehdi Malekzadeh, *Tarikh-e Enghelab-e Mashrutiyat-e Iran* [The History of the Constitutional Revolution in Iran], Vol. IV (Tehran: Elmi Press, 1363/1984), p. 215.
[30] Hairi, "Shaykh Fazl Allah Nuri's Refutation of the Idea of Constitutionalism," p. 336.
[31] Ibid., p. 328.

112   Liberation without Liberalism

Nuri's thoughts about the indispensability of the clergy to the propagation of a just and strong Islamic polity – not to mention his death by
hanging at the hands of constitutionalist forces – were exceedingly influential in shaping Khomeini's beliefs about the intersection of politics and
Islam in Shia theology. Still, his justifications for the necessity of *velayat-e
faqih* went much deeper than Nuri's antipathies against constitutionalism. For Khomeini, Islamic government was premised on the principle of
towhid (oneness of God and the universe), which in turn necessitated the
application of divine law or Sharia. True justice may only be rendered
under a government fully based on Sharia law since, according to
Khomeini, the ultimate purpose of the latter is to improve the moral
condition of humankind. In a rare and extensive interview shortly before
his return to Iran from exile in Neauphle-le-Chateau outside of Paris,
Khomeini explained the crux of this especially monistic political philosophy thusly:

> There is a great difference between all the various manmade forms of government
> in the world, on the one hand – whatever their precise nature – and a divine
> government, on the other hand, which follows divine law. Governments that do
> not base themselves on divine law conceive of justice only in the natural realm;
> you will find them concerned only with the prevention of disorder and not with the
> moral refinement of the people. Whatever a person does in his own home is of no
> importance, so long as he causes no disorder in the street. In other words, people
> are free to do as they please at home. Divine governments, however, set them-
> selves the task of making man into what he should be. In his unredeemed state,
> man is like an animal, even worse than the other animals . . . . As originally created,
> man is superior to all other beings, but at the same time, his capacities for passion,
> anger, and other forms of evil are virtually boundless . . . . The prophets came to
> tame this unbridled beast and to make it subject to certain restraints . . . . Their task
> was extremely difficult, but whatever good does exist in the world proceeds from
> them. If we were to exclude the prophets from the world, it would collapse, and
> everyone would see what chaos would ensue . . . . The law of Islam is restricted
> neither to the unseen realm nor to the manifest dimension, in the same way that
> man himself is not restricted to a single dimension. Islam came to refashion true
> and complete human beings, complete in all their dimensions. It did not cultivate
> exclusively either the spiritual dimension of man, which would have fostered in
> him an aversion to the natural realm, or the natural dimension, which would have
> made him satisfied with the natural realm. The natural dimension is the means,
> and the spiritual, the end. Stated differently, it was the task of the prophets to
> reform the natural dimension of man in order that it might become the means of
> his ascent.[32]

This exposition is noteworthy for three reasons. First, it plainly and
concisely explains the central mission of Islamic law in society to be that

[32] Algar, *Islam and Revolution*, pp. 330–332.

Monism and the Islamic Republic 113

of "the moral refinement of the people." Certainly, combatting injustice, tyranny, and disorder would be high priorities of Islamic government, but they are second-order implications of a morally refined people. By drawing a contrast to "manmade forms of government," Khomeini clearly intends to show that the normative ideals of Islam – that is, "making man into what he should be" – are more fundamental than the "natural" inclination to merely reduce disorder. Second, Khomeini is keen to underline the pivotal role of "the prophets" in mitigating the moral deficiency of humankind. The irony in his explanation here, however, seems to be lost on him since he interprets the function of the prophets – that is, the reduction of "chaos" – in the same way as those of manmade governments. Even after accounting for humankind's spiritual shortcomings (in addition to their natural deformations), the general task is "to tame this unbridled beast and to make it subject to certain restraints." Last and most significant, the passage features Khomeini's characteristically blunt and succinct representation of Islam as a decidedly *monistic* enterprise.[33] In his reading, all earthly matters and anthropocentric values are but a "means" to the "spiritual end." The ultimate task of Islamic government is to facilitate this teleological journey – to ensure that "manmade" strictures and values are not treated as ends or viewed as on par with Islamic law.

The concept of *velayat-e faqih* was Khomeini's attempt to realize these normative presuppositions in a concrete political form capable of exercising power. Over the objections of quietist senior Shia clerics such as the Grand Ayatollah Mohammad Kazem Shariatmadari – who preferred a democratic system over a theocratic one – Khomeini instructed the newly elected Assembly of Experts (Majles-e Khobregan) tasked with the drafting of the constitution to ensure that "the constitution and other laws in this Republic must be based one hundred percent in Islam."[34] The decisive factor in shifting the balance of power in favor of the Khomeinist faction, however, was the takeover of the American embassy and hostage-taking by a cohort of radical Islamic students (known as the Students Following the Line of the Imam [Khomeini]) on November 4, 1979. The hostage crisis forced the democratic-nationalist government of Bazargan to resign in protest,[35] which in turn

---

[33] By "monism," once again, I mean here the philosophical notion that there is only one source for the good life, and that there is one overriding value around which life ought to be organized. The opposite of this is the notion of "pluralism," which posits that there are multiple pathways to the good life, and that competing value systems, not just one value, undergird human life. These concepts are richly discussed in Berlin, "On the Pursuit of the Ideal."

[34] Ruhollah Khomeini, "Message to the Assembly of Experts," *Kayhan*, 28 Mordad 1358 [August 19, 1979].

[35] In an impassioned farewell message addressed to the public and various transitional governmental organs, Bazargan noted that the embassy takeover was not the sole cause

114   Liberation without Liberalism

cleared the way for the takeover of the machinery of government and other state institutions by Khomeini loyalists and other radical activists.[36] The confrontation with the United States, moreover, effectively neutralized radical leftist political parties such as the Tudeh Party, the Fadai'yun, and the Mojahedin-e Islam, each of whom were keener on rooting out "liberal collaborators" and Western imperialism than curbing the concentration of power in favor of arbitrary theocratic rule under Khomeini's leadership. Together, these events and their implications in the first year after Khomeini's return from exile amounted to a "clerical coup d'état"[37] that in the ensuing months, and certainly after the outbreak of war with Iraq, decisively hijacked the aims and prerogatives of the revolution and placed them in the service of a new labyrinthine theocratic system of rule.[38]

The Constitution of the Islamic Republic of Iran was adopted in a nationwide referendum (with much lower rate of participation than the previous one) on December 2–3, 1979. The highly polemical preamble to the constitution is remarkable in its framing of the new political order explicitly in the image of Khomeini's political vision.[39] Recognizing Khomeini as "the vanguard the Islamic Revolution," the preamble notably underlines the extra-territoriality of Islamic government: "the Constitution provides the basis for trying to perpetuate this revolution both at home and abroad."[40] Yet despite the universal scope of ambition for exporting the revolution, the preamble also limits the range of

---

of his resignation, but rather the repeated patterns of "interference," "harassment," and "arbitrary decision-making" by "unseen" and "unaccountable" elements that made a mockery of his government's mandate. He concluded his remarks by warning those tasked with drafting the new constitution to "in the final stages [of putting the final draft together], rethink and change key provisions so that popular sovereignty is secured and that the government belongs both to God and the people, not one based on class or discrimination leading to problems in the future." Mehdi Bazargan, "Farewell Address," Tehran, Iran, 16 Aban 1358 [November 7, 1979]. Bazargan's public speeches are collected in Mehdi Bazargan, *Masa'el va Moshkelat-e Nakhostin Sal-e Enghelab* [Issues and Difficulties in the First Year of Revolution], ed. Abdol-Ali Bazargan (Tehran: 1362/1983).

[36] For a detailed overview of the provisional government led by Bazargan and the LMI, see Chehabi, *Iranian Politics and Religious Modernism*, chapter 7.

[37] This widely accepted characterization is detailed in Amir Arjomand, *The Turban for the Crown*, pp.137–141.

[38] For analysis and comprehensive details of key political developments after the fall of the Bazargan government and the hostage crisis, see Milani, *The Making of Iran's Islamic Revolution*, chapter 9; Keddie and Richard, *Modern Iran*, chapter 9; Amir Arjomand, *The Turban for the Crown*, pp. 141–146; and Chehabi, *Iranian Politics and Religious Modernism*, chapter 8.

[39] The translation I rely on here is by Ruhollah K. Ramazani, "Constitution of the Islamic Republic of Iran," *Middle East Journal*, Vol. 34, No. 2 (Spring 1980): 181–204.

[40] Ibid., p. 185.

Monism and the Islamic Republic

participation in governmental affairs to "pious men"; that is, "Until the ground has been prepared and the talents have blossomed to glorify the dimensions of God's ways and have become known to the people (to emulate God's morality), this cannot be active participation by all social elements in the process of transforming society."[41] Furthermore, the preamble obliges different segments of the population (the merchant classes, women, religious minorities, the downtrodden, etc.), branches of the armed forms, organs of government, and the communications media to devote themselves to the task of propagating Islamic revolutionary values.[42] These preliminary qualifications and injunctions are significant since they lay out the ideological framework within which the actual articles of the constitution – especially its "republican" elements – ought to be interpreted. In practice, they arguably were most instrumental in securing the foundations of the Islamic Republic during its tumultuous first decade by furnishing the Khomeinist elite ("pious men") with the necessary political clout to fortify the power of the insiders (*khodi-ha*) and cleanse "the system" (Nezam) of outsiders (*gheyr-e khodi-ha*).

The structure of government in the constitution is an admixture of representative, consultative, and arbitrary institutions that reflect the republican and Islamic dual character of the Islamic state envisioned by Khomeini.[43] Articles 5 and 110 in the constitution invest supreme authority in the office of the Rahbar (the Leader). His powers include: determining and supervising the implementation of the overall policies of the state; issuing referenda; commanding the armed forces; appointing the jurists of the Guardian Council, the head of the judiciary, the head-of-state broadcasting (radio and television) corporation, the chief of general staff, the commander-in-chief of the Islamic Revolutionary Guards Corps (IRGC), and the supreme commanders-in-chief of the security and armed forces; supervising the ties between all branches of government; ratifying the appointment, as well as the dismissal (if necessary), of the president of the Islamic Republic; ratifying the qualifications of candidates for the presidency, as first confirmed by the Guardian Council; and issuing pardons or reductions in criminal penalties in accordance with

---

[41] Ibid.   [42] Ibid., pp. 185–188.

[43] After Khomeini's death in 1989, the constitution was revised and amended to reflect more clearly the duties, qualifications, and the general prerogative of the office of Rahbar (the Leader). The new constitution also eliminated the position of the prime minister and strengthened the role of the president, as well as more clearly delineating the separation of powers between the judiciary, the legislature, and the executive branches. The revised constitution was adopted through a national referendum on July 28, 1989. The major provisions in both the original and the revised versions of the constitution are reproduced in Negin Nabavi, *Modern Iran: A History in Documents* (Princeton, NJ: Markus Wiener Publishers, 2016), chapter 8.

116   Liberation without Liberalism

Islamic criteria.[44] The republican elements of the constitution are represented in the popular elections of the president, Majlis deputies, the Assembly of Experts, as well as all municipal and provincial offices. However, in practice the powers and prerogatives of these republican institutions are severely undermined by the constitutional powers of the leader and the Guardian Council to approve the eligibility and fitness of candidates for these positions. The Guardian Council is a twelve-member body consisting of six religious jurists appointed by the supreme leader and six appointed by the Majlis. It adheres to very strict religious and revolutionary criteria for approving the candidacy of eligible officeholders, thereby significantly reducing the possibility of liberal or reformist candidates getting on the ballot. Moreover, the Guardian Council is also invested with judicial powers to interpret the Constitution of the Islamic Republic, acting in effect as a constitutional court of sorts.[45]

In the main, Khomeini's monistic vision of an Islamic state administered by *fuqaha* (religious jurists) according to the principles of *towhid* is well reflected in the Constitution of the Islamic Republic of Iran. The discernment and prerogatives of a supreme jurist and his council of deputies are accorded priority over that of popular will and democratic institutions. All rights are subject to discernment by Islamic authorities and, crucially, perennially at the mercy of what may be in the best interests of the Nezam (system). The leader's power over the intelligence and security establishments, combined with the clerical authority over key *bonyad*s (nontransparent public foundations), effectively guarantees the power of the arbitrary networks of the state over its representative institutions. In practice, this underlying dynamic renders the Islamic Republic a competitive authoritarian regime – that is, a hybrid system whereby competitive elections are combined with, and ultimately constrained by, varying authoritarian practices.[46] In essence, however, both the

[44] Ibid., pp. 212–213.

[45] For an in-depth consideration of the political debates and circumstances shaping the drafting of the constitution and its ratification, see Martin, *Creating and Islamic State*, chapter VII.

[46] The literature in comparative politics uses these categories often in comparison with democratic or liberal-democratic regimes, eschewing sui generis analyses of specific regimes. For instance, see Steven Levitsky and Lucan A. Way, *Competitive Authoritarianism: Hybrid Regimes after the Cold War* (Cambridge: Cambridge University Press, 2010); Pejman Abdolmohammadi and Gianpiero Cama, "Iran as a Peculiar Hybrid Regime: Structure and Dynamics of the Islamic Republic," *British Journal of Middle Eastern Studies*, Vol. 42, No. 4 (2015): 558–578; and Naser Ghobadzadeh and Lily Zubaidah Rahim, "Electoral Theocracy and Hybrid Sovereignty in Iran," *Contemporary Politics*, Vol. 22, No. 4 (2016): 450–468. The journalist and dissident intellectual Akbar Ganji has described the system of *velayat-e faqih* as a "sultanist" regime. See Akbar Ganji, "The Latter-Day Sultan: Power and Politics in Iran," *Foreign Affairs*, Vol. 87, No. 6 (November/December 2008): 45–62, 64–66; see also

authoritarian and competitive aspects of the Islamic Republic are based on a highly monistic reading of Islamic theology, history, and sociology that admit of very little by way of alternative perspectives even within the Islamic tradition. That this exclusivist vision succeeded over secular-liberal views of constitutionalism after the fall of the Pahlavis can be attributed to the dominant narrative of the revolution as a collective reckoning with legacies of Western-backed secular autocracy. From the outset, Khomeini understood the power of discrediting political opponents by merely using the labels "Western," "liberal," "anti-Islamic," and even "intellectual" – and he was aided in this endeavor by a range of leftist and nationalist political groups who, as outlined in Chapter 3, viewed liberalism as a major impediment to liberation from Western imperial control. This rhetorical tactic, however, had the paradoxical effect of aligning secular-liberal critiques of arbitrary power with more pluralist readings of political Islam, even if these ideas remained substantively distant from each other. It is to a consideration of these challenges to the Khomeinist vision of Islamic governance that I shall turn next.

Pluralist Visions of Islamic Governance

Khomeini's death on June 3, 1989, was a watershed moment in the political trajectory of the Islamic Republic. If the first decade of the Nezam – bookended by the clerical takeover of government in November 1979 and the conclusion of the eight-year war against Iraq in 1988 – had succeeded in establishing and consolidating clerical rule, the ensuing two decades (1989–2009) featured the political emergence, electoral triumph, and demise of a movement to reform the system from within. Of course, the reform movement had its intellectual roots in the early political struggles of religious modernists – such as Bazargan, Ayatollah Mahmoud Taleqani, Yadollah Sahabi, and other National Front and LMI veterans – against the Khomeinist faction at the time of the revolution. Although different in the breadth of their concerns, not to mention historical context, in essence they both envisioned a democratic constitution rooted in Islamic pluralism. Since the political and intellectual histories of these currents have been well mined in recent scholarship, my aim in this section is to make clear the distinctions between pluralist readings of Islam and political liberalism. While the two overlap in certain values such as toleration and civic freedoms, they nevertheless entail vastly different constitutional structures and justificatory political

Akbar Ganji, "Iran's Peculiar Election: The Struggle against Sultanism," *Journal of Democracy*, Vol. 16, No. 4 (2005): 38–51.

118   Liberation without Liberalism

principles. These differences are mostly overlooked in existing accounts of reformist thought-practices, resulting in the false attribution of principles and values to Islamic pluralist and politically liberal actors alike. Accordingly, in this section I focus on two highly influential Islamic pluralist critiques of *velayat-e faqih* (one political, by Bazargan; another philosophical, by Soroush) as a demonstration of the limited appropriation of liberal arguments that fall decidedly short of endorsements of political liberalism.

Bazargan and the Idea of Freedom

"Are religion and freedom essentially mutually exclusive?" Mehdi Bazargan (1907–1995) was compelled to rhetorically pose and address this question in a disquisition entitled "Din va Azadi" ["Religion and Liberty"] shortly after his political marginalization by Khomeini.[47] In many respects, Bazargan's life and political career stand as admirable endeavors to advance a pluralist reading of political Islam in harmony with civic rights and basic freedoms. Born in the midst of the Constitutional Revolution of 1906–1911, Bazargan's religiosity was from the outset tempered by a sense of practical worldliness characteristic of most upbringings in merchant-class (*bazari*) families.[48] His elementary and secondary education were a mixture of religious and polytechnical schooling, culminating in his development as an elite student. Subsequently, Bazargan was among the top performers in a national competition in 1928 that selected students for further study at European universities. He moved to Nantes, France, and after just a few months of preparation he became the first Iranian ever to gain entry into a grande école, studying thermodynamics and attaining an engineering degree from the École Centrale des Arts et Manufactures.[49] Upon his return to Iran, Bazargan joined the Faculty of Engineering at the University of Tehran and in 1945 was elected as its dean. In this capacity, Bazargan experienced firsthand the political reach of the Tudeh Party on

[47] Mehdi Bazargan, "Din va Azadi," in *Bazyabi-ye Arzash'ha* [The Recovery of Values] (Tehran: Nehzat-e Azadi-e Iran, 1364/1983), pp. 59–88. I rely on Mahmoud Sadri's translation of the piece in this section, which was itself published in Charles Kurzman, ed., *Liberal Islam: A Sourcebook* (New York: Oxford University Press, 1998), pp. 73–84.

[48] The fullest sketch of Bazargan's life is provided by himself in *Modafe'at dar Dadgah-e Gheir'e Saleh-e Tajdid-e Nazar-e Nezami* (Tehran: Entasharat-e Modarres, 1350/1971). For a critical overview of his life and thought, see Dabashi, "Mehdi Bazargan: The Devout Engineer," in *Theology of Discontent*, pp. 324–366. The most relevant passages from his autobiographical sketch are translated and recounted in Chehabi, *Iranian Politics and Religious Modernism*. For purposes of consistency and concision, I rely on the latter volume here.

[49] See Chehabi, *Iranian Politics and Religious Modernism*, pp. 107–110.

Pluralist Visions of Islamic Governance

119

university campuses following Reza Shah's abdication in 1941, and became especially concerned about the ideological purchase that Marxism had gained among students, faculty, and organized labor in society.[50] After six years in university administration, Bazargan transitioned into the private sector but also became very active in efforts to counter the challenge posed to Mosaddeq's political party by the communist left.[51]

It was at this juncture in his career that Bazargan – alongside Yadollah Sahabi and the modernist cleric Mahmoud Taleqani[52] – became especially interested in the imperative for a reinvigorated Islamic coalition as an alternative to the anti-traditionalist and materialist agenda of the Tudeh Party.[53] Bazargan's time in France had impressed on him the compatibility (even complementarity) of a democratic political culture with religious identity. France's secular constitution may have unambiguously restricted the exercise of religion to the private realm, but Catholicism did not strain for believers, nor was its imprint on culture and public life any less discernible in modern times. While his impressions were no doubt colored by an "exaggerated sense of the importance of religion in pre-World War II France,"[54] the lessons Bazargan drew from his time there were nonetheless significant in shaping his views on how religion and politics might accommodate one another in the public sphere.[55] Accordingly, and through his subsequent political travails as a founding member of the Iran Party, minister and deputy premier in Mosaddeq's government, prominent National Front politician, co-founder of the LMI, and pivotal figure in the coalition against Mohammad Reza Shah, Bazargan forged a democratic political outlook anchored in Islamic principles. The basic political elements of this religious-pluralist view are exemplified in the first clauses of the 1961 party program of the LMI:

---

[50] Ibid., pp. 117–119.

[51] Bazargan was a founding member of both the Engineers' Association and the Iran Party, which were steadfast supporters of Mosaddeq.

[52] For brief political biographies of Taleqani and Sahabi, see Chehabi, *Iranian Politics and Religious Modernism*, pp. 103–107 and 110, respectively.

[53] As Chehabi notes, "For Taleqani and Bazargan the lesson of this state of affairs [i.e. the metastasizing support for Tudeh combined with the general public wariness of its anti-religious tendencies] was that for the struggle against the Tudeh to be efficient it had to take three forms: founding associations to counter Tudeh's influence, preparing an ideological alternative to Tudeh's attractive materialism, and supporting Mosaddeq's National Movement." Ibid., p. 119.

[54] Most of Bazargan's time in France, Chehabi observes, was spent in "traditionally Catholic Brittany" and "a Catholic enclave in Paris." Ibid., p. 109.

[55] See Bazargan, *Modafe'at*, pp. 55–58.

120   Liberation without Liberalism

… To revive the fundamental rights of the Iranian people and install the rule of law and thereby delimit the powers and responsibilities of the different branches of government for the purpose of establishing the rule of the people by the people …

To spread moral, social, and political principles based on the exalted religion of Islam with due attention to the political and cultural conditions of the present age …[56]

Like other prominent devout political dissidents during the Pahlavi years, Bazargan viewed Islam as a marker of national heritage, and therefore a decidedly more authentic resource for political and national identity than those on offer from Western secular ideologies. Unlike the radical leftist-Islamist supporters of Khomeini and idiosyncratic anti-modern intellectuals such as Ahmad Fardid, however, Bazargan was deeply skeptical of clerical authority in politics. His outlook in this regard had been shaped immensely by the role of Ayatollah Abol-Qasem Kashani in the 1953 coup that deposed Mosaddeq and sidelined his political movement thereafter.[57] Kashani, an erstwhile ally of Mosaddeq against British imperial control of Iran's oil, had betrayed him and the cause of nationalization by disavowing his support of Mosaddeq's premiership and even lending his support to the coup against him.[58] To Bazargan and most National Front members, Kashani's opportunism reflected the clergy's foremost priority for their own status as sui generis power brokers in the political arena.[59] This meant that the Mosaddeqist aims of constitutionalism, democracy, and national independence were perpetually at risk of clerical sabotage if Islamic principles and clerical authority were not decoupled. For this reason, Bazargan and other leaders of the LMI nearly always made simultaneous mention of their fealties to Islam and the Mosaddeqist agenda. For instance, as Khomeini's singular grip on

---

[56] The Liberation Movement of Iran, "The Party Program of the Liberation Movement of Iran," Tehran, 25 Ordibehesht 1340 [May 15, 1961]. I use the translation in Chehabi, *Iranian Politics and Religious Modernism*, p. 314.

[57] On the domestic dimensions of the coup, see Azimi, *Iran, The Crisis of Democracy*, chapter 20. See also Fakhreddin Azimi, "The Configuration and Role of Domestic Forces," in Gasiorowski and Byrne, eds., *Mohammad Mosaddeq and the 1953 Coup in Iran*, pp. 27–101; and Rahnema, *Behind the 1953 Coup in Iran*, chapter 15.

[58] On Kashani's role specifically, see Azimi, *Iran, The Crisis of Democracy*, pp. 332–333. Kashani's receipt of foreign funds in exchange for his support of the coup was recently corroborated in previously neglected declassified material published by the National Security Archive; see British Foreign Office, "Persia: Political Review of the Recent Crisis," September 2, 1953, Top Secret. For a summary of new findings, see Malcolm Byrne and Mark Gasiorowski, eds., "New Findings on the Clerical Involvement in 1953 Coup in Iran," *Briefing Book #619*, March 7, 2018 (https://nsarchive.gwu.edu/briefing-book/iran/2018–03–07/new-findings-clerical-involvement-1953-coup-iran, last accessed August 15, 2019).

[59] Abrahamian, *Iran between Two Revolutions*, p. 458.

Pluralist Visions of Islamic Governance 121

political power became more imminent after the passage of the Constitution of the Islamic Republic, the LMI underlined its broader aims, declaring: "we are Muslims, Iranians, constitutionalists, and Mosaddeqists: Muslim because we refuse to divorce our [religious] principles from our politics; Iranians because we respect our national heritage; constitutionalists because we demand freedom of thought, expression, and association; Mosaddeqists because we want national independence."[60] It must be noted, however, that the LMI was composed of a diverse and highly dynamic set of factions, spanning the political-religious spectrum from socialist, social-democratic, liberal-democratic, and conservative ideologies both inside Iran and abroad among university students and intellectual circuits. As such, the statements and aims of the organization are significant only as a reflection of the relative position of the LMI to political winds and other movements in time.[61] Bazargan's pluralist approach was in many respects informed by the quest for an equilibrium position between all the various viewpoints represented within the LMI.

Khomeini's swift ascent to and consolidation of power in the post-Shah transitional period was more than a political shock to Bazargan – it represented the culmination of all that he had viewed with suspicion and dread, yet never quite believed would be possible, in religion-based movements throughout his political career.[62] The ruthless installment of clerical rule was not only a blow to the democratic character of the revolution, but especially an affront to the pluralist vision of political Islam represented by the LMI.[63] After his resignation and forced

[60] "The Formation of the Liberation Movement," *Ette'alat*, May 16, 1979. Quoted in ibid., p. 460.

[61] The LMI's 1980 "Statement of Aims," for instance, pledges not only to advance "the lofty principles of Islam," but further "[t]o accept the leadership of the Imam [Khomeini] and to struggle against all acts that might weaken his leadership" and "[t]o cooperate with the informed, committed, and authentic clergy that moves along the path of unity." The stark contrast between this statement and the earlier statements of the LMI clearly reflects the changing political trajectories and circumstances of the country in the post-revolutionary period. See Chehabi, *Iranian Politics and Religious Modernism*, pp. 318–319.

[62] As Chehabi notes, "His tenure as prime minister was a traumatic experience for Mehdi Bazargan." Ibid., p. 275.

[63] Bazargan's bewilderment at Khomeini's rise, popularity, and autocratic tendencies is famously on display in his interviews with Oriana Fallaci and Hamid Algar, respectively. In each, he complains incessantly of the constant interference by Khomeini and those carrying out his orders through various revolutionary outfits, and of the growing gulf between clerical authority and democratic principles in the postrevolutionary period. Yet throughout these interviews he is more bewildered than coherent. At one point during his interview with Fallaci, he compares Khomeini's habitual unsolicited intercessions to Mosaddeq's leadership style, clearly in an attempt to dismiss comparisons between Khomeini and Mussolini or Hitler. See Oriana Fallaci, "'Everybody Wants To Be

122   Liberation without Liberalism

marginalization into domestic exile by Khomeini, Bazargan reflected more broadly on the relationship between revolution, politics, Islam, and constitutionalism.[64] The striking aspect of his writings and interviews in this period (up until his death) was the clear articulation of an alternative, nonclerical conception of Islamic government based on individual rights and basic freedoms. Bazargan's essay "Religion and Liberty" (cited at the beginning of this section) is the most concrete expression of these views, and to some observers the clearest statement of his liberalism.[65]

The essay explores the relationship between religion and liberty through a highly stylized set of comparisons (e.g. with Western Christendom), anecdotal reasoning (e.g. paternalism and family relations), and analogies (e.g. the natural world) that are meant to illuminate the natural affinity between human reason, freedom, and faith in God, on the one hand, and underline the perils of fundamentalism and arbitrary religious guardianship, on the other. Bazargan begins by arguing that "the mission of the prophets has been to liberate human beings, not to enslave them." They are to be emancipated "... from the illusion of idolatry ... from compulsive worship of worldly goods ... from religious imposters, false guardians of temples and religions who propagated idolatry and opposed the prophets ... [and] from the kings, louts, and possessors of the power and the riches, and the oppressors of our time."[66] But the liberationist mission of the prophets, Bazargan continues, is explicitly circumscribed by God (in the Qur'an) to only serve "as witness and example, bearing glad tidings and admonishment, calling God, and providing light. It [the Qur'an] recommends tolerance in the face of harassment by the infidels and the hypocrites and reliance upon God."[67] This limitation is due to the God-given "gift" of free will bestowed on human beings, which Bazargan describes in the following manner:

Boss': An Interview with Mehdi Bazargan, Prime Minister of Iran," *The New York Times*, October 28, 1979, Section SM, p. 5; Mehdi Bazargan, "Mosahebe-ye Hamid Algar ba Mohandes Bazargan," in *Enghelab-e Eslami-ye Iran, Majmou'eh-ye Asar* (Tehran: Bonyad-e Farhangi-ye Mohandes Mehdi Bazargan, 1389/2010), pp. 198–225. The interview was conducted on 12 Bahman 1359 [February 1, 1981].

[64] The bulk of his political thinking on these subjects were collected in *Bazyabi-ye Arzash'ha* and *Enghelab-e Eslami Dar Do Harekat* [The Islamic Revolution in Two Movements] (Tehran: Naraghi, 1363/1984). Other LMI veterans similarly reflected on these questions, albeit in typically fragmentary and allegorical terms given the regime's heavy-handed censorship of such material.

[65] Mahmoud Sadri, for instance, in his translation of Bazargan's essay notes that "A subtext of Bazargan's speech is a defense of liberalism against the left wing of the Freedom [or Liberation] Movement, as well as against anti-democratic forces in the Islamic Republic." Mehdi Bazargan, "Religion and Liberty," trans. Mahmoud Sadri, in Kurzman, ed., *Liberal Islam*, p. 74, n. 4.

[66] Bazargan, "Din va Azadi," p. 76.   [67] Ibid.

Freedom is essential for our creativity and spiritual evolution. Had free will been denied to us we would follow an inevitable path guided by animal instincts. Protected by doubt we would remain as stationary in our position as ants, horses, and pigeons. Free will and liberty, fraught with weakness, confusion, and concerns as they are, provoke us to concentrate, think, decide, and move. As such, they are the tools of extraordinary evolution and progress among human beings as compared to animals. Reason, perception, will, and morality are all results of fee will and liberty. Freedom is God's gift to His steward on earth, humankind. Whoever takes away this freedom is guilty of the greatest treason against humankind.[68]

Bazargan's framing of free will, reason, and toleration as divine offerings worthy of utmost respect is clearly meant as a challenge to monistic conceptions of Islam that subordinate individual freedom to divine injunctions (as interpreted by religious jurists). The moral and political implications of this grounding are of course immense. In moral terms, it entails a view of Islamic community as irreducibly varied and dynamic. Since Muslims, by virtue of their varied life circumstances, have reasons to live and act differently, then there can be multiple pathways to living the good (i.e. faithful) life.[69] Politically, it necessitates a form of government based on consultation (*shura*), respect for majority opinion, and toleration of oppositional viewpoints. Citing the consultative and tolerant approach of the Prophet Muhammad and his disciples, Bazargan argued that "Islamic government cannot help but be at once consultative, democratic, and divinely inspired."[70] However, Bazargan conceded that a key conundrum marks conflicting interpretations of Islamic government in modern times, namely: how must the guidance and advice of religious authorities or the "sources of emulation" be incorporated into the political institutions of the modern state?

Although Bazargan does not propose a resolution of his own to this tension in Shia jurisprudence – and notes the absence of clear thinking on the matter by religious scholars – he is keen to demonstrate that Khomeini's concept of *velayat-e faqih*, "[which] is now being propagated with the help of state propaganda, is an important and subtle issue that needs to be scrutinized from religious, legal, historical, social, and political viewpoints."[71] To Bazargan, the formal institutionalization of religion in the political structures proposed by Khomeini not only substituted

---

[68] Ibid., p. 77.
[69] Bazargan notes, "Islam permits differences of opinion even within the realm of the tenets of religion, let along in administration and governmental issues. Shiite theology, under the rubric of *ijtihad* [Islamic interpretation], has left the gate of such debates open until the end of time and the resurrection of the Messiah (may God hasten his rise)." Ibid., p. 79.
[70] Ibid. [71] Ibid., p. 78.

124   Liberation without Liberalism

religious authority for the technocratic competence required of governmental officials, but more importantly facilitated the conditions for corruption and autocracy since it entwined the political legitimacy with divine sovereignty. The latter move in fact ensured that secular interests and abuses of power could always be justified and excused by appeals to divine sovereignty. Indeed, the censorship, increasing harassment, and violence committed against journalists and dissidents in the weeks and months following the ratification of the new theocratic constitution confirmed this.[72] For Bazargan, then, under Khomeini's *velayat-e faqih* basic freedoms, rights, and democratic values were at the mercy and interpretation of clerical authorities, and not recognized as inherently inviolable. Those adhering to the monistic precepts of Khomeini's vision, Bazargan cautioned, "are deluded and naïve about their own monopoly of the truth and about the notion of freedom." Adding, "Freedom is not a luxury; it is a necessity. When freedom is banished, tyranny will take its place."[73]

The intensity with which Bazargan inveighs against Islamic monism has certainly left the impression on many of his political supporters and historians of a liberal champion of natural rights and perhaps even secular constitutionalism. But in the same essay on freedom, Bazargan is adamant on an Islamic basis for rights and constitutionalism. In probing the boundaries between religion and politics, his fealty to Qur'anic instructions are clear:

The world-view and the ideology, the philosophical anthropology, and the constitutional laws – that is, the foundation of the government – should be based on and inspired by the Book [the Qur'an] and *sunna*. Ordinary laws, too, should not contradict those ordinances. It is entirely proper, even necessary, that the parliament of an Islamic country is comprised of people's representatives who are acquainted with the tenets of Islam, and who are God-fearing, reasonable, prudent, and trustworthy; so they legislate in accordance with Islam's fundamental tenets and ultimate goals.[74]

It is important to note that unlike constitutional-era liberal reformers – such as Malkum Khan and Mostashar al-Dowleh – Bazargan was not merely paying lip service to Islam when reflecting on the composition of Islamic government in this manner. Nor was he insincere about his fealties to democratic institutions and politics. The central organizing principle of his political vision was the belief in the possibility of a politics that is both Islamic and democratic; namely, an Islamic belief

---

[72] Bazargan's routine complaints about such "interferences" are cataloged in his public speeches and interviews during his turbulent tenure as prime minister. See Bazargan, *Masa'el va Moshkelat.*
[73] Bazargan, "Din va Azadi," p. 82.   [74] Ibid., pp. 78–79.

Pluralist Visions of Islamic Governance 125

system that is sufficiently pluralistic and given to toleration, on the one hand, and a representative form of government anchored in the liberationist mission of the prophets, on the other. Indeed, this composite vision is at the core of the political project associated with the LMI and later reform movements in the Islamic Republic. But is it accurate to characterize it as a liberal vision?

Bazargan's Islamic pluralism certainly lends itself to the practice of liberal politics – that is, the emphasis on respect for and toleration of oppositional perspectives means that individual Muslims could wholeheartedly endorse liberal constitutional precepts. But as the preceding makes clear, its elemental principles are Islamic, not liberal. Put simply, under Islamic government sovereignty belongs to God, not individuals. Justifications for free will and toleration may well emanate from worldly affairs and even the ends they seek are open to multiple interpretations, but the moral source of such license can only be divine power, not human life itself.[75] In contrast, individual personhood constitutes the moral core of political liberalism. Under a liberal-constitutional regime, equal respect for persons is derived not from divine sovereignty but rather from the Enlightenment notion that each human life possesses an intrinsic value in and of itself – by the simple virtue of it being a human life. Here, the Kantian principle of treating individual human beings as ends in themselves and not as means either in the employ of, or toward, higher purposes is absolutely central to political liberalism.[76] As such, the conception of freedom offered by Bazargan, though it certainly allows for greater expressive liberties and diversity of opinions within the Islamic community, nonetheless subordinates individual will to divine sovereignty.

Moreover, this tension poses a fundamental challenge to the practice of Islamic democracy itself: whose interpretation of divine doctrine should prevail when disagreements arise? This is no small matter since, precisely because they have reason to think and act differently, human beings are bound to clash in their viewpoints, interests, and values. In such cases, on the basis of whose final authority should disputes be settled? Bazargan's response to this riddle is decidedly incoherent: "the Qur'an has envisioned, without censure, the existence and expression of disagreements and differences of opinion among the faithful. It recommends the disagreements with the rulers to be referred to the Prophet and to God;

---

[75] As Bazargan notes, "God not only leaves people free to be 'either thankful or ungrateful' [Qur'an 76:3] and gives a grace period when they sin; He also assists believers and unbelievers alike on their chosen path." Ibid., p. 76.

[76] The fullest and best-known expression of the moral basis of political liberal is presented in Larmore, "Political Liberalism."

126   Liberation without Liberalism

which in our days, would mean the body of religious knowledge."[77] This statement is incoherent in light of Bazargan's explicit preference for an unmediated relationship between individual Muslims and God. Disagreements arise *precisely because individuals differ on how a given "body of religious knowledge" ought to be interpreted.* It follows, then, that in a government premised on Islamic principles either religious authorities must act as the arbiters of disputes between individuals, or that the final arbiter of disputes must be a secular authority (in which case the Islamic basis of government is tenuous at best). Bazargan's attempt at addressing this inconsistency is equally vague and incomplete. "Being free and autonomous is one thing," he argues, and "being responsible for one's beliefs and actions quite another .... Thus freedom exists; so do responsibility and restraint. The choice is ours."[78] He concludes his essay by adding that the religious scholars and the clergy "have no rights or responsibilities save those delegated to them within the democratic system of the Islamic government."[79]

The incoherence at the heart of Bazargan's reflections on the relationship between freedom and Islamic government is especially instructive as an insight into the bewilderingly swift manner in which the parameters of debate about representative government narrowed after Khomeini's successful consolidation of power. Bazargan's appropriation of liberal concepts such as individual autonomy, equal respect, and toleration is necessarily limited and incomplete because the object of his critique is Khomeini's concept of *velayat-e faqih* and not radical-leftist, socialist, or liberal-democratic perspectives on government. Compared to Khomeini's, his moral and political justifications of Islamic government are certainly more pluralistic and representative. But in their deference to divine sovereignty as the ultimate source of the good, and the central arbiter of disputes in cases of disagreement about the terms of citizenship under Islamic government, Bazargan's prescriptions are decidedly non-liberal. To reiterate, this does not mean that Islamic pluralist views are fundamentally irreconcilable with liberal constitutionalism – Muslim pluralists such as Bazargan can easily marshal interpretations of Islamic doctrine in support of liberal-democratic principles (as is the case with Muslims in all liberal democracies today). Rather, the point here is that Islamic pluralism, by virtue of its split commitments to divine and popular sovereignty, could not accommodate liberal views free of religious oversight. Similar, but more philosophically oriented, difficulties marked later reformist thinking about Islamic democracy, as exemplified in the political thought of Abdolkarim Soroush.

---

[77] Bazargan, "Din va Azadi," p. 83.   [78] Ibid., p. 84.   [79] Ibid.

Pluralist Visions of Islamic Governance 127

Soroush and the Idea of Islamic Democracy

In the pantheon of postrevolutionary Islamic pluralist thought, no thinker has received more attention than the religious intellectual Hossein Haj Farajollah Dabbagh, better known by his pen name, Abdolkarim Soroush. Since the mid-1990s, he has been variously labeled as "the Martin Luther of Islam," an "Islamic mystic," an "Islamic liberal," and "the philosopher of Islamic reform," among other epithets.[80] Soroush's intellectual trajectory, however, is not dissimilar to that of other Islamic reformers before and after the revolution.[81] Born in 1945 to a middle-class religious family in Tehran, he attended a traditional public school in south Tehran before getting accepted into the highly selective Alavi School, a rigorous private religious institution overseen by devout educators with roots in the merchant community. He obtained his undergraduate degree in pharmacology from the University of Tehran in 1969, followed by two-year postgraduate study of analytical chemistry and the history of science at Chelsea College in London. His time in London proved to be a formative experience as he was for the first time exposed to the cannon of Western analytical philosophy (especially works by Karl Popper, Paul Feyerabend, and Imre Lakatos, as well as debates between logical positivists and their detractors) and found himself increasingly engaged in diaspora politics among Iranian students.[82] During this period, Soroush established a reputation as a serious religious critic of Marxism, building an impressive corpus of written works and public lectures.[83] His interventions especially endeared him to clerical leaders such as Ayatollahs Tabatabaie, Motahari, Montazeri, and Khomeini, and

---

[80] See Robin Wright, "Scholar Emerges as the Martin Luther of Islam," *The Seattle Times*, February 12, 1995; Brumberg, *Reinventing Khomeini*, pp. 202–213; Mahmoud Sadri, "Sacral Defense of Secularism: The Political Theologies of Soroush, Shabestari, and Kadivar," *International Journal of Politics, Culture and Society*, Vol. 15, No. 2 (Winter 2001): 258–260; and Behrooz Ghamari-Tabrizi, *Islam and Dissent in Post-revolutionary Iran: Abdolkarim Soroush, Religious Politics and Democratic Reform* (London: I.B Tauris & Co. Ltd., 2008), chapter 7.

[81] Michaelle Browers and Charles Kurzman, "Introduction," in Michaelle Browers and Charles Kurzman, eds., *An Islamic Reformation?* (Lanham, NJ: Lexington, 2003), pp. 1–17.

[82] For an autobiographical account of Soroush's intellectual journey, see his interview with Mahmoud and Ahmad Sadri in Soroush, *Reason, Freedom, and Democracy in Islam*, pp. 3–25. Laura Secor provides the most contextual narrative of Soroush's intellectual ascent and eclipse in *Children of Paradise*, pp. 57–81.

[83] His works in this period include *Nahad-e Na-Aram-e Jahan* [The Dynamic Nature of the Universe] (Tehran: Entesharat-e Qalam, 1356/1977); *Tazad-e Dialiktiki* [Dialectical Contradiction] (Tehran: Entesharat-e Hekmat, 1357/1978); *Falsafeh-ye Tarikh* [The Philosophy of History] (Tehran: Entesharat-e Hekmat, 1358/1979); and *Elm Chist, Falsafeh Chist?* [What Is Science, What Is Philosophy?] (Tehran: Entesharat-e Hekmat, 1358/1979).

128   Liberation without Liberalism

his public renown further grew after the revolution as he publicly took on Tudeh Party ideologues and even the ousted president Abolhassan Banisadr.[84]

Soroush's early fervent support for the Islamic Republic had earned him an appointment on the infamous seven-member Setad-e Enghelab-e Farhangi [The Committee on Cultural Revolution] in 1980 (later renamed the Council on Cultural Revolution). The committee's functions ranged from the rewriting of school textbooks, the policing of public and cultural institutions, to the realignment of university curricula and faculty with Islamic principles. In practice, this meant the systematic cultural cleansing of all traces of secular Western influences in the social sciences and humanities, including the mass purging of faculty and staff suspected of harboring liberal and Marxist views.[85] As the clerical establishment's power became more entrenched and the approach to oppositional viewpoints more violent and severe, however, Soroush became disillusioned with the turn toward absolute theocracy in the Islamic Republic. In 1983, he resigned his post on the Council on Cultural Revolution and retreated into academic and intellectual life, returning to his earlier preoccupations with philosophies of history, religion, and science.[86] In this period, his subtle but increasingly dissonant writings began to appear in the publication *Kayhan-e Farhangi*, a cultural supplement of the state-run *Kayhan* newspaper that was at the time overseen by Mohammad Khatami, the future reformist president. Most important among these writings were the germs of his later more comprehensively elaborated philosophy of religion in his magnum opus, *Qabz va Bast-e Teorik-e Shari'at: Ya Nazariyeha-ye Takamol-e Ma'refat-e Dini* [The Theoretical Contraction and Expansion of Sharia: Or, Thoughts on the Evolution

---

[84] He debated Tudeh leaders Ehsan Tabari and Nourodin Kiyanouri in a series of televised prime-time debates, and warned supporters of Banisadr to be grateful to the Islamic Republic, "Otherwise, God forbid, they will suffer retributions if they show no gratitude towards God's benevolence." Secor, *Children of Paradise*, p. 68.

[85] The extent and impact of Soroush's involvement in the purging of university faculty and rewriting of education curricula is immensely controversial and as of this writing still not entirely clear. See Ghamari-Tabrizi, *Islam and Dissent in Post-revolutionary Iran*, pp. 105–129. A more recent assessment appears in Sadeghi-Boroujerdi, *Revolution and Its Discontents*, pp. 207–212.

[86] After joining the Institute for Cultural Research and Studies in 1983, Soroush published a series of articles (based on his lectures) on the humanities, the philosophy of history, and the philosophy of social and physical sciences, later collected in *Tafarroj-e Son'a: Goftarha-i dar Akhlagh va San'at va Elm-e Ensani* [Promenading Creation: Essays on Ethics, Technology, and the Human Sciences] (Tehran: Serat Cultural Institute, 1373/1994). He also translated works by Edwin Brutt (*Metaphysical Foundations of Modern Physical Sciences*), Daniel Little (*Varieties of Social Science Explanation: An Introduction to the Philosophy of Social Science*), and Alan Ryan (*The Philosophy of the Social Sciences*).

Pluralist Visions of Islamic Governance   129

of Religious Knowledge].[87] The central and explosive (to the religious establishment) claim in these discourses was the distinction Soroush drew between religion (*din*) and religious knowledge (*ma'refat-e dini*). Soroush argued that while the essence of religion is fundamentally immutable and constant, religious knowledge is conditioned by historical contingency, context, and the limits of human reason.[88] As such, human knowledge of religion is deeply entangled in what Clifford Geertz (building on Max Weber's insights) called "webs of significance" that are both reflective and generative of underlying power structures in society.[89] The obvious implication of this reading was that no single interpretation of the Sharia could ever be absolute or incontestable. Indeed, interpretive authority and religious expertise are important accompaniments of religious belief; but their contributions do not constitute the final, unassailable word of God.[90]

Soroush's reflections in *Kayhan-e Farhangi* – and after the closure of the latter, in the intellectual journal *Kiyan* – built on his earlier disquiet with Ali Shariati's conception of Islam as merely a mobilizing ideology for political and social change.[91] Shariati's liberation theology regarded Shiism as an especially potent political force precisely because of the knowability of its central, universal truth as encapsulated by the principle of *towhid* (the oneness of God).[92] In Shariati's calls to action that prefigured the Iranian revolution, *towhid* was the basis for a confident, assertive, and public religion. For Soroush, in contrast, the instrumentalization of religion in this manner reduced it to the level of a worldly ideology,[93] which by demeaning the mystical essence of Islam (i.e. the mystery of the true essence of Islam) could only lead to corruption and social degeneration at the hands of those who would arrogate to themselves the absolute

---

[87] Published in Tehran (Serat, 1373/1994), the book has undergone four revisions and reprints.

[88] Ibid., p. 52.

[89] Clifford Geertz, *The Interpretation of Cultures* (New York: Basic Books, 1973), p. 89.

[90] Soroush, *Qabz va Bast-e Teorik-e Shari'at*, pp. 485–490.

[91] For a comparison between Shariati and Soroush, see Behrooz Ghamari-Tabrizi, "Contentious Public Religion: Two Conceptions of Islam in Revolutionary Iran: Ali Shari'ati and Abdolkarim Soroush," *International Sociology*, Vol. 19, No. 4 (December 2004): 504–523.

[92] See Chapter 3 for an elaboration of this principle and its resonance in Khomeini's political philosophy.

[93] Soroush's critique of Islam as ideology and of ideological society is outlined in his collection of essays *Farbehtar az Idiolozhi* [Loftier than Ideology] (Tehran: Serat, 1372/1993). For a thorough summary of Soroush's repudiation of religion as ideology, see Sadeghi-Boroujerdi, *Revolution and Its Discontents*, pp. 213–226.

130   Liberation without Liberalism

right of interpretation.[94] Indeed, at the political level, Soroush's rejection of Shariati's reading of Islam as a revolutionary ideology led by qualified guardians of the faith emerged out of the recognition that the arbitrary authority granted to a *vali-ye faqih* (supreme jurist) and attendant vanguard institutions in the Islamic Republic ultimately advanced the political agenda of a self-interested elite under the guise of safeguarding Islamic values.

In this gradual reckoning with the nature of the Nezam, moreover, Soroush was not alone. The end of the eight-year Iran-Iraq War, followed by the death of Khomeini, occasioned the emergence of a cross section of revolutionaries-turned-reformists – religious thinkers and journalists such as Mohammad Mojtahed-Shabestari, Saeed Hajjarian, Mohsen Kadivar, Akbar Ganji, Mostafa Tajzadeh, Abbas Abdi, Alireza Alavi-Tabar, and Hassan Yousefi Eshkevari – whose reflections, as a collective, expounded on more pluralistic, participatory, and democratic alternatives to the reigning orthodoxies in the Islamic Republic.[95] Many of these figures became known through their writings in the intellectual periodicals and newspapers such as *Kiyan, Iran-e Farda, Salam,* and *Ayin* – outlets which served as the collective brain trusts of reform- and dissident-minded political thinkers around Ayatollah Montazeri, the pragmatist president Akbar Hashemi Rafsanjani, and the would-be reformist president Mohammad Khatami.[96] Together, their interventions reflected not only the anxieties of transition into the post-Khomeini era, but even more acutely the eagerness to chart and embrace a modus vivendi between their religious values and a resurgent post–Cold War global discourse of liberal triumphalism. The latter trend was perhaps most evident in the frequency and depth of engagement of these thinkers with canonical works in liberal and critical political thought, which were complemented by invited lectures and visits by notable

---

[94] As Soroush argued, "The secret of the finality of Islam lies in the continuity of the revelation." Soroush, *Farbehtar az Idiolozhi,* p. 78. Ghamari-Tabrizi sums up the core difference between Shariati's and Soroush's visions thusly: "Whereas Shari'ati believed that selected vanguard intellectuals were capable of comprehending the truth of Islam, Soroush introduced an epistemological pluralism in the context of which any absolute truth-claim was suspect." Ghamari-Tabrizi, "Contentious Public Religion," p. 516.
[95] For an account of the "intellectual revolution" inaugurated by the entry of these ideas into the postrevolutionary public sphere, see Kamrava, *Iran's Intellectual Revolution,* chapter 5; and Brumberg, *Reinventing Khomeini,* chapters 6–8.
[96] Many veterans of the LMI were also active participants in these circles. For a comprehensive historical account and exegetical retelling of the currents of thought emerging out of the so-called Kiyan Circle, the Center for Strategic Research, and the Ayin Circle, see Sadeghi-Boroujerdi, *Revolution and Its Discontents,* pp. 46–48, 136–186, and 207–240. For a concise overview, see Mohammad Ayatollahi Tabaar, *Religious Statecraft: The Politics of Islam in Iran* (New York: Columbia University Press, 2018), pp. 214–222.

Pluralist Visions of Islamic Governance 131

Western intellectuals such as Jürgen Habermas, Agnes Heller, Richard Rorty, Anthony Giddens, Antonio Negri, Ashis Nandy, Paul Ricoeur, Noam Chomsky, John Keane, Timothy Garton Ash, Michael Ignatieff, among others.[97]

Soroush's profile and interventions, however, were nearly always at the forefront and a step above these discussions. This itself was also reflective of the general anxieties of Western liberal and intellectual discourses about the imperative of seeking out pluralistic, accommodationist, and reformist viewpoints from the Islamic world.[98] In a post–Cold War intellectual landscape encased by highly reductive and binary-ridden, yet tremendously influential, arguments about "the end of history" and "clash of civilizations," both the orientalist yearning for the arrival of a "Martin Luther of Islam" and a corrective to that impulse were most palpable among Western academics and journalists.[99] By virtue of his exposure to, and affiliations with, Western academic institutions, Soroush's pluralistic interventions were capaciously engaged with and disseminated relatively widely within Western intellectual circles, even if the nuances (i.e. contradictions, inconsistencies, as well as subtle qualifications) of his arguments were often glossed over.[100] Among his published works, his thoughts on the possibility of a religious democratic government were of most interest in the 1990s, which corresponded

---

[97] It is important to note that nonreligious intellectuals and university professors were most instrumental in facilitating these exchanges, even as they relied on religious reformers and their connections for the necessary permissions and political cover against conservative critics. Most instrumental in facilitating such visits was the liberal philosopher Ramin Jahanbegloo, who was later arrested on charges of seeking to foment a "color revolution" and subsequently forced into exile in Canada. He provides an account of his imprisonment and subsequent exile in Ramin Jahanbegloo, *Time Will Say Nothing: A Philosopher Survives an Iranian Prison* (Saskatchewan: University of Regina Press, 2014). For an example of the depth of intellectual engagements with Habermas's work during this period, see Ali Paya and Mohammad Amin Ghaneirad, "Habermas and Iranian Intellectuals," *Iranian Studies*, Vol. 40, No. 3 (June 2007): 305–334.

[98] These anxieties are captured well in Hashemi, *Islam, Secularism, and Liberal Democracy*, which is in equal parts a thoughtful rumination on the relationship between Islam and democracy and the challenge to prevailing orthodoxies of the time that reduced the complex of democratization into such binaries.

[99] As Mahmoud and Ahmad Sadri note, "Whatever the aptness of such analogies, they are notable not so much for their historical accuracy as for their power of historical imagination and intercultural understanding, otherwise woefully lacking in the Western media's voyeuristic and orientalist interest in the Islamic world." Soroush, *Reason, Freedom, and Democracy in Islam*, p. xv.

[100] References to Soroush's thought and writings are too numerous to reproduce here, but within comparative political theory influential introductions were made in Fred Dallmayr, *Dialogue among Civilizations: Culture and Religion in International Relations* (New York: Palgrave Macmillan, 2002), pp. 167–184; and Abdolkarim Soroush, "The Evolution and Devolution of Religious Knowledge," trans. Mahmoud Sadri, in Kurzman, ed., *Liberal Islam*, pp. 244–251.

132   Liberation without Liberalism

with the rise of the reform movement under the political leadership of Mohammad Khatami in Iran.

Soroush's thoughts on Islamic democracy were first published in the pages of *Kiyan*, [101] and especially in critical exchanges with the journalist and future dissident-exile Akbar Ganji (then writing under the pseudonym Hamid Paidar) and the former intelligence ministry agent-turned-reformist strategist Saeed Hajjarian (pseudonym Jahangir Salehpour). [102] The most lucid explanation of Soroush's position, however, emerged in his response to Ganji, who provocatively argued against the compatibility of democratic and Islamic principles. [103] Soroush used the provocation as an opportunity to push back against, in his view, three common misconceptions in debates about the compatibility of Islam and democracy. The first issue was the commonplace conflation of democracy with what he called "extreme liberalism."[104] "Democracy," Soroush observed, "is comprised of a method of restricting the power of the rulers and rationalizing their deliberations and policies, so that they will be less vulnerable to error and corruption, more open to exhortation, moderation, consultation; and so that violence and revolution will not become necessary."[105] In contrast to this mere "method" for devolving power, adjudicating rights, and ensuring accountability, however, stood the far more complex enterprise of liberalism. As a comprehensive view of life in its own right, liberalism fundamentally reflects the preference for a society organized around scientific as opposed to religious knowledge. [106] "Liberal philosophers," Soroush argued, "consider metaphysical arguments unverifiable and unfalsifiable. Consequently, they deem controversy over the truth or falsehood of religious beliefs futile and interminable."[107] But crucially for Soroush, while the recognition of the incommensurability of different religious views of life forced political expressions of liberalism to treat religious beliefs with impartiality (i.e. the right to religious freedom), it did not compel the same response toward scientific knowledge. As such, in liberal societies, the essence of "[l]liberal freedom was freedom from the fetters of religion and metaphysics. It was freedom from divine guardianship. This freedom had an epistemological and rational basis. Liberal philosophers did not discover man's fallibility and free will. They

---

[101] Abdolkarim Soroush, "Hokumat-e demokratik-e dini?" [Religious Democratic Government?], *Kiyan*, Vol. 3, No. 11 (1372/1993).

[102] On Hajjarian's political trajectory and thoughts, see Eskandar Sadeghi-Boroujerdi, "From Etela'ati to Eslahtalabi: Sa'id Hajjarian, Political Theology and the Politics of Reform in Post-revolutionary Iran," *Iranian Studies*, Vol. 47, No. 6 (2014): 987–1009.

[103] Akbar Ganji [Hamid Paidar, pseud.], "Paradox-e Eslam va Demokrasi" [The Paradox of Islam and Democracy], *Kiyan*, Vol. 4, No. 19 (1373/1994).

[104] Soroush, *Reason, Freedom, and Democracy in Islam*, p. 134.   [105] Ibid.

[106] Ibid., pp. 136–137.   [107] Ibid., p. 136.

Pluralist Visions of Islamic Governance 133

discovered the irrelevance of metaphysics."[108] Clarifying liberalism's epistemological commitments, Soroush implies, would enable us to see it as merely one among many other comprehensive views of the good life that could work alongside democracy, not the only one or even the most optimal one.

The second issue Soroush addresses in this response is the distortion of the Sharia in the form of the most monistic interpretations of it by fundamentalist adherents of Islam. Here he reiterates the distinction between the mystical essence of religion and mutable, contextual nature of religious knowledge, which forms the basis of his theology. Yet interestingly, in connection with his discussion of democracy, Soroush goes further by noting that "religious knowledge is potentially as open to criticism as scientific knowledge; [hence,] the authority of religion in religious knowledge is as invalid as the authority of science in the scientific knowledge."[109] What Soroush wishes to highlight here is the legitimacy of subjecting religious knowledge, and hence religious authority, to democratic criticism. If knowledge of religion in society is variable and dynamic, then any temporal claims on behalf of religion must be subjected to debate based on rational dialogue and reciprocal recognition of others' rights and freedoms. "Therefore," Soroush concludes, "the religious attitude (relegating judgment to the shared religious knowledge) maintains the same epistemological relationship to democracy as does the scientific attitude (relegating judgment to the shared wisdom of practitioners)."[110] A reductive understanding of Islam based only on the monistic, ahistorical interpretations of its fundamentalist adherents overlooks its variable function and practice in the daily lives of Muslims, whose differences must inevitably be resolved according to a set of representative and fair principles.

The conflation of democracy and liberalism, coupled with the reductive understanding of Islam, led to the third and most important "error" in Ganji's incompatibility thesis, according to Soroush: the equation of religious democratic government (*hokumat-e demokratik-e dini*) with religious jurisprudential government (*hokumat-e feqhi*). The latter, Soroush argues, had no pretensions to democracy or representative government. He notes that proponents of *hokumat-e feqhi*, as in the case of *velayat-e faqih*, "themselves avoid the title of democracy; they even take great pride and delight in opposing it, because they consider democracy as a fruit of the secular Western culture."[111] Yet, Soroush continues, "religious law [Sharia] is not synonymous with the entirety of religion; nor is the debate over the democratic religious government a purely jurisprudential

---

[108] Ibid., p. 137.   [109] Ibid.   [110] Ibid.   [111] Ibid., p. 134.

134   Liberation without Liberalism

argument. Moreover, jurisprudential statements are different from epistemological ones, and no methodic[al] mind should conflate the two realms."[112] Religious democratic government, in contrast, is concerned with facilitating debate and dialogue – through equal and free representation – around different interpretations of Islamic principles. Islamic democracy thus takes seriously the mutability of religious knowledge and especially the plurality of human reason that fuel disagreements and dynamism in the first place. While such a political system certainly demands a "religious understanding that needs to undergo constant examination," it does not, Soroush reassures, "require believers to abandon their convictions, secularize their creed, and lose faith in divine protection."[113] In this way, the democratic method would strengthen religion by facilitating open and equitable debate about the vicissitudes of belief in perennially changing Islamic societies. This vision, Soroush argues, stands in stark contrast to theocratic conceptions of Islam, as in the case of *velayat-e faqih*, that envision "the imposition of a particular belief or punishment of disbelief ... [which] are impermissible and undesirable in a democratic religious society."[114]

Soroush's objections to Ganji's incompatibility thesis lead to a key question regarding the substantive differences between his vision of religious democratic government and liberal democracy, since the latter also guarantees state neutrality and a robust set of rights and freedoms. In an earlier article on "The Idea of Democratic Religious Government"[115] (which prefigured the exchange with Ganji), Soroush argues that Islamic democracy must grapple with three complex normative issues: "to reconcile people's satisfaction with God's approval; to strike a balance between the religious and the nonreligious; and to do right by both the people and by God, acknowledging at once the integrity of human beings and of religion."[116] These challenges could be met, he proposes, if a pluralist reading of religion were combined with religious respect for modern human rights. Soroush is adamant that such a process does not entail "a surrender to relativistic liberalism," and that, at any rate, "liberalism is not the fount of human rights, nor is religion their antithesis."[117] Such misconceptions, Soroush notes, stem from the delayed embrace of the discourse of human rights by religious thinkers and lay persons alike, for whom "the language of religion and religious law is the language of duties, not rights." Consequently, the faithful are habituated to "look among their duties to find their rights, not vice versa."[118] Post-Enlightenment liberal discourses, in contrast, have adopted a discourse of rights in

---

[112] Ibid.   [113] Ibid., p. 135.   [114] Ibid.   [115] Ibid., pp. 122–130.   [116] Ibid., p. 122.
[117] Ibid., p. 129.   [118] Ibid., p. 129–130.

Pluralist Visions of Islamic Governance   135

a conscious effort to curtail any justifications of arbitrary powers of government or religion on the basis of obligations owed by citizens. For Soroush, however, the differential emphasis on duties versus rights in these discourses is not evidence of their mutual exclusivity. The task of a religious democratic government is to demonstrate the harmonious cohabitation of duties and rights by reframing their respective contributions to democratic citizenship.[119]

The absence of a detailed, substantive discussion of just how such philosophical vision might be *politically* achieved is a striking omission in Soroush's collective writings on these matters. Certainly, articulating a philosophical view is itself a most important endeavor, and Soroush is to be credited for having created an intellectual space within religious circles for discussions about the demands placed on religious thinking and practice by pluralism – and his interventions there, as respectful and judicious in their framing as they are, still of course elicited a harsh reaction from conservative and traditionalist factions that resulted in his forced exile to Europe and the United States. But Soroush's elliptical approach to the political implications of his vision for Islamic democracy is not only on account of these factors. Rather, his reluctance to delve into the political dimensions of Islamic democracy is due to a fundamental tension at the heart of his view of society. Bluntly stated, in Soroush's view society may at once be composed of autonomous individuals (with various degrees of religiosity and nonbelief) and be a coherent religious unit capable of justifying its customs, values, and rules to all of its members. The crucial presupposition here – and it is a very significant assumption since without it there would be no need for a democratic religious governmental scheme in the first place – is that Iran is essentially a religious society whose democratic aspirations spring out of the pluralistic nature of religious knowledge, not nonreligious claims or pursuits. This is an extraordinarily sweeping assumption. Soroush is himself aware of the tension it sets up in his concept, and yet his response betrays the complex array of considerations a viable political program would have to address:

There is no doubt that a democracy is engaged in an interminable process of choosing and examining, while a religious society believes that it has made a crucial choice and that it has the answer within its reach: it has chosen the path of religiosity and has determined to live in the shade of a religious belief. However, this preliminary decision of religious societies paves the way to innumerable subsequent decisions and arduous trials. From there on, it is religious

---

[119] As Soroush concludes his essay, "In the elusive and delicate balance between the two realms lies the rare elixir that the contemporary world, because of its neglect, finds unattainable or undesirable." Ibid., p. 130.

136   Liberation without Liberalism

understanding that needs to undergo constant examination. It will have to pass through difficult cycles of contraction, expansion, modification, and equilibrium:
On the path of love, a hundred hazards lie, beyond oblivion, yet;
So you won't say: once I reach my life's end, I'll have escaped. [Hafez, *Ghazaliyat* 314][120]

Soroush's characteristic reliance on poetry, literary witticisms, and mystical wisdom at precisely those junctures where further analytical elaboration of justificatory principles and political procedures are necessary is a telling sign of the limited nature, and selective scope, of his democratic vision. For instance, how precisely is the claim that "a religious society believes that it has made a crucial choice and that it has the answer within its reach" to be reconciled with the notion of an ever-changing "religious understanding" perennially engulfed in "difficult cycles of contraction, expansion, modification, and equilibrium," let alone the sanctity of individual autonomy so prized by Soroush? Such unresolved tensions reappear throughout Soroush's writings on religious democratic government, much to the chagrin of his critics. Ali Mirsepassi's critical reflections on these shortcomings capture the common frustrations with Soroush's ideas in this realm rather well: "Perhaps if Soroush could identify some of the religious-political institutions of democracy and the practical outcome of their implementation, instead of laying out general philosophical principles for his religious politics, one could have a better understanding of his goals. For example, if he could elaborate on the institution of the 'council' within Islamic tradition and how it could be adapted to broad popular participation in matters political."[121]

These limitations are in fact symptomatic of a more fundamental flaw in Soroush's thinking on democracy, which is laid bare in an analogy he employs – in response to Ganji's objections – to describe his rationale for combining religion and democracy. Soroush argues, "The idea of democratic religious society is a result of logical decoupling of democracy and liberalism. As such, it is analogous to the attempts of the social democrats to separate democracy from capitalism."[122] The first clear implication of

---

[120] Ibid., p. 135.
[121] Mirsepassi believes that Soroush's inability to delve into the practicalities of his vision stems from his underlying devotion to a mercurial sense of religiosity. As he puts the case bluntly, "The problem stems from the fact that Soroush believes in the discourse of political Islam and wishes to salvage an ideology that has been bankrupt for some time now. His refusal to recognize any distinction between the private sphere (including religious affiliations and convictions) and the public sphere, his insistence on incorporating his own religious and intellectual prerogatives into a broad social agenda, and his habitual 'augmentation' of all sociological concepts with religious pre- and post-fixes, cannot help the cause of democracy in Iran." Mirsepassi, *Democracy in Modern Iran*, pp. 88–89.
[122] Soroush, *Reason, Freedom, and Democracy in Islam*, p. 138.

Pluralist Visions of Islamic Governance

this statement is that Soroush clearly believes that *the* precondition for religious democracy is the nullification of the liberal attributes of democracy. In other words, while religion and democracy can coexist happily, religion and liberalism cannot. This is a curiously strong statement given Soroush's earlier appraisal of liberal-pluralist values and his admiration of the works of modern and contemporary liberal philosophers.[123] The choice of analogy is also striking, given the centrality of liberal values, rights, and procedures to both social democracy and capitalist society. The differences in each case have to do with the distributive dimensions of social and economic policy, while maintaining strict adherence to the bedrock principles of equality of interests, political autonomy, and reciprocity, whose substance is essentially liberal.[124]

It is indeed true, as Soroush never tires of repeating, that democracy is but a "method" of government based on popular consent and representation. He also seems aware that liberalism's imprint on democracy is revealed in constitutional protections for individual rights and freedoms, through appeals to justifiable reasons in resolving disputes, and in the priority granted to pluralism. Yet, by arguing that a rejection of liberalism is a necessary condition for the establishment of religious democratic government, he seems unaware of the intricate linkages between liberalism and democracy in modern times. Put simply, in modern and contemporary iterations of democracy it is difficult to discern where democratization of liberalism ends and liberalization of democracy begins. This is not merely a Western liberal democratic conceit, but a reflection of the simultaneous diffusion of both liberal and democratic principles around the globe since the end of modern European empires and the expansion of membership in international society based on the principle of self-determination.[125] It also explains why even in debates among critical democratic theorists, liberalism and democracy are hardly ever spoken of in binary terms, and instead are held to account in

---

[123] Ibid., 137. For a comprehensive normative study on the "ideal ethical encounter" and coexistence between Islam and democracy, see March, *Islam and Liberal Citizenship*. For a general account of the liberal accommodation of religious beliefs, see Lucas Swaine, *The Liberal Conscience: Politics and Principles in a World of Religious Pluralism* (New York: Columbia University Press, 2006).

[124] As Corey Brettschneider has explained, "These values are central to the idea of democracy because they support the notion of democratic citizens as free, equal, and reasonable rulers." Corey Brettschneider, *Democratic Rights: The Substance of Self-government* (Princeton, NJ: Princeton University Press, 2007), p. 9.

[125] For insightful recent works on the tortuous path of these developments, see Manela, *The Wilsonian Moment*; and Adom Getachew, *Worldmaking after Empire: The Rise and Fall of Self-determination* (Princeton, NJ: Princeton University Press, 2019).

138   Liberation without Liberalism

reference to their conjoined capacities for accommodating difference and mitigating injustice.[126]

In the final analysis, the tensions and contradictions in Soroush's explanation of the relationship between liberalism and democracy spring from the paradoxical disposition on his part, on the one hand, to appropriate liberal principles in constructing a pluralistic conception of religious knowledge and, on the other, arguing that a religious democratic government based on religious pluralism is mutually exclusive of liberalism. This paradox ultimately reflects Soroush's desire to reframe political liberal values such as individual autonomy, political equality, and reciprocity in religious-pluralist terms for a society that he believes has collectively chosen the path of belief over unbelief.[127] It is clear from his labyrinthine writings on the subject that he is fundamentally concerned about the impact of liberalism on religious values in the absence of an overarching commitment to religious heritage and foundations – as is the case in the once religious but increasingly secular Western liberal democracies. But unlike religious and communitarian Western critics of liberalism,[128] Soroush is not merely content with arguing for more robust constitutional protections against liberal and secular impositions on the faithful. Rather, his conception of Islamic democracy seeks to maintain the privileged status of religious values over democratic – and, by extension, liberal – principles and norms. He envisions a democratic society based on a pluralism of values as defined by religion, not on the basis of natural rights. As he emphatically declares, "Belief is a hundred times more diverse and colorful than disbelief. If the pluralism of secularism makes it suitable for democracy, the faithful community is a thousand times more suitable for it …. [Therefore,] religious government over a faithful and alert society that respects liberty and dynamism of religious understanding cannot help but be a democratic society."[129] However, as

---

[126] For a collection of influential interventions by leading critical and liberal-democratic theorists, see Seyla Benhabib, ed., *Democracy and Difference: Contesting the Boundaries of the Political* (Princeton, NJ: Princeton University Press, 1996).

[127] That his conservative religious critics accuse him of attempting to smuggle liberal principles under the guise of religious pluralism is perhaps the best indication of how transparent Soroush's appropriations are. But from a scholarly standpoint, it is Soroush's *mis*appropriation of liberal values that is manifest, since he never qualifies how the priority of religious interpretations – however diverse and dynamic they may be – would not in each case supersede the liberal substance of individual autonomy and political equality.

[128] See, for instance, Alasdair MacIntyre, *After Virtue: A Study in Moral Philosophy* (Notre Dame, IN: University of Notre Dame Press, 1981); Michael Sandel, *Liberalism and the Limits of Justice* (Cambridge: Cambridge University Press, 1982); and Michael Walzer, *Spheres of Justice: A Defense of Pluralism and Equality* (Oxford: Blackwell, 1983).

[129] Soroush, *Reason, Freedom, and Democracy in Islam*, p. 144–145.

Conclusion: Religious Pluralism contra Liberalism

it has been repeatedly asked of Soroush in different ways: if what is meant by "liberty and dynamism of religious understanding" is not enshrined in constitutional principles that do not privilege a particular reading of the faith, then is not such a conception of government bound to be nondemocratic, even theocratic?[130] After all, even in democratic societies with robust guarantees of basic rights of freedoms, the ebb and flow of constitutional interpretation is to a great extent at the mercy of power politics.

Conclusion: Religious Pluralism contra Liberalism

The set of political and intellectual dispositions examined in the previous section obviously do not qualify as endorsements of political liberalism, much less comprehensive liberalism. They certainly correspond to aspects of a Shklarian "liberalism of fear," as Sadeghi-Boroujerdi has recently argued.[131] Judith N. Shklar's evocative framework envisioned an essentially negative (in the Berlinian sense of the concept) form of liberalism limited to "politics and to proposals to restrain potential abusers of power in order to lift the burden of fear and favor from the shoulders of adult women and men, who can then conduct their lives in accordance with their own beliefs and preferences, as long as they do not prevent others from doing so as well."[132] In the context of Iran's postrevolutionary dissident politics, this framework has assuredly some explanatory purchase. As Sadeghi-Boroujerdi demonstrates, it "was borne out of lived experience of precarity, as several of Iran's postrevolutionary religious intellectuals shifted subject position from ideological legitimators of the revolutionary Islamist regime to more ambivalent internal critics on the outskirts of political power and thereby subject to the state apparatus', and its agents', wanton encroachments."[133] In the cases of Bazargan, Soroush, and their dissident-intellectual fellow

---

[130] Ziba Mir-Hosseini offers perhaps the most concrete implications of Soroush's unwillingness to address this core issues in the case of Islamic jurisprudential rulings and interpretations on gender norms and relations. Her indictment of Soroush's pluralistic vision centers on his avoidance of jurisprudence (*fiqh*) altogether and lack of specificity regarding the constitutional provisions that ought to uphold women's rights as human rights. See Ziba Mir-Hosseini, *Islam and Gender: The Religious Debate in Contemporary Iran* (Princeton, NJ: Princeton University Press, 2000), pp. 213–246.

[131] As Sadeghi-Boroujerdi notes, religious-pluralist intellectual discourses "in the late 1980s and 1990s gradually came to represent a *liberal turn* in Iranian politico-religious thought; i.e., broadly speaking, they held that state power should be limited, the rule of law guaranteed, and civil and human rights protected." Sadeghi-Boroujerdi, *Revolution and Its Discontents*, pp. 187–188 (italics in the original).

[132] Judith N. Shklar, "The Liberalism of Fear," in Nancy Rosenblum, ed., *Liberalism and the Moral Life* (Cambridge, MA: Harvard University Press, 1989), p. 31.

[133] Sadeghi-Boroujerdi, *Revolution and Its Discontents*, p. 188.

140   Liberation without Liberalism

travelers, the minimal emphasis on representative government, basic human rights, and pluralism, in the absence of any programmatic vision for liberal constitutionalism, certainly testify to the adherence to this limited sense of liberalism. Notable, too, is the circumspect method of communicating inconvenient or taboo ideas in public forums by adopting pseudonyms, engaging in doublespeak, and other hidden liberal tactics of yore.

As the preceding sections also make clear, however, these intellectuals' commitments to some version of religious-constitutionalist framework, no matter how pluralistic or representative its foundations, places them at odds with even a minimalist rendering of liberalism.[134] This is not because religious and liberal values are incompatible with each other. But rather because to the extent that these intellectuals incorporate liberal values in their political writings, it is in order to present a more pluralistic version of *Islam* and not to advocate for models of liberal government and rights that are fundamentally untethered to assumptions about the religious character of society and individual religiosity. Their reluctance to endorse more robust liberal-secular visions, moreover, cannot be solely attributed to the repressive conditions of public life under the Islamic Republic, since many religious intellectuals – such as Soroush – endorse similar views even while leading a life of exile in Western democratic societies.[135] It would be more accurate, therefore, to characterize their views as embodying and promoting certain liberal antipathies (e.g. anti-absolutism and anti-imperialism) and prescriptions (e.g. constitutionalism and pluralism) *strictly within* the Islamic tradition, and not attempting to promote liberalism as a social and political program in its own right. This point bears emphasis because it speaks to the long-standing tradition of progressive thought that I have alluded to in the previous chapters, and which especially accounts for the circumspect expression of liberal values and ideals in Iranian society. Indeed, in the case of religious intellectuals this proclivity is less the case of disguising liberal values as more capacious religious beliefs – as, for instance, was the case at the time of the Constitutional Revolution – and more so the case of a forthright and confident belief in the mutual exclusivity of comprehensive visions of

[134] To be sure, this is more the case with Soroush and Khatami-era reformists than Bazargan and some other LMI veterans, who were more open about their preference for a secular-democratic order than an outright religious one.

[135] A prominent exception to this cohort is Akbar Ganji, whose writings and activism in exile have decisively moved in the direction of secularism and liberal-democratic government. Since the scope of this inquiry is limited to the twentieth century, I do not explore Ganji's political thinking here. For a concise elaboration of his views on Islam, democracy, and liberalism, however, see Akbar Ganji, *The Road to Democracy in Iran* (Cambridge, MA: MIT Press, 2008).

Conclusion: Religious Pluralism contra Liberalism 141

liberalism and Islamic identity. As Mohammad Khatami, whose reformist platform and triumph in the presidential elections in 1997 was staked on this religious-pluralist vision conveyed bluntly in an interview before his landslide victory, "I believe that a true human being who believes and has accepted Islam cannot be a liberal .... [Whereas] liberalism is based on man's wants, wishes, and his materialistic needs, [Islam focuses on] the spiritual and ethical improvement of man."[136]

---

[136] "Khatami Interview on Elections," *Jomhouri-ye Eslami*, February 25, 1997, FBIS-NES -97–047. Quoted in Brumberg, *Reinventing Khomeini*, p. 228.

5   Conclusion
(In)visible Liberalisms

Something which has often surprised me is the realization that these Persians knew as much as I did about the customs and way of life of our nation; they had grasped even the subtlest points, and noticed things which, I am sure, have escaped many a German who has travelled through France. I attribute this to the length of their stay here, apart from the fact that it is easier for an Asian to learn about the habits of Frenchmen in a year than for a Frenchman to learn about the habits of Asians in four, because the latter's readiness to talk about himself is equaled only by the reticence of the former. [1]

SL: *Do you think that liberalism is . . . essentially European, then? Or Western?*
IB: *It was certainly invented in Europe.*
SL: *Historically, of course. But, I mean now – is it an essentially Western principle?*
IB: *Yes. I suspect that there may not be much liberalism in Korea. I doubt if there is much liberalism even in Latin America. I think liberalism is essentially the belief of people who have lived on the same soil for a long time in comparative peace with each other. An English invention. The English have not been invaded for a very very long time. That's why they can afford to praise these virtues. I see that if you were exposed to constant pogroms you might be a little more suspicious of the possibility of liberalism.* [2]

Conventional accounts of modern liberalism take it for granted that liberal thought-practices are differentiated from their counterparts by their public affirmation of recognizably liberal aims or values. It may well be that those invoking or appealing to liberal values are not conscious of the substance of the ideology behind their inclinations, but the mere *visibility* of them partaking in such familiar activities qualifies them as liberal political thought-practices. Indeed, political theorists regularly cite expressions of unfettered individuality and political equality, reason-based dialogue, and everyday manifestations of steadfast adherence to core principles of value pluralism as indications of the readily

---

[1] Charles-Louis de Secondat, Baron de Montesquieu, *Persian Letters*, trans. Christopher Betts (London: Penguin, 2004), p. 40.
[2] Isaiah Berlin and Steven Lukes, "Isaiah Berlin: In Conversation with Steven Lukes," *Salmagundi*, No. 120 (Fall 1998): 121.

142

Conclusion 143

recognizable diffusion of liberal values in Western democratic societies. In each instance, the essential qualities of liberalism at work are gleaned not only from a perceptible liberal vocabulary but also from the public manner in which such activities attest to and promote underlying liberal values. But what of those thought-practices that are deliberately disguised to seem non-liberal, yet whose purpose and effects are unmistakably liberal? Contemporary political theorists and intellectual historians are well-accustomed to seeing through such prudential acts of concealment or iterations of liberal concepts inflected by context in the works of canonical thinkers in the Western liberal tradition.[3] Indeed, we unhesitatingly interpret the rhetorical deference shown to religion, national identity, cultural heritage, commercial society, or even hereditary rule in the classic works of modern liberal thought as evidence of the liberal tradition's elasticity, heterogeneity, and adaptability over time.[4] Yet, the same courtesy is not extended to liberalism's developmental course outside of the Western experience. Instead, the standards applied to non-Western contexts seem to be exclusively drawn from the prevailing signifiers and languages of Western liberalism.

There are a number of reasons for the persistence of the visibility bias in studies of modern liberalism. The first and most obvious reason is that much liberal theorizing concerns ideal types that prescribe more just and equitable improvements to *existing* liberal-democratic regimes. In *Political Liberalism*, for instance, John Rawls is explicit from the outset about the aim of his theory "to work out a political conception of justice for a (liberal) constitutional democratic regime that a plurality of reasonable doctrines, both religious and non-religious, liberal and nonliberal, may

---

[3] The entire corpus of "the Cambridge School" in intellectual and political history certainly attests to this awareness. From among the most notable works in this genre, see Berlin, "Two Concepts of Liberty," the University of Oxford, October 31, 1958; John Dunn, *The Political Thought of John Locke: An Historical Account of the Argument of the 'Two Treatises of Government'* (Cambridge: Cambridge University Press, 1969); Hannah Pitkin, "Are Freedom and Liberty Twins?" *Political Theory*, Vol. 16 (1998): 523–552; Quentin Skinner, "Meaning and Understanding in the History of Ideas," *History and Theory*, Vol. 8, No. 1 (1969): 3–53; Quentin Skinner, *Liberty before Liberalism* (Cambridge: Cambridge University Press, 1998); James Tully, *An Approach to Political Philosophy: Locke in Contexts* (Cambridge: Cambridge University Press, 1993); Stefan Collini, *Liberalism and Sociology: L. T. Hobhouse and Political Argument in England, 1880–1914* (Cambridge: Cambridge University Press, 1979); Michael Freeden, *Liberalism Divided: A Study in British Political Thought, 1914–1939* (New York: Oxford University Press, 1986); Jeremy Waldron, *God, Locke, and Equality: Christian Foundations in Locke's Political Thought* (Cambridge: Cambridge University Press, 2002); and Ryan, *The Making of Modern Liberalism.*

[4] Hobhouse, *Liberalism*, was perhaps the first systematic theoretical treatment of liberalism that allowed for the imprint of historical context on liberal ideas. For more recent scholarly treatments of the liberal tradition as a historical enterprise, see Freeden, *Liberal Languages*; and Ryan, *The Making of Modern Liberalism.*

144   Conclusion

endorse for the right reasons."[5] In *The Law of Peoples*, Rawls does indeed reflect on what he calls "decent" non-liberal societies, but the main subject of concern for him is "a particular conception of right and justice that applies to the principles and norms of international law and practice,"[6] not the practice of liberal norms inside the boundaries of non-liberal states. Other major works of liberal political theory are similarly delimited in their respective inquiries.[7] That such luminous works operate on the assumption of exiting liberal institutional settings, however, does not render them in the least deficient. By envisioning the reasonable potential of certain norms and principles, ideal theory performs an indispensable function in spurring deeper reflections about our real-world difficulties (not to mention the essential service it renders to the development of theory itself).[8] But an unacknowledged yet significant implication of such efforts has been the privileging of a "specialized language," in Michael Freeden's acute diagnosis, that seemingly has absolved political theorists from being "in touch with the political and cultural constraints that ensure the viable flexibility liberalism requires, as it competes in the real-world arena of policymaking, of reform, of social inspiration, and of political mobilization."[9] Hidden liberal practices, the preceding chapters have hopefully demonstrated, are evidence of precisely such "viable flexibility" required of liberal actors in contexts where the hegemony of non-liberal doctrines is overriding.

The second factor, also related to the first, has to do with the widespread conflation of liberalism as a universal philosophical creed with the practice of liberalism as a contextual activity. The former has to do with the normative content of liberalism as a moral and political doctrine, whereas the latter is chiefly about *how* that content is articulated, received, and sustained over time. Some of the fault for this confusion rests with liberal theorists themselves, most of whom too often neglect elaborating

[5] John Rawls, *Political Liberalism* (New York: Columbia University Press, 1996), p. xli.
[6] John Rawls, *The Law of Peoples* (Cambridge, MA: Harvard University Press, 1999), p. 3.
[7] For a representative sample, see Ronald Dworkin, *Taking Rights Seriously* (Cambridge, MA: Harvard University Press, 1977); Amy Gutmann, *Liberal Rights* (Cambridge: Cambridge University Press, 1980); Nancy L. Rosenblum, *Liberalism and the Moral Life* (Cambridge, MA: Harvard University Press, 1989); Jeremy Waldron, *Liberal Rights: Collected Papers, 1981–1991* (Cambridge: Cambridge University Press, 1993); Amy Gutmann and Dennis Thompson, *Democracy and Disagreement* (Cambridge, MA: Harvard University Press, 1996); Wall, ed., *The Cambridge Companion to Liberalism*.
[8] Indeed, the spate of "liberal egalitarian" works in political theory and philosophy in the second half of the twentieth century were most influential in terms of their impact on thinking about institutions and public policy in many Western democratic societies. For a comprehensive critical appraisal of this impact, see Katrina Forrester, *In the Shadow of Justice: Postwar Liberalism and the Remaking of Political Philosophy* (Princeton, NJ: Princeton University Press, 2019).
[9] Freeden, *Liberal Languages*, p. 6.

Conclusion

on the practical implications of liberal prescriptions for different contexts.[10] As a result, reflections on the encounter between certain liberal values (e.g. individual autonomy) and non-liberal principles (e.g. religious customs) tend to ignore myriad hybrid practices in which elements of both doctrines may (un)easily coexist. This oversight has made liberalism vulnerable to charges of ahistoricism and universal abstraction, which have further obscured its variable manifestations across a range of cultural and political orders.[11] To communitarian and agonistic critics, liberalism's imposition of rational criteria for social cooperation leads to the construction of a universal model of citizenship, whereby the identities of and differences between citizens are deliberately kept out of the political process, consigned to the private realm.[12] As a result, modern liberal ideals of autonomy and equality are envisioned independently of contestation, antagonism, and active participation – dynamics that provide the normative foundations and ethical character of democratic life.[13] I do not wish to relitigate here what has been a long-standing debate in political theory between liberals and their detractors, except to note that such exchanges end up further reifying the image of liberalism as a universally visible, self-avowed form of political practice for the reasons mentioned above.

Hidden liberal practices, however, significantly undermine these criticisms by demonstrating how liberalism, far from discriminating between beliefs on the basis of their "reasonableness," in fact arguably offers the most effective practical strategies for a great variety of belief systems to counter arbitrary forms of power. In non-liberal democratic societies,

---

[10] An exception to this rule has been the work of William A. Galston on the practical implications of value pluralism: Galston, *Liberal Pluralism*; and Galston, *The Practice of Liberal Pluralism*. But here, too, the scope of liberal practices is limited to societies in which liberal institutions and values are established and widely absorbed.

[11] For the most lucid and philosophically rigorous critique of liberalism's ahistoricity, see Raymond Geuss, *History and Illusion in Politics* (Cambridge: Cambridge University Press, 2001), pp. 69–109.

[12] The arguments of communitarian critics of liberalism are best discerned in the context of the so-called liberal-communitarian debate. For helpful summaries, see Simon Caney, "Liberalism and Communitarianism: A Misconceived Debate," *Political Studies*, Vol. XL (1992): 273–289; Amy Gutmann, "Communitarian Critics of Liberalism," *Philosophy & Public Affairs*, Vol. 14, No. 3 (Summer 1985): 308–322; and Will Kymlicka, "Liberalism and Communitarianism," *Canadian Journal of Philosophy*, Vol. 18, No. 2 (June 1988): 181–204. The most influential account of the agonistic critique of liberalism can be found in Mouffe, *The Return of the Political*, especially the introduction and chapters 3 and 9.

[13] For a representative summation of these criticisms, see Walzer, *Spheres of Justice*; Michael Walzer, *Thick and Thin: Moral Argument at Home and Abroad* (Notre Dame, IN: University of Notre Dame, 1994); Charles Taylor, "The Politics of Recognition," in Amy Gutmann, ed., *Multiculturalism: Examining the Politics of Recognition* (Princeton, NJ: Princeton University Press, 1994), pp. 25–73; Chantal Mouffe, "Politics and the Limits of Liberalism," in *The Return of the Political* (London: Verso, 2005).

146   Conclusion

hidden liberalism is premised not only on the notion that "the personal is political" but also on the understanding that constructive political change is often the result of private acts prudently impressed upon others. As such, in contrast to the visible operation of liberal practices that rely on institutional and procedural guarantees, hidden liberalism almost solely relies on the agency of individuals. This does not make it merely the private practice of liberalism, however. To the contrary, its inadmissibility as a public standpoint forces its practitioners to engage with and examine more deeply the reasons behind the appeal of other public standpoints in order to rearticulate liberal aims in terms most resonant to others. Such painstaking, yet notably effective, bridge-building efforts also stand as noteworthy counterexamples to an especially influential interpretation of liberalism as "an art of separation."[14] In its subterranean and appropriated form, as the case of Iran has shown, liberalism is in fact first and foremost concerned with breaking down barriers and arbitrary separations, and to the extent that it may advocate in favor of certain divisions (e.g. between church and state or public and private domains) it does so on the basis of common moral principles such as equal respect for persons. Indeed, this is a major reason why liberalism has always been expressed and experienced differently across time and space, and according to the most effective means to its realization. Universal fealty to liberal principles and aims need not necessitate universal means and approaches to attaining them.[15]

The propensity to blend abstract ideals and contextual practices is most glaringly discernible in the study of liberalism in non-Western contexts. Precisely because liberal practices do not manifest themselves in similar terms to Western-centric conceptions of them, their cumulative impact on the development of more open and transparent political forms has largely been overlooked. To the extent that historians of political thought, and especially works in intellectual history, have contemplated the fate of liberalism in non-Western contexts, they have almost universally modeled their inquiries on preconceptions about existing public expressions of

---

[14] Michael Walzer, "Liberalism and the Art of Separation," *Political Theory*, Vol. 12, No. 3. (August 1984): 315. Walzer emphatically observes, "Liberalism is a world of walls, and each one creates a new liberty."

[15] Here I follow Charles Larmore's incisive distinction between the "universal content" of moral ideals and their "universal justifiability." The former refers to "a set of (categorical) duties that obligate each person with regard to all other persons as such," while the latter merely posits "that this system of duties is such that each person, simply by virtue of being rational, has good reason to accept them as his duties." Larmore proposes that we "reject the idea of *universal justifiability* . . . while keeping that of a *universalist content*. That is, why can we not affirm a set of duties binding on all without supposing they must be justifiable to all?" Larmore, *The Morals of Modernity*, p. 57 (emphasis in the original).

Conclusion 147

liberal norms and values in Western contexts. This tendency, moreover, is not wholly unrelated to erstwhile liberal associations with Western imperial interests across the globe. The legacy of "liberal imperialism" has been much studied in the literature on the history of Western political thought, and debates about its content and range still continue in political theory;[16] but nearly all of these studies have been about *Western* liberalism, not its *non-Western* variants.[17] Curiously, there has been little by way of scholarly investigations into the implications of liberal imperialism for the reception and development of liberalism during and after the retreat of formal imperial practices in non-Western contexts.[18] The present study, especially in Chapters 2 and 3, has underlined how this legacy has had a profound effect on the practical iterations of liberalism in Iran against the backdrop of resurgent anti-liberal doctrines and practices.

Yet, just as suspicions about the purposes of Western liberalism have impeded its open reception in postimperial societies, confidence in the essential superiority and universality of the Western model of liberal democracy has been at its highest among Western liberal democrats for much of the twentieth and early twenty-first centuries. From Woodrow Wilson's avowal to "make the world safe for democracy," to the anti-communist panegyrics of "liberal Cold Warriors," to the designation of liberal democracy as "the end of history," to the militarization of democracy promotion in the form of George W. Bush's "Freedom Agenda," the seemingly unshakable faith in the redeeming qualities of liberal democracy has confirmed liberalism's global posture as a "fighting creed."[19] Given the selective nature of this advocacy according to the imperatives of geopolitics, however, it has resulted in further deepening the impression of liberalism as a tool of statecraft in the service of Western cultural and political supremacy.[20] Furthermore, although today most Western liberals vehemently oppose the exploitation of liberal ideals for geostrategic

[16] See, for example, Mehta, *Liberalism and Empire*; Pitts, *A Turn to Empire*; Mantena, *Alibis of Empire*; Muthu, ed., *Empire and Modern Political Thought*; Bell, *Reordering the World*.

[17] Regardless of how much they may have enhanced our understanding of "the ideological complexity and internal variability of liberalism." Bell, *Reordering the World*, p. 5.

[18] The sole exception to this oversight is the case of India. There exist a few histories of Indian liberal thoughts that seek to move beyond Anglo-centric preoccupations about India's place in the minds of British liberals to more comprehensive examinations of Indian liberalism itself. But even in these studies the focus is almost exclusively on the public expressions of liberal beliefs commensurate with existing Western formulations. See, for example, Bayly, *Recovering Liberties*; Buch, *Rise and Growth of Indian Liberalism*; and Kumar, "Liberalism and Reform in India."

[19] "All this is to say," Taylor has convincingly argued, "that liberalism can't and shouldn't claim complete cultural neutrality. Liberalism is also a fighting creed." Taylor, "The Politics of Recognition," p. 62.

[20] Manela comprehensively catalogues this effect in the rise of anti-colonial nationalist movements after the retreat of European empires and the subsequent rise of American

148   Conclusion

ends, their own utter lack of curiosity about the varieties of non-Western doctrines and practices has left them, as Daniel A. Bell argues in reference to East Asian societies, "de facto, as secular preachers of the democratic faith, blind to the possibility of defensible alternatives that may be worth learning from."[21] The same observation, of course, can be made of postcolonial societies, where notably a key aspect of liberation struggles has been to draw attention to the discrepancies between Western rhetoric on liberal democracy and the aims of Western foreign policy.[22]

This has especially been the case with liberal political theories and practices. Indeed, a central implication of the account presented in this book is that Western liberalism's disinterest in the variable reception and mutation of liberal ideals beyond its own shores has placed a dual burden on postcolonial liberals: to advance liberal claims *against both the arbitrary exercises of state power and the legacy of Western imperialism partially liable for the disfigurement of the state*. Hidden liberalism, as a pragmatic political thought-practice, is largely born out of this fraught historical inheritance. Nevertheless, it is also critical not to characterize the imperial background as all-encompassing. Despite Western imperialism's indelible imprint on the national identities, systems of knowledge, socioeconomic and political development, and institutional capacities of postcolonial states, zones of resistance and possibilities for authentic communal life abound. As the late Edward Said once observed, "No social system, no historical vision, no theoretical totalization, no matter how powerful, can exhaust all the alternatives or practices that exist within its domain. There is always the possibility to transgress."[23] In point of fact, it is my contention that hidden liberalism constitutes just such a transgression. It is not by any means the only form of transgression, as other ideologies – Islamism, nativism, socialism, communism – have and continue to struggle for recognition. But, crucially, even in postcolonial considerations of such transgressive thought-practices liberalism is largely overlooked. Here, the issue is less the case of the invisibility of liberalism as a familiar ideology than its deliberate dismissal as, at best, a compromised mode of thought.

---

military and economic power in *The Wilsonian Moment*. See also Mishra, *From the Ruins of Empire*.

[21] Bell goes on to point out: "Here the asymmetry with East Asia is most striking. Since the late nineteenth century, the dominant trend has been to recognize (and act upon) the importance of learning from Western political theories and practices." Daniel A. Bell, *Beyond Liberal Democracy: Political Thinking for an East Asian Context* (Princeton, NJ: Princeton University Press, 2006), p. 6.

[22] See Manela, *The Wilsonian Moment*, part III.

[23] Edward W. Said, *Musical Elaborations* (New York: Columbia University Press, 1991), p. 55.

Conclusion 149

In much postcolonial writing, liberalism is simply *ideologia non grata*, except as an object of critique.[24] Within political theory, the postcolonial treatments of liberalism have largely followed the same lines of criticism as those of radical/agonistic, communitarian, Marxist, and post-structuralist perspectives, which take to task liberalism for its abstract and universalist model of rationalism, its privileging of individuals over groups, its insular (Western) and limited view of distributive justice, and its neglect of the irreducible variety of cultural identities.[25] These substantive deficits, postcolonial critics conclude, render liberalism insufficiently inclusive or emancipatory to offer a constructive agenda for recovering indigenous identities and achieving equal sovereign status in world politics. These concerns, although certainly not immaterial, are nonetheless secondary to the paradox raised in this book: that despite liberalism's history of complicity with ideologies and practices of Western imperialism, it has also been a powerful influence on the substance and shape of social and political struggles in a semicolonial society. Moreover, as Chapter 2 made clear, the range of liberal antipathies and prescriptions that have been either championed, rearticulated, or appropriated by liberals and non-liberals alike may well cumulatively amount to a form of *liberal postcolonial* response to the legacies of imperialism. The neglect of these subversive modes of liberal thought-practices is a conspicuous blind spot of much contemporary

---

[24] Exploring the reasons behind this is too historically complex and theoretically varied to fit within the scope of the present study. Suffice it to say that it is centered fundamentally on the relationship between liberalism and continued Western dominance, especially in the realm of global political economy. For representative inquiries, see James Tully, "Lineages of Informal Imperialism," in Duncan Kelly, ed., *Lineages of Empire* (Oxford: Oxford University Press, 2009), pp. 3–30; Hobson, *The Eurocentric Conception of World Politics*; Halperin and Palan, eds., *Legacies of Empire*; Robert Vitalis, *White World Order, Black Power Politics* (Ithaca, NY: Cornell University Press, 2015). For two recent works focusing specifically on the relationship between Islam and liberalism in this domain, see Joseph A. Massad, *Islam in Liberalism* (Chicago, IL: University of Chicago Press, 2015); and Faisal Devji and Zaheer Kazmi, eds., *Islam after Liberalism* (Oxford: Oxford University Press, 2017).

[25] These criticisms are best summarized by Duncan Ivison, who discusses them in reference to the exclusion of indigenous communities in North America and Australasia in chapter 2 of his book *Postcolonial Liberalism* (Cambridge: Cambridge University Press, 2002). But individual strands of these critiques can be found in Partha Chaterjee, *The Nation and Its Fragments: Colonial and Postcolonial Histories* (Princeton, NJ: Princeton University Press, 1993); Homi Bhaba, *The Location of Culture* (New York: Routledge, 1994); Gayatri Chakravorty Spivak, *A Critique of Postcolonial Reason: Toward a History of the Vanishing Present* (Cambridge, MA: Harvard University Press, 1999); Dipesh Chakrabarty, *Provincializing Europe* (Princeton, NJ: Princeton University Press, 2000); Bhikhu Parekh, *Rethinking Multiculturalism: Cultural Diversity and Political Theory*, 2nd ed. (London: Palgrave Macmillan, 2006); and James Tully, *Public Philosophy in a New Key, Volume II: Imperialism and Civic Freedom* (Cambridge: Cambridge University Press, 2008).

150   Conclusion

postcolonial theorizing. What is more, in the polemical iterations of its second- and third-generation exponents this oversight has metamorphosed into an orthodoxy that evaluates any thought, practice, or norm as either in the service of or resistance to liberal imperialism.[26] This reflexive determinism has complemented Western liberalism's visibility bias toward indigenous liberal movements by portraying them as mere facsimiles of Western liberalism without a natural domestic constituency, and as mostly the purview of out-of-touch, inauthentic Westernized elites.[27]

Mercifully, within political theory the emergence of "cross-cultural" and "comparative" approaches has moved the discipline beyond the aforementioned postcolonial orthodoxies by proposing an alternative hermeneutics premised on, in the words of Fred Dallmayr, "reciprocal questioning and critique."[28] These efforts have resulted in a number of influential studies about a variety of indigenous and hybrid political thought-practices in Islamic, Confucian, and cosmopolitan contexts.[29] There is much value to these inquiries, and indeed the present study

---

[26] Massad's *Islam in Liberalism* is a good example of this.

[27] For an incisive critique of the intersection of American social scientific knowledge, liberalism, and imperial designs characteristic of these complementary studies, see Lisa Wedeen, "Scientific Knowledge, Liberalism, and Empire: American Political Science in the Middle East," in Seteny Shami and Cynthia Miller-Idriss, eds., *Middle East Studies for the New Millennium: Infrastructures of Knowledge* (New York: New York University Press, 2016), pp. 31–81.

[28] Fred Dallmayr, "Introduction: Toward a Comparative Political Theory," *The Review of Politics*, Vol. 59, No. 3 (Summer 1997): 421–427.

[29] Roxanne L. Euben, "Comparative Political Theory: An Islamic Fundamentalist Critique of Rationalism," *Journal of Politics*, Vol. 59, No. 1 (1997): 28–55; Roxanne L. Euben, *Journeys to the Other Shore* (Princeton, NJ: Princeton University Press, 2006); Farah Godrej, *Cosmopolitan Political Thought: Method, Practice, Discipline* (New York: Oxford University Press, 2011); Leigh Jenco, "'What Does Heaven Ever Say?': A Methods-Centered Approach to Cross-cultural Engagement," *American Political Science Review*, Vol. 101, No. 4 (2007): 741–755; Leigh Jenco, *Changing Referents: Learning across Space and Time in China and the West* (New York: Oxford University Press, 2015); Leigh Jenco, "New Pasts for New Futures: A Temporal Reading of Global Thought," *Constellations*, Vol. 23, No. 3 (2016): 436–447; and Loubna El Amine, *Classical Confucian Political Thought: A New Interpretation* (Princeton, NJ: Princeton University Press, 2015). For introductory surveys of, and critical engagements with, comparative political theory, see Anthony J. Parel and Ronald C. Keith, *Comparative Political Philosophy: Studies under the Upas Tree*, 2nd ed. (Lanham, MD: Lexington Books, 2003); Andrew F. March, "What Is Comparative Political Theory?" *The Review of Politics*, Vol. 71, No. 4 (2009): 531–565; Farah Godrej, "Response to 'What Is Comparative Political Theory?,'" *The Review of Politics*, Vol. 71, No. 4 (2009): 567–582; Antony Black, "The Way Forward in Comparative Political Thought," *Journal of International Political Theory*, Vol. 7, No. 2 (2011): 221–228; Diego von Vacano, "The Scope of Comparative Political Theory," *Annual Review of Political Science*, Vol. 18 (2015): 465–480; and Melissa D. Williams and Mark E. Warren, "A Democratic Case for Comparative Political Theory," *Political Theory*, Vol. 42, No.1 (February 2014): 26–57.

Conclusion   151

draws on key conceptual and interpretive insights derived from comparative case studies of predominant ideologies in postcolonial contexts. That said, there is no singular methodology that binds comparative inquiries in political theory; and the scope and objectives of scholarly endeavors in this domain are more often subject to debate than agreement.[30] While some have questioned the utility of the "Western/non-Western" binary that grounds much discussion in this area, others have argued that unless comparative inquiry is reconceived "as an immanent critique" of political theory's pretensions to global knowledge then such binaries will continue to be reproduced in new discursive forms.[31] In the wake of these criticisms as well as the immense diversity of topical and thematic concerns that are contained within this body of literature, it would perhaps be more accurate to conceive of comparative and cross-cultural approaches as a specific *genre of inquiry* within political theory, as opposed to a subdiscipline with clearly delineated conceptual or methodological boundaries of its own.

The term "genre" here is meant to denote a particular *interpretative composition* of conceptual and contextual concerns as the basis for scholarly inquiry into the overlapping, intersecting, and generally fluid interplay of political ideas.[32] Viewed in this light, comparative political theory's distinction lies primarily in its more *spatially inclusive* range of concerns and subject matter that, through contextual exposition (and not merely comparison), may yield more capacious understandings of specific political thought-practices.[33] What all this entails for a comparative

---

[30] The very term "comparative," for instance, is problematic since the substance or merits of political concepts cannot be assessed in parallel fashion and based on standardized qualitative methodologies, as is the case in the subfield of comparative politics. Similar issues of method and scope are raised in Michael Freeden, "Editorial: The Comparative Study of Political Thinking," *Journal of Political Ideologies*, Vol. 12, No. 1 (2007): 1–9.

[31] On the former critique, see Loubna El Amine, "Beyond East and West: Reorienting Political Theory through the Prism of Modernity," *Perspective on Politics*, Vol. 14, No. 1 (2016): 102–120. The latter critical take is offered in Murad Idris, "Political Theory and the Politics of Comparison," *Political Theory* (2016): 1–20.

[32] Adrian Little has recently argued that concept analysis and contextual methods can be combined to form a coherent methodology for comparative political thought. Adrian Little, "Contextualizing Concepts: The Methodology of Comparative Political Theory," *The Review of Politics*, Vol. 80, No. 1 (2018): 87–113. Yet, not all works in comparative political theory engage in conceptual analysis, and neither is contextual analysis always illuminating in understanding the breadth and scope of particular concepts, theories, norms, or practices in different settings. The latter may still fall within the bounds of this genre, but it is difficult to distill a common methodology from them.

[33] As Little argues, "The point of conducting comparative political theory is that it is generative of new dimensions of political concepts or systems of knowledge that would hitherto have been more difficult to identify if the comparison had not taken place." Ibid., p. 94.

152   Conclusion

study of liberalism is best summed up by Freeden in a rare theoretical treatment in political theory, worth quoting in full:

> Many scholars of political thought may be attracted by the seemingly solid values liberalism promotes but, irrespective of those values, liberalism is an unusually complex set of ideas, traditions and concepts for scholars to tackle. For a system of ideas purporting to be rational and even harmonious, it offers an extraordinary range of internal divergences within that rational compass; moreover, it is usually, but wrongly, described as lacking the passionate intensity associated with the movers and shakers among twentieth-century ideologies. Yet to point out that there are liberalisms rather than a single liberalism hardly begins to do the work. The differences begin long before we attempt to distinguish between, say, Italian and Hungarian liberal varieties, or different British liberal ones over time and space, or libertarian and social liberal ones. The internal battleground is not only occupied by practicing liberals who compete over what liberalism is, but is the site of contesting methods of analysis and interpretation that are not always consciously held, yet produce widely diverging understandings of what we look at whenever we assume we are looking at liberalism. That is the challenge facing any well-thought-out program of comparative political thought.[34]

Although Freeden himself is concerned with the comparative studies of European liberalisms, the challenge he lays out equally applies to varieties of non-Western, postcolonial liberalism as well. It also speaks to two distinct but complementary aims that have motivated *Hidden Liberalism*: (i) to articulate the "battleground" of ideas in which liberalism has been engaged with and challenged over time in the Iranian context, and (ii) to examine the context-specific reasons behind liberalism's (un)conscious invisibility as a political ideology. My hope is that the general discussion of the main aspects of liberal political thinking in the case of modern Iran, combined with the critical examination of the obstacles to their public expression and development, can add to an expanding repository of "liberal languages" in circulation across the globe, which in turn might enrich our study of political thought in general.

---

[34] Michael Freeden, "European Liberalisms: An Essay in Comparative Political Thought," *European Journal of Political Theory*, Vol. 7, No. 1 (2008): 9–30.

Bibliography

Abdolmohammadi, Pejman, "The Iranian Constitutional Revolution and the Influence of Mirza Āqā Khan Kermani's Political Thought," in Ali M. Ansari, ed., *Iran's Constitutional Revolution of 1906: Narratives of the Enlightenment* (London: Gingko Library, 2016), pp. 116–128.

Abdolmohammadi, Pejman and Gianpiero Cama, "Iran as a Peculiar Hybrid Regime: Structure and Dynamics of the Islamic Republic," *British Journal of Middle Eastern Studies*, Vol. 42, No. 4 (2015): 558–578.

Abou El Fadl, Khaled, *Islam and the Challenge of Democracy* (Princeton, NJ: Princeton University Press, 2004).

Abrahamian, Ervand, *Iran between Two Revolutions* (Princeton, NJ: Princeton University Press, 1982).

Radical Islam: The Iranian Mojahedin (London: I.B. Tauris & Co. Ltd., 1989).

Khomeinism: Essays on the Islamic Republic (Berkeley, CA: University of California Press, 1993).

Tortured Confessions: Prisons and Public Recantations in Modern Iran (Berkeley, CA: University of California Press, 1999).

A History of Modern Iran (New York: Cambridge University Press, 2008).

The Coup: 1953, the CIA, and the Roots of Modern US-Iranian Relations (New York: The New Press, 2013).

Adamiyat, Fereydoun, *Fekr-e Azadi va Moqaddame-ye Nehzat-e Mashrutiyat* [The Idea of Liberty and the Beginning of the Iranian Constitutional Movement] (Tehran: Payam, 1342/1961).

Andishehay-e Mirza Agha Khan Kermani [The Ideas of Mirza Aqa Khan Kermani] (Tehran: Tahuri, 1346/1967).

Andishe-ye Mirza Fath'Ali Akhundzadeh [The Ideas of Mirza Fath'ali Akhundzadeh] (Tehran: Khawrazmi Press, 1349/1970).

Andishe-ye Taraqi va Hokoumat-e Qanun: Asr-e Sepahsalar [The Idea of Progress and the Rule of Law: The Age of Sepahsalar] (Tehran: Payam, 1351/1972).

Ideoluzhi-ye Nehzat-eh Mashrute-ye Iran [The Ideology of the Iranian Constitutional Movement] (Tehran: Payam, 1355/1976).

Andisheha-ye Talebof Tabrizi [Talebof Tabrizi's Thoughts], 2nd ed. (Tehran: Damavand, 1363/1984).

Adib-Moghaddam, Arshin, "The Pluralistic Momentum in Iran and the Future of the Reform Movement," *Third World Quarterly*, Vol. 27, No. 4 (2006): 665–674.

154   Bibliography

"Islamic Secularism and the Question of Freedom," in Faisal Devji and Zaheer Kazmi, eds., *Islam after Liberalism* (New York: Oxford University Press, 2017), pp. 189–202.

Psycho-nationalism: Global Thought, Iranian Imaginations (Cambridge: Cambridge University Press, 2018).

Afary, Janet, *The Iranian Constitutional Revolution, 1906–1911: Grassroots Democracy, Social Democracy, and the Origins of Feminism* (New York: Columbia University Press, 1996).

Afary, Janet and Kevin B. Anderson, *Foucault and the Iranian Revolution: Gender and the Seductions of Islamism* (Chicago, IL: The University of Chicago Press, 2005).

al-Afghani, Sayyid Jamal al-Din, "The Reign of Terror in Persia," *The Contemporary Review*, Vol. LXI (1892), pp. 238–248.

"Letter to the Chief Mujtahid [Mirza Hasan Shirazi], Written from Basra to Samara," in Edward G. Browne, *The Persian Revolution of 1905–1909* (London: Frank Cass & Co. Ltd., 1966), pp. 15–30.

"Answer of Jamal al-Din to Renan," in Nikki R. Keddie, *An Islamic Response to Imperialism: Political and Religious Writings of Sayyid Jamal al-Din al-Afghani* (Berkeley, CA: University of California Press, 1983), pp. 181–187.

"Lecture on Teaching and Learning," in Nikki R. Keddie, *An Islamic Response to Imperialism: Political and Religious Writings of Sayyid Jamal al-Din al-Afghani* (Berkeley, CA: University of California Press, 1983), pp. 101–108.

Afkhami, Gholam Reza, *The Life and Times of the Shah* (Berkeley, CA: University of California Press, 2009).

Afshar, Iraj, "Kāva Newspaper," *Encyclopædia Iranica*, Vol. XVI, Fasc. 2 (May 31, 2013), pp. 132–135.

Afshar, Iraj, ed., *Mosaddeq va Masa'il-e Hoquq va Siasat* [Mosaddeq and Issues in Law and Politics] (Tehran: Zamineh, 1358/1979).

Akhavi, Shahrough, "'Ali Shari'ati," in John L. Esposito and Emad El-Din Shahin, eds., *The Oxford Handbook of Islam and Politics* (New York: Oxford University Press, 2013), pp. 169–179.

Akhundzadeh, Fath'ali Mirza, *Maqalat* [Essays], ed. Baqer Momeni, trans. Ahmad Taheri Araghi and Mohammad Ali Farzaneh (Tehran: Ava, 1351/ 1972).

"Akhundzadeh to Mirza Yusuf Khan," March 29, 1871, *Alifba*, repr. (Tabriz: 1357/1978).

Maktubat: Nameha-ye Kamal al-Dowleh be Shahzadeh Jamal al-Dowleh [Correspondences of Kamal al-Dowleh to Prince Jamal al-Dowleh], ed. Bahram Chubineh (Frankfurt: Alborz, 2006).

Alam, Asadollah, *The Shah and I: The Confidential Diary of Iran's Royal Court, 1968–77*, ed. Alinaghi Alikhani (London: I.B. Tauris & Co. Ltd., 2008).

Al-e Ahmad, Jalal, *Dar Khedmat va Khiyanat-e Rowshanfekran* [On the Service and Betrayal of Intellectuals] (Tehran: Ravaq Publishers, 1356/1977).

Occidentosis: A Plague from the West (Berkeley, CA: Mizan Press, 1984).

Algar, Hamid, "Malkum Khan, Akhundzada and the Proposed Reform of the Arabic Alphabet," *Middle Eastern Studies*, Vol. 5, No. 2 (1969): 116–130.

Bibliography

Mirza Malkum Khan: A Study in the History of Iranian Modernism (Berkeley, CA: University of California Press, 1973).

Islam and Revolution: Writings and Declarations of Imam Khomeini, 1941–1980 (North Haledon, NJ: Mizan Press, 1981).

Roots of the Islamic Revolution in Iran (Oneonta, NY: Islamic Publications International, 2001).

Alvandi, Roham, *Nixon, Kissinger, and the Shah: The United States and Iran in the Cold War* (Oxford: Oxford University Press, 2016).

Amanat, Abbas, *Pivot of the Universe: Naser al-Din Shah Qajar and the Iranian Monarchy, 1831–1896* (Berkeley, CA: University of California Press, 1997).

Iran: A Modern History (New Haven, CT: Yale University Press, 2017).

Amir Arjomand, Said, "The 'Ulama's Traditionalist Opposition to Parliamentarianism: 1907–1909," *Middle Eastern Studies*, Vol. 17, No. 2 (1981): 174–190.

The Turban for the Crown: The Islamic Revolution in Iran (New York: Oxford University Press, 1988).

"Constitution of the Islamic Republic," *Encyclopædia Iranica*, Vol. VI, Fasc. 2 (1992), pp. 150–158.

Anderson, Benedict, *Imagined Communities: Reflections on the Origin and Spread of Nationalism* (New York: Verso, 1991).

An-Na'im, Abdullahi Ahmed, *Toward an Islamic Reformation: Civil Liberties, Human Rights, and International Law* (Syracuse, NY: Syracuse University Press, 1996).

Ansari, Ali M., *Iran, Islam, and Democracy: The Politics of Managing Change* (London: Royal Institute of International Affairs, 2000).

"The Myth of the White Revolution: Mohammad Reza Shah, 'Modernization', and the Consolidation of Power," *Middle Eastern Studies*, Vol. 37, No. 3 (2001): 1–24.

The Politics of Nationalism in Modern Iran (Cambridge: Cambridge University Press, 2012).

"Mohammad Ali Foroughi and the Construction of Civic Nationalism in Early Twentieth-Century Iran," in H. E. Chehabi, Peyman Jafari, and Maral Jefroudi, eds., *Iran in the Middle East: Transnational Encounters and Social History* (London: I.B. Tauris & Co. Ltd., 2015), pp. 11–26.

"Taqizadeh and European Civilization," *Iran*, Vol. 54, No. 1 (2016): 47–58.

Ansari, Ali M., ed., *Iran's Constitutional Revolution of 1906: Narratives of the Enlightenment* (London: Gingko Library, 2016).

Aqeli, Baqer, "Dāvar, 'Alī-Akbar," *Encyclopædia Iranica*, Vol. VIII, Fasc. 2 (November 18, 2011), pp. 133–135.

Ashraf, Ahmad and Ali Banuazizi, "Iran's Tortuous Path Toward 'Islamic Liberalism'," *International Journal of Politics, Culture, and Society*, Vol. 15, No. 2 (Winter 2001): 237–256.

Azimi, Fakhreddin, *Iran, The Crisis of Democracy: From the Exile of Reza Shah to the Fall of Musaddiq* (London: I.B. Tauris & Co. Ltd., 1989).

"The Configuration and Role of Domestic Forces," in Mark J. Gasiorowski and Malcolm Byrne, eds., *Mohammad Mosaddeq and the 1953 Coup in Iran* (Syracuse, NY: University of Syracuse Press, 2004), pp. 27–101.

156   Bibliography

Bahar, Mohammad-Taqi Malek al-Sho'ara, *Tarikh-e Mokhtasar-e Ahzab-e Siasi-ye Iran* [A Brief History of Political Parties in Iran], Vol. I (Tehran: 1323/1945).

Bakhash, Shaul, *The Reign of the Ayatollahs: Iran and the Islamic Revolution* (New York: Basic Books, 1984).

Baron de Montesquieu, Charles-Louis de Secondat, *Persian Letters*, trans. Christopher Betts (London: Penguin, 2004).

Bayat, Asef, "Shariati and Marx: A Critique of an 'Islamic' Critique of Marxism," *Alif: Journal of Comparative Poetics*, Vol. 9 (1990): 19–41.

Making Islam Democratic: Social Movements and the Post-Islamist Turn (Stanford, CA: Stanford University Press, 2007).

Bayat Philipp, Mangol, "The Concepts of Religion and Government in the Thought of Mirza Aqa Khan Kermani, a Nineteenth-Century Persian Revolutionary," *International Journal of Middle East Studies*, Vol. 5, No. 4 (1974): 381–400.

"Mirza Agha Khan Kermani: A Nineteenth-Century Persian Nationalist," *Middle Eastern Studies*, Vol. 10 (1974): 36–59.

"Shi'ism in Contemporary Iranian Politics: The Case of Ali Shariati," in E. Kedourie and S. G. Haim, eds., *Towards a Modern Iran* (London: Frank Cass, 1980), pp. 155–168.

Iran's First Revolution: Shi'ism and the Constitutional Revolution of 1905–1909 (Oxford: Oxford University Press, 1991).

Bayly, C. A., *The Birth of The Modern World, 1780–1914* (Oxford: Blackwell Publishing, 2004).

Recovering Liberties: Indian Thought in the Age of Liberalism and Empire (Cambridge: Cambridge University Press, 2012).

Bazargan, Mehdi, *Modafe'at dar Dadgah-e Gheir'e Saleh-e Tajdid-e Nazar-e Nezami* (Tehran: Entasharat-e Modarres, 1350/1971).

"Farewell Address," Tehran, Iran, 16 Aban 1358 [November 7, 1979].

"Jaryan-e ta'sis-e nehzat-e Azadi-ye Iran," *Safahati az tarikh-e mo'aser-e Iran: Asnad-e nehzat-e Azadi-ye Iran* [A few pages from contemporary Iranian history: The documents of the Freedom Movement of Iran], Vol. 1, No. 1 (1982): 13–17.

Bazyabi-ye Arzash'ha [The Recovery of Values] (Tehran: Nehzat-e Azadi-e Iran, 1364/1983).

Masa'el va Moshkelat-e Nakhostin Sal-e Enghelab [Issues and Difficulties in the First Year of Revolution], ed. Abdol-Ali Bazargan (Tehran: 1362/1983).

Enghelab-e Eslami Dar Do Harekat [The Islamic Revolution in Two Movements] (Tehran: Naraghi, 1363/1984).

"Religion and Liberty," trans. Mahmoud Sadri, in Charles Kurzman, ed., *Liberal Islam: A Sourcebook* (New York: Oxford University Press, 1998), pp. 73–84.

"Mosahebe-ye Hamid Algar ba Mohandes Bazargan," in *Enghelab-e Eslami-ye Iran, Majmou'eh-ye Asar* (Tehran: Bonyad-e Farhangi-ye Mohandes Mehdi Bazargan, 1389/2010), pp. 198–225.

Bell, Daniel A., *Beyond Liberal Democracy: Political Thinking for an East Asian Context* (Princeton, NJ: Princeton University Press, 2006).

Bell, Duncan, "What Is Liberalism?" *Political Theory*, Vol. 42, No. 6 (2014): 1–34.

Reordering the World: Essays on Liberalism and Empire (Princeton, NJ: Princeton University Press, 2016).

Benhabib, Seyla, *The Claims of Culture: Equality and Diversity in the Global Era* (Princeton, NJ: Princeton University Press, 2002).

Benhabib, Seyla, ed., *Democracy and Difference: Contesting the Boundaries of the Political* (Princeton, NJ: Princeton University Press, 1996).

Berlin, Isaiah, "Two Concepts of Liberty," in *Four Essays on Liberty* (Oxford: Oxford University Press, 1969).

"The Bent Twig: A Note on Nationalism," *Foreign Affairs*, Vol. 51, No. 1 (1972): 11–30.

The Crooked Timber of Humanity (Princeton, NJ: Princeton University Press, 1998).

"The First and the Last," *New York Review of Books*, Vol. 45 (1998): 52–60.

"On the Pursuit of the Ideal," *New York Review of Books*, Vol. 35, No. 4 (1998): 11–18.

Berlin, Isaiah and Steven Lukes, "Isaiah Berlin: In Conversation with Steven Lukes," *Salmagundi*, No. 120 (Fall 1998): 52–134.

Bhaba, Homi, *The Location of Culture* (New York: Routledge, 1994).

Black, Antony, "The Way Forward in Comparative Political Thought," *Journal of International Political Theory*, Vol. 7, No. 2 (2011): 221–228.

Blunt, W. W., *The Secret History of the English Occupation of Egypt* (London: T. F. Unwin, 1907).

Boroujerdi, Mehrzad, *Iranian Intellectuals and the West: The Tormented Triumph of Nativism* (Syracuse, NY: Syracuse University Press, 1996).

"Triumphs and Travails of Authoritarian Modernization in Iran," in Stephanie Cronin, ed., *The Making of Modern Iran: State and Society under Riza Shah, 1921–1941* (New York: Routledge, 2003), pp. 152–160.

Bourdieu, Pierre, *The Logic of Practice* (Stanford, CA: Stanford University Press, 1990).

Brettschneider, Corey, *Democratic Rights: The Substance of Self-government* (Princeton, NJ: Princeton University Press, 2007).

British Foreign Office, "Persia: Political Review of the Recent Crisis," September 2, 1953, Top Secret.

Browers, Michaelle and Charles Kurzman, "Introduction," in Michaelle Browers and Charles Kurzman, eds., *An Islamic Reformation?* (Lanham, NJ: Lexington, 2003), pp. 1–17.

Browne, Edward G., *The Persian Revolution of 1905–1909* (London: Frank Cass & Co. Ltd., 1966).

Brumberg, Daniel, *Reinventing Khomeini: The Struggle for Reform in Iran* (Chicago, IL: The University of Chicago Press, 2001).

Buch, Maganlal A., *Rise and Growth of Indian Liberalism [from Ram Mohun to Gokhale]* (Baroda: Atmaram Printing Press, 1938).

Buzan, Barry and George Lawson, *The Global Transformation: History, Modernity and the Making of International Relations* (Cambridge: Cambridge University Press, 2015).

158   Bibliography

Byrne, Malcolm and Mark Gasiorowski, eds., "New Findings on the Clerical Involvement in 1953 Coup in Iran," *Briefing Book #619*, March 7, 2018 (http s://nsarchive.gwu.edu/briefing-book/iran/2018–03-07/new-findings-clerical-inv olvement-1953-coup-iran, last accessed August 15, 2019).

Caney, Simon, "Liberalism and Communitarianism: A Misconceived Debate," *Political Studies*, Vol. XL (1992): 273–289.

Césaire, Aime, *Discourse on Colonialism* (New York: Monthly Review Press, 2000).

Cesari, Jocelyn, *When Islam and Democracy Meet: Muslims in Europe and in the United States* (London: Palgrave Macmillan, 2006).

Chakrabarty, Dipesh, *Provincializing Europe* (Princeton, NJ: Princeton University Press, 2000).

Chakravorty Spivak, Gayatri, *A Critique of Postcolonial Reason: Toward a History of the Vanishing Present* (Cambridge, MA: Harvard University Press, 1999).

Chaterjee, Partha, *The Nation and Its Fragments: Colonial and Postcolonial Histories* (Princeton, NJ: Princeton University Press, 1993).

Chehabi, Houchang E. , "Society and State in Islamic Liberalism," *State, Culture, and Society*, Vol. 3, No. 1 (Spring 1985): 85–101.

Iranian Politics and Religious Modernism: The Liberation Movement of Iran under the Shah and Khomeini (Ithaca, NY: Cornell University Press, 1990).

"Staging the Emperor's New Clothes: Dress Codes and Nation-Building under Reza Shah," *Iranian Studies*, Vol. 26, Nos. 3–4 (1993): 209–229.

"The Banning of the Veil and Its Consequences," in Stephanie Cronin, ed., *The Making of Modern Iran: State and Society under Riza Shah, 1921–1941* (London: Routledge, 2003), pp. 193–210.

Chehabi, Houchang E. and Vanessa Martin, eds., *Iran's Constitutional Revolution: Popular Politics, Cultural Transformations and Transnational Connections* (London: I.B. Tauris & Co. Ltd., 2010).

Collier, David R., *Democracy and the Nature of Influence in Iran, 1941–1979* (Syracuse, NY: University of Syracuse Press, 2017).

Collini, Stefan, *Liberalism and Sociology: L. T. Hobhouse and Political Argument in England, 1880–1914* (Cambridge: Cambridge University Press, 1979).

Cox, Robert W., "Social Forces, States, and World Orders: Beyond International Relations Theory," *Millennium: Journal of International Studies*, Vol. 10, No. 2 (June 1981): 126–155.

Cronin, Stephanie, *The Army and Creation of the Pahlavi State in Iran, 1921–1926* (London: I.B. Tauris & Co. Ltd., 1997).

Soldiers, Shahs, and Subalterns in Iran: Opposition, Protest and Revolt, 1921–1941 (New York: Palgrave Macmillan, 2010).

Cronin, Stephanie, ed., *The Making of Modern Iran: State and Society under Riza Shah, 1921–1941* (London: Routledge, 2003).

Dabashi, Hamid, *Theology of Discontent: The Ideological Foundation of the Islamic Republic* (New Brunswick, NJ: Transaction Publishers, 1993).

Dallmayr, Fred, "Introduction: Toward a Comparative Political Theory," *The Review of Politics*, Vol. 59, No. 3 (Summer 1997): 421–427.

Dialogue among Civilizations: Culture and Religion in International Relations (New York: Palgrave Macmillan, 2002).

Bibliography 159

Devji, Faisal and Zaheer Kazmi, eds., *Islam after Liberalism* (Oxford: Oxford University Press, 2017).

Devos, Biana and Christoph Werner, eds., *Culture and Cultural Politics under Reza Shah: The Pahlavi State, the New Bourgeoisie and the Creation of a Modern Society in Iran* (New York: Routledge, 2014).

Dowlatabadi, Mahmoud, *The Colonel*, trans. Tom Patterdale (London: Haus Publishing Ltd., 2011).

Doyle, Michael W., "Liberalism and World Politics," *American Political Science Review*, Vol. 80, No. 4 (December 1986): 1151–1169.

Dunn, John, *The Political Thought of John Locke: An Historical Account of the Argument of the 'Two Treatises of Government'* (Cambridge: Cambridge University Press, 1969).

Dworkin, Ronald, *Taking Rights Seriously* (Cambridge, MA: Harvard University Press, 1977).

El Amine, Loubna, *Classical Confucian Political Thought: A New Interpretation* (Princeton, NJ: Princeton University Press, 2015).

"Beyond East and West: Reorienting Political Theory through the Prism of Modernity," *Perspective on Politics*, Vol. 14, No. 1 (2016): 102–120.

Enayat, Hadi, *Law, State, and Society in Modern Iran: Constitutionalism, Autocracy, and Legal Reform, 1906–1941* (New York: Palgrave Macmillan, 2013).

Enayat, Hamid, *Modern Islamic Political Thought: The Response of the Shi'i and Sunni Muslims to the Twentieth Century* (London: Bloomsbury Publishing, 2005).

Esposito, John L. and John O. Voll, *Islam and Democracy* (New York: Oxford University Press, 1996).

Ettehadieh, Mansoureh [Nezam Mafi, pseud.], "Concessions (Emtīāzāt)," *Encyclopædia Iranica*, Vol. VI, Fasc. 2 (October 28, 2011), pp. 119–122.

Euben, Roxanne L., "Comparative Political Theory: An Islamic Fundamentalist Critique of Rationalism," *Journal of Politics*, Vol. 59, No. 1 (1997): 28–55.

Enemy in the Mirror: Islamic Fundamentalism and the Limits of Modern Rationalism (Princeton, NJ: Princeton University Press, 1999).

Journeys to the Other Shore (Princeton, NJ: Princeton University Press, 2006).

Fallaci, Oriana, "'Everybody Wants To Be Boss': An Interview with Mehdi Bazargan, Prime Minister of Iran," *The New York Times*, October 28, 1979.

Fanon, Franz, *Wretched of the Earth* (New York: Grove Press, 1963).

Fardid, Ahmad, "Pasokh be Chand Porsesh Dar Bab-e Farhang-e Shargh" [Response to a Few Questions Regarding Eastern Culture], transcribed by Reza Davari, *Farhang va Zendegi*, Vol. 7 (January 1972): 32–39.

Didar-e Farrahi va Fotouhat-e Akhar al-Zaman [Divine Encounter and Apocalyptic Revelations], 2nd ed. (Tehran: Nashr-e Nazar, 1378/2008).

Gharb va Gharbzadegi [The West and Westoxication], unpublished.

Forrester, Katrina, *In the Shadow of Justice: Postwar Liberalism and the Remaking of Political Philosophy* (Princeton, NJ: Princeton University Press, 2019).

Freeden, Michael, *Liberalism Divided: A Study in British Political Thought, 1914–1939* (New York: Oxford University Press, 1986).

"Editorial: The Comparative Study of Political Thinking," *Journal of Political Ideologies*, Vol. 12, No. 1 (2007): 1–9.

160 Bibliography

"European Liberalisms: An Essay in Comparative Political Thought," *European Journal of Political Theory*, Vol. 7, No. 1 (2008): 9–30.

Liberal Languages: Ideological Imaginations and Twentieth-Century Progressive Thought (Princeton, NJ: Princeton University Press, 2009).

Fukuyama, Francis, *The End of History and the Last Man* (New York: Simon & Schuster, 1992).

Galston, William A., *Liberal Pluralism: The Implications of Value Pluralism for Political Theory and Practice* (Cambridge: Cambridge University Press, 2002).

The Practice of Liberal Pluralism (Cambridge: Cambridge University Press, 2005).

Ganji, Akbar [Hamid Paidar, pseud.], "Paradox-e Eslam va Demokrasi" [The Paradox of Islam and Democracy], *Kiyan*, Vol. 19 (1373/1994).

"Iran's Peculiar Election: The Struggle against Sultanism," *Journal of Democracy*, Vol. 16, No. 4 (2005): 38–51.

"The Latter-Day Sultan: Power and Politics in Iran," *Foreign Affairs*, Vol. 87, No. 6 (November/December 2008): 45–66.

The Road to Democracy in Iran (Cambridge, MA: MIT Press, 2008).

Gasiorowski Mark J. and Malcolm Byrne, eds., *Mohammad Mosaddeq and the 1953 Coup in Iran* (Syracuse, NY: University of Syracuse Press, 2004).

Geertz, Clifford, *The Interpretation of Cultures* (New York: Basic Books, 1973).

Getachew, Adom, *Worldmaking after Empire: The Rise and Fall of Self-determination* (Princeton, NJ: Princeton University Press, 2019).

Geuss, Raymond, *History and Illusion in Politics* (Cambridge: Cambridge University Press, 2001).

Ghamari-Tabrizi, Behrooz, "Contentious Public Religion: Two Conceptions of Islam in Revolutionary Iran: Ali Shari'ati and Abdolkarim Soroush," *International Sociology*, Vol. 19, No. 4 (December 2004): 504–523.

Islam and Dissent in Post-revolutionary Iran: Abdolkarim Soroush, Religious Politics and Democratic Reform (London: I.B. Tauris & Co. Ltd., 2008).

Foucault in Iran: Islamic Revolution after the Enlightenment (Minneapolis, MN: University of Minnesota Press, 2016).

Gheissari, Ali, *Iranian Intellectuals in the 20th Century* (Austin, TX: University of Texas Press, 1998).

"Constitutional Rights and the Development of Civil Law in Iran, 1907–41," in H. E. Chehabi and Vanessa Martin, eds., *Iran's Constitutional Revolution: Popular Politics, Cultural Transformations and Transnational Connections* (London: I.B. Tauris & Co. Ltd., 2010), pp. 69–79.

"Shadman, Fakhr-al-Din," *Encyclopædia Iranica*, March 15, 2010 (www .iranicaonline.org/articles/shadman, last accessed June 15, 2018).

"Iranian Intellectuals, Past and Present," interview by Ali Ahmadi Motlagh, *Muftah*, March 10, 2011 (http://muftah.org/?p=923, last accessed December 12, 2018).

"Iran's Dialectic of the Enlightenment: Constitutional Experience, Transregional Connections, and Conflicting Narratives of Modernity," in Ali Ansari, ed., *Iran's Constitutional Revolution of 1906: Narratives of the Enlightenment* (London: Gingko Library, 2016), pp. 15–47.

Bibliography

Gheissari, Ali and Vali Nasr, *Democracy in Iran: History and the Quest for Liberty* (New York: Oxford University Press, 2006).

Ghobadzadeh, Naser and Lily Zubaidah Rahim, "Electoral Theocracy and Hybrid Sovereignty in Iran," *Contemporary Politics*, Vol. 22, No. 4 (2016): 450–468.

Godrej, Farah, "Response to 'What Is Comparative Political Theory?'," *The Review of Politics*, Vol. 71, No. 4 (2009): 567–582.

   Cosmopolitan Political Thought: Method, Practice, Discipline (New York: Oxford University Press, 2011).

Gong, Gerrit W., *The Standard of "Civilization" in International Society* (Oxford: Clarendon Press, 1984).

Gutmann, Amy, *Liberal Rights* (Cambridge: Cambridge University Press, 1980).

   "Communitarian Critics of Liberalism," *Philosophy & Public Affairs*, Vol. 14, No. 3 (Summer 1985): 308–322.

Gutmann, Amy and Dennis Thompson, *Democracy and Disagreement* (Cambridge, MA: Harvard University Press, 1996).

Hairi, Abdul-Hadi, "Shaykh Fazl Allah Nuri's Refutation of the Idea of Constitutionalism," *Middle Eastern Studies*, Vol. XXIII, No. 3 (1977): 327–339.

Hajjarian, Saeed, "Velayat-e Motlaqeh-ye Faqih va Qanun-e Asasi" [The Absolute Rule of the Jurist and Constitutionalism], *Asr-e Ma*, No. 61 (February 7, 1997).

Halperin, Sandra and Ronen Palan, eds., *Legacies of Empire: Imperial Roots of the Contemporary Global Order* (Cambridge: Cambridge University Press, 2015).

Hashemi, Nader, *Islam, Secularism, and Liberal Democracy: Toward a Democratic Theory in Muslim Societies* (New York: Oxford University Press, 2009).

Hobhouse, L. T., *Liberalism* (Oxford: Oxford University Press, 1964).

Hobsbawm, Eric J., *Nations and Nationalism since 1780*, 2nd ed. (Cambridge: Cambridge University Press, 2012).

Hobson, Christopher, "Liberal Democracy and Beyond: Extending the Sequencing Debate," *International Political Science Review*, Vol. 33, No. 4 (September 2012): 441–454.

Hobson, J. A., *Imperialism: A Study* (Ann Arbor, MI: University of Michigan Press, 1965 [1902]).

Hobson, John M., *The Eurocentric Conception of World Politics: Western International Theory, 1760–2010* (Cambridge: Cambridge University Press, 2012).

Hourani, Albert, *Arabic Thought in the Liberal Age, 1798–1939* (Cambridge: Cambridge University Press, 1983).

Huntington, Samuel P., *The Clash of Civilizations and the Remaking of World Order* (New York: Simon & Schuster, 1998).

Idris, Murad, "Political Theory and the Politics of Comparison," *Political Theory* (2016): 1–20.

Ivison, Duncan, *Postcolonial Liberalism* (Cambridge: Cambridge University Press, 2002).

Jahanbegloo, Ramin, "Two Concepts of Secularism," *Comparative Studies of South Asia, Africa, and the Middle East*, Vol. 31, No. 1 (2011): 13–22.

162   Bibliography

Democracy in Iran (New York: Palgrave Macmillan, 2013).

The Gandhian Moment (Cambridge, MA: Harvard University Press, 2013).

Time Will Say Nothing: A Philosopher Survives an Iranian Prison (Saskatchewan: University of Regina Press, 2014).

Jahanbegloo, Ramin, ed., *Iran: Between Tradition and Modernity* (Lanham, MD: Lexington Books, 2004).

Civil Society and Democracy in Iran (Lanham, MD: Lexington Books, 2012).

Jahanbegloo, Ramin and Isaiah Berlin, *Recollections of a Historian of Ideas: Conversations with Isaiah Berlin* (New York: Charles Scriber's Sons, 1991).

Jansen, Jan C. and Jürgen Osterhammel, *Decolonization: A Short History* (Princeton, NJ: Princeton University Press, 2017).

Jenco, Leigh, "'What Does Heaven Ever Say?': A Methods-Centered Approach to Cross-cultural Engagement," *American Political Science Review*, Vol. 101, No. 4 (2007): 741–755.

Changing Referents: Learning across Space and Time in China and the West (New York: Oxford University Press, 2015).

"New Pasts for New Futures: A Temporal Reading of Global Thought," *Constellations*, Vol. 23, No. 3 (2016): 436–447.

Kadivar, Mohsen, *Hokumat-e Vela'iy: Andishe-ye Siasi Dar Eslam* [Government by the Guardian: An Exercise in Islamic Political Thought] (Tehran: Nashr-e Ney, 1377/1998).

Kamrava, Mehran, *Iran's Intellectual Revolution* (Cambridge: Cambridge University Press, 2008).

Kapuściński, Ryszard, *Shah of Shahs* (London: Penguin Books, 1985).

Kasravi, Ahmad, *A'yin* [Guidelines] (Tehran: 1311–1312/1932–1933).

Ma Cheh Mikhahim? [What Do We Want?] (Tehran: Paydar, 1319/1940].

Dar Piramun-e Islam [About Islam] (Tehran: 1322/1943).

Katouzian, Homa, "European Liberalisms and Modern Concepts of Liberty in Iran," *Journal of Iranian Research and Analysis*, Vol. 16, No. 2 (2000): 16–17.

Sadeq Hedayat: The Life and Legend of An Iranian Writer (London: I.B. Tauris & Co. Ltd., 2002).

State and Society in Iran: The Eclipse of the Qajars and the Emergence of the Pahlavis (London: I.B. Tauris & Co. Ltd., 2006).

Mosaddeq and the Struggle for Power in Iran (London: I.B. Tauris Co. & Ltd., 2009).

Keddie, Nikki R., *Religion and Rebellion in Iran: The Tobacco Protest of 1891–92* (London: Frank Cass & Co. Ltd., 1966).

Sayyid Jamal al-Din al-Afghani: A Political Biography (Berkeley, CA: University of California Press, 1972).

An Islamic Response to Imperialism: Political and Religious Writings of Sayyid Jamal al-Din al-Afghani (Berkeley, CA: University of California Press, 1983).

Keddie, Nikki R. and Yann Richard, *Modern Iran: Roots and Results of Revolution* (New Haven, CT: Yale University Press, 2006).

Kedouri, Eli, *Afghani and 'Abduh: An Essay on Religious Unbelief and Political Activism in Modern Islam* (London: Frank Cass Co. Ltd., 1997).

Bibliography 163

Kelly, Paul, "Liberalism and Nationalism," in Steven Wall, ed., *The Cambridge Companion to Liberalism* (Cambridge: Cambridge University Press, 2015), pp. 329–351.

Kermani, Mirza Agha Khan, *Se Maktub* [Three Letters], Bahram Chubineh, ed. (Frankfurt: Alborz, 2005).

Sad Khatabeh [A Hundred Lectures], ed. Haroun Vohouman (Los Angeles, CA: Ketab Corp., 1386/2007).

Kermani, Nazem al-Islam, *Tarikh-e Bidari-ye Iranian* [History of Iranians' Awakening] (Tehran: 1328/1910).

Khamenei, Sayyed Ali, "Remarks to the Member of the Basij in Kermanshah Province," October 14, 2011 (http://farsi.khamenei.ir/newspart-index?ti d=1703#14379, last accessed June 6, 2018).

Khomeini, Ruhollah, *Kashf al-Asrar* [The Unveiling of Secrets] (Tehran: 1322/ 1943).

Hokoumat-e Eslami [Islamic Government] (Tehran: 1357/1978).

"Message to the Assembly of Experts," *Kayhan*, 28 Mordad 1358 [August 19, 1979].

Kia, Mehrdad, "Mirza Fath Ali Akhundzade and the Call for Modernization of the Muslim World," *Middle Eastern Studies*, Vol. 31, No. 3 (1995): 422–448.

"Persian Nationalism and Language Purification," *Middle Eastern Studies*, Vol. 34, No. 2 (1998): 12–16.

Kukathas, Chandran, *The Liberal Archipelago: A Theory of Diversity and Freedom* (Oxford: Oxford University Press, 2003).

Kumar, Ravinder, "Liberalism and Reform in India," in Guy S. Mértaaux and François Crouzet, eds., *The New Asia* (New York: New American Library, 1965), pp. 177–202.

Kurzman, Charles, *The Unthinkable Revolution in Iran* (Cambridge, MA: Harvard University Press, 2004).

Kurzman, Charles, ed., *Liberal Islam: A Sourcebook* (New York: Oxford University Press, 1998).

Modernist Islam, 1840–1904: A Sourcebook (New York: Oxford University Press, 2002).

Kymlicka, Will, "Liberalism and Communitarianism," *Canadian Journal of Philosophy*, Vol. 18, No. 2 (June 1988): 181–204.

Lambton, Ann, K. S., *Qajar Persia: Eleven Studies* (London: I.B. Tauris & Co. Ltd., 1987).

Larmore, Charles, "Political Liberalism," *Political Theory*, Vol. 18, No. 3 (1990): 339–360.

The Morals of Modernity (Cambridge: Cambridge University Press, 1996).

The Autonomy of Morality (Cambridge: Cambridge University Press, 2008).

Levitsky, Steven and Lucan A. Way, *Competitive Authoritarianism: Hybrid Regimes after the Cold War* (Cambridge: Cambridge University Press, 2010).

Little, Adrian, "Contextualizing Concepts: The Methodology of Comparative Political Theory," *The Review of Politics*, Vol. 80, No. 1 (2018): 87–113.

MacIntyre, Alasdair, *After Virtue: A Study in Moral Philosophy* (Notre Dame, IN: University of Notre Dame Press, 1981).

164 Bibliography

Madani, S. J., *Hoquq-e Asasi dar Jomhouri-ye Eslami-e Iran* [Constitutional Laws of the Islamic Republic of Iran], Vol. II (Tehran: Soroush, 1365/1986).

Makki, Hossein, *Tarikh-e Bist Saleh-ye Iran* [Twenty-Year History of Iran], Vols. I & II (Tehran: Elmi, 1374/1995).

Malekzadeh, Mehdi, *Tarikh-e Enghelab-e Mashrutiyat-e Iran* [The History of the Constitutional Revolution in Iran], Vol. IV (Tehran: Elmi Press, 1363/1984).

Manafzadeh, Ali Reza, "Ahmad Kasravi," *Encyclopædia Iranica*, Vol. XVI, Fasc. 1, p. 97.

Manela, Erez, *The Wilsonian Moment: Self-determination and the International Origins of Anticolonial Nationalism* (New York: Oxford University Press, 2007).

Mansuri, Javad, ed., *Tarikh-e Qiyam-e Panzdah-e Khordad be Ravayat-e Asnad* [Documentary History of the June 5 Uprising] (Tehran: Markaz-e Asnad-e Enghelab-e Eslami, 1377/1998).

Mantena, Karuna, *Alibis of Empire: Henry Maine and the Ends of Liberal Imperialism* (Princeton, NJ: Princeton University Press, 2010).

Marashi, Afshin, "Performing the Nation: The Shah's Official State Visit to Kemalist Turkey, June to July 1934," in Stephanie Cronin, ed., *The Making of Modern Iran: State and Society under Riza Shah, 1921–1941* (London: Routledge, 2003), pp. 99–120.

Nationalizing Iran: Culture, Power, and the State, 1870–1940 (Seattle, WA: University of Washington Press, 2008).

March, Andrew F., *Islam and Liberal Citizenship: The Search for an Overlapping Consensus* (New York: Oxford University Press, 2009).

"What Is Comparative Political Theory?" *The Review of Politics*, Vol. 71, No. 4 (2009): 531–565.

Martin, Vanessa, *Islam and Modernism: The Iranian Revolution of 1906* (London: I.B. Tauris & Co. Ltd., 1989).

Creating an Islamic State: Khomeini and the Making of a New Iran (London: I.B. Tauris & Co. Ltd., 2010).

Iran between Nationalism and Secularism: The Constitutional Revolution of 1906 (London: I.B. Tauris & Co. Ltd., 2013).

Marx, Karl, "The Eighteenth Brumaire of Louis Bonaparte," in *Selected Works* (Moscow: Progress Publishers, 1958).

Masroori, Cyrus, "European Thoughts in Nineteenth-Century Iran: David Hume and Others," *Journal of the History of Ideas*, Vol. 61, No. 4 (2000): 657–674.

"French Romanticism and Persian Liberalism in Nineteenth-Century Iran: Mirza Agha Khan Kirmani and Jacques-Henri Bernardine de Saint-Pierre," *History of Political Thought*, Vol. 28, No. 3 (2007): 542–556.

Massad, Joseph A., *Islam in Liberalism* (Chicago, IL: University of Chicago Press, 2015).

Matin-Asgari, Afshin, "The Pahlavi Era: Iranian Modernity in Global Context," in Touraj Daryaee, ed., *The Oxford Handbook of Iranian History* (New York: Oxford University Press, 2012), pp. 346–364.

Bibliography   165

Both Eastern and Western: An Intellectual History of Iranian Modernity (Cambridge: Cambridge University Press, 2018).

Matin, Kamran, "Decoding Political Islam: Uneven and Combined Development and Ali Shariati's Political Thought," in Robbie Shilliam, ed., *International Relations and Non-Western Thought: Imperialism, Colonialism, and Investigations of Global Modernity* (London: Routledge, 2010), pp. 124–140.

Matthee, Rudi, "Jamal al-Din al-Afghani and the Egyptian National Debate," *International Journal of Middle East Studies*, Vol. 21, No. 2 (1989): 151–169.

"Transforming Dangerous Nomads into Useful Artisans, Technicians, Agriculturalists: Education in the Reza Shah Period," *Iranian Studies*, Vol. 26, Nos. 3–4 (1993): 313–336.

Mayall, James, *Nationalism and International Society* (Cambridge: Cambridge University Press, 1990).

Mazinani, Mehran, "Liberty in Akhundzadeh's and Kermani's Thoughts," *Middle Eastern Studies*, Vol. 51, No. 6 (2015): 883–900.

Mehta, Uday Singh, *Liberalism and Empire: A Study in Nineteenth-Century British Liberal Thought* (Chicago, IL: University of Chicago Press, 1999).

Menashri, David, *Education and the Making of Modern Iran* (Ithaca, NY: Cornell University Press, 1992).

Merat Amini, Parvin, "A Single-Party State in Iran, 1975–78: The Rastakhiz Party – The Final Attempt by the Shah to Consolidate His Political Base," *Middle Eastern Studies*, Vol. 38, No. 1 (2002): 131–168.

Milani, Abbas, *Lost Wisdom: Rethinking Modernity in Iran* (Washington, DC: Mage Publishers, 2004).

Eminent Persians: The Men and Women Who Made Modern Iran, 1941–1979, Vol. I (Syracuse, NY: Syracuse University Press, 2008).

The Shah (New York: Palgrave Macmillan, 2011).

Milani, Mohsen, *The Making of Iran's Islamic Revolution: From Monarchy to Islamic Republic* (Boulder, CO: Westview Press, 1988).

Mill, John Stuart, *On Liberty and Other Writings*, ed. Stefan Collini (Cambridge: Cambridge University Press, 1989).

Mir-Hosseini, Ziba, *Islam and Gender: The Religious Debate in Contemporary Iran* (Princeton, NJ: Princeton University Press, 2000).

Mirsepassi, Ali, *Intellectual Discourse and the Politics of Modernization: Negotiating Modernity in Iran* (New York: Cambridge University Press, 2000).

Democracy in Modern Iran (New York: New York University Press, 2010).

Political Islam, Iran, and Enlightenment: Philosophies of Hope and Despair (New York: Cambridge University Press, 2011).

Transnationalism in Iranian Political Thought: The Life and Thought of Ahmad Fardid (Cambridge: Cambridge University Press, 2017).

Iran's Quiet Revolution: The Downfall of the Pahlavi State (Cambridge: Cambridge University Press, 2019).

Mirsepassi, Ali and Mehdi Faraji, "De-politicizing Westoxification: The Case of *Bonyad Monthly*," *British Journal of Middle East Studies*, Vol. 45, No. 3 (2018): 355–375.

166   Bibliography

Mishra, Pankaj, *From the Ruins of Empire: The Revolt against the West* (New York: Farrar, Straus and Giroux, 2012).

Moaddel, Mansoor, "Shi'i Political Discourse and Class Mobilization in the Tobacco Movement of 1890–1892," *Sociological Forum* Vol. 7, No. 3 (September 1992): 447–468.

Moghissi, Haideh, *Populism and Feminism in Iran: Women's Struggle in a Male-Defined Revolutionary Movement* (New York: St. Martin's Press Inc., 1996).

Mojtahed Shabestari, Mohammad, "Demokrasi va din-dari" [Democracy and Religious Piety], in *Naqdi bar Qara'at-e Rasmi az Din: Bohran-ha, Chalesh-ha, Rah-e Hal-ha* [A Critique of Literal Interpretations of Religion: Crises, Debates, and Solutions] (Tehran: Tarh-e Now, 1379/2000).

Mosaddeq, Mohammad, *Kapitulasion va Iran* [Capitulation and Iran] (Tehran: 1293/1914).

Mouffe, Chantal, *The Return of the Political* (London: Verso, 1993).

   The Democratic Paradox (London: Verso, 2000).

   "Politics and the Limits of Liberalism," in *The Return of the Political* (London: Verso, 2005).

Muthu, Sankar, *Enlightenment against Empire* (Princeton, NJ: Princeton University Press, 2003).

Muthu, Sankar, ed., *Empire and Modern Political Thought* (Cambridge: Cambridge University Press, 2012).

Nabavi, Negin, *Intellectuals and the State in Iran: Politics, Discourse, and the Dilemma of Authenticity* (Gainesville, FL: University of Florida Press, 2003).

   Modern Iran: A History in Documents (Princeton, NJ: Markus Wiener Publishers, 2016).

Na'ini, Mohammad Hussein, *Tanbih al-umma wa tanzih al-milla, hokumat az nazar-e eslam* [On the Admonition and Refinement of the Nation: Or, Government from the Perspective of Islam], 6th ed. (Tehran: Sherkat-e Sahami-e Enteshar, 1339/1960).

Naipaul, V. S., *A Bend in the River* (New York: Vintage, 1979).

Najmabadi, Afsaneh, *Women with Mustaches and Men without Beards: Gender and Sexual Anxieties of Iranian Modernity* (Berkeley, CA: University of California Press, 2005).

Nezam al-Dowleh, Mirza Malkum Khan, "God Has Blessed Iran," *Qanun*, Vol. 1, No. 2 (1890): 1–2.

   "Persian Civilization," *The Contemporary Review*, Vol. LIX (1891), pp. 238–244.

   Resaleha-ye Mirza Malkum Khan Nazem al-Dowleh [The Treatises of Mirza Malkum Khan Nazem al-Dowleh], ed. Hojatollah Aseel (Tehran: Nashr-e Ney, 1381/2002).

Nosrat Mozaffari, Nahid, "An Iranian Modernist Project: Ali Akbar Dehkhoda's Writings in the Constitutional Period," in H. E. Chehabi and Vanessa Martin, eds., *Iran's Constitutional Revolution: Popular Politics, Cultural Transformations, and Transnational Connections* (London: I.B. Tauris & Co. Ltd., 2012), pp. 193–212.

Bibliography 167

Nuri, Sheikh Fazlollah, *Ketab-e Tadhkirat-e al-Ghafil va-Irshad al-Jahil* [The Book of Admonition to the Misinformed and Guidance for the Ignorant] (Tehran: 1287/1908).

Osterhammel, Jürgen, *The Transformation of the World* (Princeton, NJ: Princeton University Press, 2014).

Paidar, Parvin, *Women and the Political Process in Twentieth-Century Iran* (Cambridge: Cambridge University Press, 1995).

Parekh, Bhikhu, *Rethinking Multiculturalism: Cultural Diversity and Political Theory*, 2nd ed. (London: Palgrave Macmillan, 2006).

Parel, Anthony J. and Ronald C. Keith, *Comparative Political Philosophy: Studies under the Upas Tree*, 2nd ed. (Lanham, MD: Lexington Books, 2003).

Parvin, Nassereddin, "Irān-e Now," *Encyclopædia Iranica*, Vol. XIII, Fasc. 5 (December 15, 2006), pp. 498–500 (www.iranicaonline.org/articles/iran-e-now, last accessed September 15, 2019).

Paya, Ali and Mohammad Amin Ghaneirad, "Habermas and Iranian Intellectuals," *Iranian Studies*, Vol. 40, No. 3 (June 2007): 305–334.

Pitkin, Hannah, "Are Freedom and Liberty Twins?" *Political Theory*, Vol. 16 (1998): 523–552.

Pitts, Jennifer, *A Turn to Empire: The Rise of Imperial Liberalism in Britain and France* (Princeton, NJ: Princeton University Press, 2006).

"Political Theory of Empire and Imperialism," *Annual Review of Political Science*, Vol. 13, No. 1 (June 2010): 211–235.

Polanyi, Karl, *The Great Transformation: The Political and Economic Origins of Our Time* (Boston, MA: Beacon Press, 1957).

Postel, Danny, *Reading Legitimation Crisis in Tehran: Iran and the Future of Liberalism* (Chicago, IL: Prickly Paradigm Press, 2006).

Rahnema, Ali, *An Islamic Utopian: A Political Biography of Ali Shari'ati* (London: I.B. Tauris & Co. Ltd., 2014).

Behind the 1953 Coup in Iran: Thug, Turncoats, Soldiers, and Spooks (Cambridge: Cambridge University Press, 2014).

Rajaee, Farhang, *Islamism and Modernism: The Changing Discourse in Iran* (Austin, TX: University of Texas Press, 2007).

Ramazani, Ruhollah K., "Constitution of the Islamic Republic of Iran," *Middle East Journal*, Vol. 34, No. 2 (Spring 1980): 181–204.

Rawls, John, *Political Liberalism* (New York: Columbia University Press, 1996).

The Law of Peoples (Cambridge, MA: Harvard University Press, 1999).

Rezvani, Mohammad-Esmail, "Ruznameh-ye Sheikh Fazlollah Nuri," *Tarikh I*, No. 2 (1977): 168–170.

Rosanvallon, Pierre, *Democracy Past and Present*, ed. Samuel Moyn (New York: Columbia University Press, 2006).

Rosenblatt, Helena, *The Lost History of Liberalism: From Ancient Rome to the Twenty-First Century* (Princeton, NJ: Princeton University Press, 2018).

Rosenblum, Nancy L., *Liberalism and the Moral Life* (Cambridge, MA: Harvard University Press, 1989).

Ryan, Alan, *The Making of Modern Liberalism* (Princeton, NJ: Princeton University Press, 2012).

168 Bibliography

Sadeghi-Boroujerdi, Eskandar, "From Etela'ati to Eslahtalabi: Sa'id Hajjarian, Political Theology and the Politics of Reform in Post-revolutionary Iran," *Iranian Studies*, Vol. 47, No. 6 (2014): 987–1009.

Revolution and Its Discontents: Political Thought and Reform in Iran (Cambridge: Cambridge University Press, 2019).

Sadri, Mahmoud, "Sacral Defense of Secularism: The Political Theologies of Soroush, Shabestari, and Kadivar," *International Journal of Politics, Culture and Society*, Vol. 15, No. 2 (Winter 2001): 258–260.

Saffari, Siavash, *Beyond Shariati: Modernity, Cosmopolitanism, and Islam in Iranian Political Thought* (Cambridge: Cambridge University Press, 2017).

Said, Edward W., *Orientalism* (New York: Vintage, 1979).

Musical Elaborations (New York: Columbia University Press, 1991).

Culture and Imperialism (New York: Vintage, 1993).

Saikal, Amin, *The Rise and Fall of the Shah: Iran from Autocracy to Religious Rule* (Princeton, NJ: Princeton University Press, 1980).

Sandel, Michael, *Liberalism and the Limits of Justice* (Cambridge: Cambridge University Press, 1982).

Sanjabi, Maryam B., "Rereading the Enlightenment: Akhundzada and His Voltaire," *Iranian Studies*, Vol. 28, Nos. 1–2 (2007): 39–60.

Scott, James C., *Domination and the Arts of Resistance: Hidden Transcripts* (New Haven, CT: Yale University Press, 1990).

Secor, Laura, *Children of Paradise: The Struggle for the Soul of Iran* (New York: Riverhead Books, 2016).

Seyed-Gohrab, A. A. and Sen McGlinn, eds., *One Word – Yek Kalameh: 19th Century Persian Treatise Introducing Western Codified Law* (Amsterdam: Leiden, 2010).

Shadman, Fakhr al-Din, *Taskhir-e Tammadon-e Farangi* [The Capture of Western Civilization] (Tehran: 1326/1948).

Tariki va Rowshana'i [Darkness and Light] (Tehran: 1328/1950).

Teragedy-e Farang [The Tragedy of the West] (Tehran: Tahuri, 1346/1967).

Shariati, Ali, *Ensan, Eslam va Marxism* [Humankind, Islam, and Marxism] (Tehran: 1356/1977).

Marxism and Other Western Fallacies: An Islamic Critique, trans. R. Campbell (Berkeley, CA: Mizan Press, 1980).

Islam and Man, trans. Fatollah Marjani (Houston, TX: Free Islamic Lit. Inc., 1981).

Shklar, Judith N., "The Liberalism of Fear," in Nancy Rosenblum, ed., *Liberalism and the Moral Life* (Cambridge, MA: Harvard University Press, 1989), pp. 21–39.

Skinner, Quentin, "Meaning and Understanding in the History of Ideas," *History and Theory*, Vol. 8, No. 1 (1969): 3–53.

Liberty before Liberalism (Cambridge: Cambridge University Press, 1998).

"A Third Concept of Liberty," *Proceedings of the British Academy*, Vol. 117 (2002), pp. 237–268.

Sohrabi, Nader, "Revolution and State Culture: The Circle of Justice and Constitutionalism in 19th-Century Iran," in George Steinmetz, ed., *State/ Culture: State-Formation after the Cultural Turn* (Ithaca, NY: Cornell University Press, 1999), pp. 253–288.

Bibliography 169

Soroush, Abdolkarim, *Nahad-e Na-Aram-e Jahan* [The Dynamic Nature of the Universe] (Tehran: Entesharat-e Qalam, 1356/1977).

Tazad-e Dialiktiki [Dialectical Contradiction] (Tehran: Entesharat-e Hekmat, 1357/1978).

Elm Chist, Falsafeh Chist? [What Is Science, What Is Philosophy?] (Tehran: Entesharat-e Hekmat, 1358/1979).

Falsafeh-ye Tarikh [The Philosophy of History] (Tehran: Entesharat-e Hekmat, 1358/1979).

Farbehtar az Idiolozhi [Loftier than Ideology] (Tehran: Serat, 1372/1993).

"Hokumat-e demokratik-e dini?" [Religious Democratic Government?], *Kiyan*, Vol. 3, No. 11 (1372/1993).

Qabz va Bast-e Teorik-e Shari'at: Ya Nazariyeha-ye Takamol-e Ma'refat-e Dini [The Theoretical Contraction and Expansion of Sharia: Or, Thoughts on the Evolution of Religious Knowledge] (Tehran: Serat, 1373/1994).

Tafarroj-e Son'a: Goftarha-i dar Akhlagh va San'at va Elm-e Ensani [Promenading Creation: Essays on Ethics, Technology, and the Human Sciences] (Tehran: Serat Cultural Institute, 1373/1994).

"The Evolution and Devolution of Religious Knowledge," trans. Mahmoud Sadri, in Charles Kurzman, ed., *Liberal Islam: A Sourcebook* (New York: Oxford University Press, 1998), pp. 244–251.

Reason, Freedom, and Democracy in Islam, trans. Mahmoud Sadri and Ahmad Sadri (Oxford: Oxford University Press, 2000).

Swaine, Lucas, *The Liberal Conscience: Politics and Principles in a World of Religious Pluralism* (New York: Columbia University Press, 2006).

Tabaar, Mohammad Ayatollahi, *Religious Statecraft: The Politics of Islam in Iran* (New York: Columbia University Press, 2018).

Talebof, Abdul-Rahim, *Safineh-ye Talebi ya Ketab-e Ahmad* [The Talebian Vessel or the Book of Ahmad] (Istanbul: 1311–1312/1893–1894).

Tamir, Yael, *Liberal Nationalism* (Princeton, NJ: Princeton University Press, 1995).

Taqizadeh, Hassan, *Ayandeh*, Vol. 1, No. 1 (1304/1925): 17–25.

Tavakoli-Tarqi, Mohamad, "Imagining Western Women: Occidentalism and Euro-eroticism," *Radical America*, Vol. 24, No. 3 (1990): 73–87.

Refashioning Iran: Orientalism, Occidentalism, and Historiography (New York: Palgrave Macmillan, 2001).

Taylor, Charles, "The Politics of Recognition," in Amy Gutmann, ed., *Multiculturalism: Examining the Politics of Recognition* (Princeton, NJ: Princeton University Press, 1994), pp. 25–73.

The Liberation Movement of Iran, "The Party Program of the Liberation Movement of Iran," Tehran, 25 Ordibehesht 1340 [May 15, 1961].

Tully, James, *An Approach to Political Philosophy: Locke in Contexts* (Cambridge: Cambridge University Press, 1993).

Public Philosophy in a New Key, Volume II: Imperialism and Civic Freedom (Cambridge: Cambridge University Press, 2008).

"Lineages of Informal Imperialism," in Duncan Kelly, ed., *Lineages of Empire* (Oxford: Oxford University Press, 2009), pp. 3–30.

Vahdat, Farzin, *God and Juggernaut: Iran's Intellectual Encounter with Modernity* (Syracuse, NY: Syracuse University Press, 2002).

170   Bibliography

Vitalis, Robert, *White World Order, Black Power Politics* (Ithaca, NY: Cornell University Press, 2015).

von Vacano, Diego, "The Scope of Comparative Political Theory," *Annual Review of Political Science*, Vol. 18 (2015): 465–480.

Waldron, Jeremy, *Liberal Rights: Collected Papers, 1981–1991* (Cambridge: Cambridge University Press, 1993).

God, Locke, and Equality: Christian Foundations in Locke's Political Thought (Cambridge: Cambridge University Press, 2002).

Wall, Steven, ed., *The Cambridge Companion to Liberalism* (Cambridge: Cambridge University Press, 2015).

Wallerstein, Immanuel, *Centrist Liberalism Triumphant, 1789–1914* (Berkeley, CA: University of California Press, 2011).

Walzer, Michael, *Spheres of Justice: A Defense of Pluralism and Equality* (Oxford: Blackwell, 1983).

"Liberalism and the Art of Separation," *Political Theory*, Vol. 12, No. 3. (August 1984): 315–330.

Thick and Thin: Moral Argument at Home and Abroad (Notre Dame, IN: University of Notre Dame, 1994).

Wedeen, Lisa, "Scientific Knowledge, Liberalism, and Empire: American Political Science in the Middle East," in Seteny Shami and Cynthia Miller-Idriss, eds., *Middle East Studies for the New Millennium: Infrastructures of Knowledge* (New York: New York University Press, 2016), pp. 31–81.

Williams, Melissa D. and Mark E. Warren, "A Democratic Case for Comparative Political Theory," *Political Theory*, Vol. 42, No.1 (February 2014): 26–57.

Wright, Robin, "Scholar Emerges as the Martin Luther of Islam," *The Seattle Times*, February 12, 1995.

Yousefi Eshkevari, Hassan, *Remembering the Days: Political Approaches of the Reformist Movement in Iran* (Tehran: Gam-eh No, 2000).

Zakaria, Fareed, "The Rise of Illiberal Democracy," *Foreign Affairs*, Vol. 96, No. 6 (November–December 1997): 22–43.

"Islam, Democracy, and Constitutional Liberalism," *Political Science Quarterly*, Vol. 119, No. 1 (Spring 2004): 1–20.

Zarakol, Ayşe, *After Defeat: How the East Learned to Live with the West* (Cambridge: Cambridge University Press, 2011).

Zia-Ebrahimi, Reza, *The Emergence of Iranian Nationalism: Race and Politics of Dislocation* (New York: Columbia University Press, 2016).

Zirinsky, Michael, "Riza Shah's Abrogation of Capitulations," in Stephanie Cronin, ed., *The Making of Modern Iran: State and Society under Riza Shah, 1921–1941* (London: Routledge, 2003), pp. 81–98.

Index

Abdi, Abbas, 130
Abrahamian, Ervand, 24, 28, 38, 43, 71, 77, 78, 81, 88, 98, 99, 100, 109, 120, 121, 153
Adamiyat, Fereydoun, 24, 30, 32, 36, 37, 50, 51, 85, 95, 153
Afary, Janet, 13, 14, 34, 35, 47, 50, 68, 69, 70, 74, 88, 154
al-Afghani, Jamal al-Din, 37, 62, 63, 64, 65, 66, 67, 68
Afghanistan, 63, 64
Akhundzadeh, Mirza Fath'ali, 30, 36, 45, 64, 84, 95, 153
   art of critique, 33–34
   as nationalist, 33
   contra traditionalism, 31–33
   Maktubat, 31–33
   Maqalat, 31–33
Alavi-Tabar, Alireza, 54, 130
Al-e Ahmad, Jalal, 60, 63
   critique of Westernism, 91–97
Algar, Hamid, 30, 31, 37, 79, 88, 92, 103, 108, 109, 121, 122, 154, 156
Amanat, Abbas, 16, 41, 65, 66, 67, 78, 155
Amir Arjomand, Said, x, 68, 69, 81, 99, 102, 103, 107, 114, 155
Amir Kabir, 29
Anderson, Benedict, 44
Anglo-Iranian Oil Company, 48, 72
Anglo-Soviet occupation, 74
anjomanha-ye melli, 14
*anjoman*s, 14, 35
Ansari, Ali, 11, 12, 30, 33, 36, 46, 47, 48, 49, 78, 105, 153, 155, 160
anti-absolutism, 17, 19, 26, 27, 35, 36, 140
anti-constitutionalism, 16, 62, 68, 111
anti-imperialism, 17, 19, 26, 27, 40, 43, 49, 98, 108, 140
anti-Semitism, 46
arbitrary rule, 15, 37, 38, 41, 50, 69
Assembly of Experts, 103, 113, 116, 163
Ataturk, Mustafa Kemal, 72

Ayandeh (periodical), 48
Ayin (periodical), 130
Azerbaijan, 43, 47
Azimi, Fakhreddin, 16, 43, 75, 120, 155

Bahar, Mohammad-Taqi, 39, 46
Banisadr, Abolhassan, 128
Bazargan, Mehdi, 20, 49, 50, 103, 104, 107, 113, 114, 118, 121, 122, 156, 159
   on Islamic pluralism, 118–126
Behbahani, Abdollah, 68
Bell, Duncan, 5, 39, 147
Berlin, Isaiah, 27, 35, 55, 113, 142, 143, 157, 161
Bourdieu, Pierre, 8
British imperialism, 65

Cambridge School, 18, 143
capitalism, 2, 20, 27, 61, 71, 98, 136
Césaire, Aime, 45
Chehabi, H. E., 13, 34, 39, 47, 51, 72, 74, 79, 106, 114, 118, 119, 120, 121, 155, 158, 160, 166
civilizing mission, 40
clash of civilizations, 106, 131
Cobden, Richard, 40
colonialism, 39, 92, 96
comparative political theory, 18
Comte, Auguste, 37
Confederation of Iranian Students in Exile, 98
Constant, Benjamin, 40
constitutionalism, 16, 17, 23, 29, 41, 50, 51, 52, 55, 68, 69, 70, 80, 85, 96, 100, 105
Constitutional Revolution, 20, 39, 46, 50, 51, 52, 68, 97
   supplementary laws, 15
   as Enlightenment dialectic, 11–14
Council of Guardians, 103, 116

172   Index

Dallmayr, Fred, 131, 150, 158
Dar al-Fonoun, 29, 47, 82, 92, 95
Davar, Ali Akbar, 41, 71
Declaration of the Rights of Man, 51
dialectics of Enlightenment, 14
Dowlatabadi, Mahmoud, 45

Egypt, 1, 38, 63, 157
Enayat, Hadi, 51
end of history, the, 106, 131, 147
Euben, Roxanne, 64
European Enlightenment, 2
Europeanism, 80
expressive liberties, 6–7

Fadai'yun, 109, 114
Fallaci, Oriana, 121
Fanon, Franz, 45, 89, 92, 159
Fardid, Ahmad, 63
    anti-modernism, 85–91
    Fardid Circle, 85
Farhangestan, 47, 73
Foroughi, Mohammad Ali, 39, 41, 47, 48,
    73, 82, 155
Foucault, Michel, 88, 154, 160
France, 40, 63, 118, 119, 142, 147, 167
Freeden, Michael, 5, 6, 7, 25, 143, 144,
    151, 152
Freedom Movement of Iran, 49, 50,
    98, 156
freethinking, 23

Galston, William, 6
Ganji, Akbar, 116, 117, 130, 132, 133, 134,
    136, 140, 160
Germany, 42
gharbzadegi, 61, 62, 70, 96, 97, 99
    definition, 61
Gharbzadegi (Al-e Ahmad), 91, 93, 94
Gheissari, Ali, x, 11, 12, 15, 23, 24, 30, 38,
    46, 51, 52, 71, 74, 75, 81, 82, 86, 88,
    89, 92, 95, 97, 160
great transformation, the, 13

Habl al-Matin (periodical), 34
Hajjarian, Saeed, 104, 130, 132, 161, 168
Hashemi Rafsanjani, Ali Akbar, 130
Heidegger, Martin, 85, 86, 87
hidden liberalism, 6–11, 148
    as reflexive practice, 8
    compared to liberalism, 8–11
Hobhouse, L. T., 143
Hobsbawm, Eric J., 45, 161
Hobson, J. A., 40
Hourani, Albert, 64

House of Oblivion (Faramoush-Khaneh),
    2, 37
Hume, David, 31, 39, 164

Ibn Bajja, 64
Ibn Rushd, 64
Ibn Sina, 64
Ibn Tufayl, 64
India, viii, 12, 15, 38, 40, 63, 65, 147, 163
individual liberty, 8, 19, 27, 32
individualism, 14, 15, 20, 21, 35, 57, 61
Iran-e Farda (periodical), 130
Iran-e Now (periodical), 34, 46, 47, 167
Iranshahr (periodical), 48
Iraq, 12, 63, 100, 109, 114, 117, 130
Islamic Association of Students, 98
Islamic democracy, 79, 100, 125, 126, 132,
    134, 135, 138
Islamic liberalism, 21, 104, 106
Islamic pluralism, 20, 117, 125, 126
Islamic reformism, 4, 17, 105
Islamism, 17, 20, 62, 88, 91, 105, 148,
    154, 167

Jahanbegloo, Ramin, 47, 55, 56, 57,
    131, 161
Jebhe-ye Meli. See National Front, the

Kadivar, Mohsen, 104, 127, 130, 162, 168
Kamrava, Mehran, 100, 105, 130, 162
Kapuściński, Ryszard, 79, 80
Kashani, Abol-Qasem, 120
Kasravi, Ahmad, 34, 38, 39, 80, 84, 85, 92,
    162, 164
Katouzian, Homa, 15, 24, 29, 33, 38, 42,
    43, 76, 162
Kaveh (periodical), 42
Kermani, Mirza Agha Khan, 31, 34, 36, 37,
    45, 50, 95, 153, 156
    on anti-absolutism, 36
    Sad Khatabeh, 36
Khatami, Mohammad, 106, 128, 130, 132,
    140, 141
Khomeini, Ruhollah, 20, 79, 98, 107,
    113, 114
    on Islamic government, 109–114
Khomeinism, 63, 98, 99, 100, 109, 153
Kiyan (periodical), 129, 130, 132, 160, 169

Lahouti, Abol-Qasem, 46
Larmore, Charles, viii, 53, 57, 58, 125,
    146, 163
liberal imperialism, 5, 20, 147, 150
liberal internationalism, 5, 40
liberalism

Index

173

aristocratic liberalism, 51
definition, 4–7
Iranian liberalism, 3, 16, 25
liberal imagination, 4
liberal intelligentsia, 16, 41, 79
liberal reformers, 16, 32, 52, 73, 93, 124
modern liberalism, 15, 53, 142, 143
political liberalism, vii, 18, 29, 60, 106, 117, 118, 125, 139
Western liberalism, 11, 16, 22, 56, 61, 90, 91, 143, 147, 148, 150
liberalization, 17, 62, 72, 106, 137
liberal nationalism, 5, 28, 44, 45, 46
Liberation Movement of Iran, 20, 39, 79, 103, 106, 107, 120, 158, 169
liberationist ideologies, 18, 20, 89, 122, 125
Locke, John, 39, 143, 159, 169, 170

majles, 15
Malkum Khan, Mirza, 19, 31, 32, 37, 50, 67, 84, 96, 97
anti-absolutism, 37–38
Qanun (periodical), 37–38
tanzimat-style reforms, 1–2
Marxism, 17, 62, 88, 89, 90, 119, 127, 156, 168
Masroori, Cyrus, 30, 31, 33, 164
materialism, 20, 61, 89, 90, 119
Matin-Asgari, Afshin, 12, 24, 78, 81, 92, 94, 164
Mehta, Uday Singh, 40, 147, 165
Milani, Abbas, 84
Mill, John Stuart, 37, 39, 50
Mirsepassi, Ali, 12, 24, 56, 57, 62, 81, 85, 87, 88, 92, 98, 105, 136, 165
modernization, 63, 64, 73
intellectual basis, 29–30
Mohammad Ali Shah, 69, 111
Mojahedin-e Islam, 109, 114
monism, 35, 113, 124
Montazeri, Hossein-Ali, 103, 127, 130
Mosaddeq, Mohammad, 16, 23, 39, 42, 62, 76, 120
Kapitulasion va Iran, 42
anti-imperialism, 42–44
self-determination, 48–50
Mosavat (periodical), 34
Mostashar al-Dowleh, Mirza Yusuf Khan, 32, 51, 52, 67, 96, 124
Yek Kalameh, 51

Na'ini, Mohammad Hussein, 110, 111, 166
Naipaul, V. S., 45
Najmabadi, Afsaneh, 72, 73, 166
Naraqi, Ehsan, 81

Naser al-Din Shah, 1, 29, 47, 65, 67, 155
National Bank of Iran, 72
National Front, the, 39, 43, 48, 75, 76, 78, 79, 98, 117, 119, 120
nationalism
and Mossadeq, 48
and the Pahlavis, 48–49
as anti-imperialism, 43–44
nationalization, 23, 43, 48, 120
Nehzat-e Azadi-ye Iran. See Liberation Movement of Iran
Nuri, Sheikh Fazlollah, 62, 68, 69, 79, 93, 96, 111

Ottoman Empire, 1, 12, 13

Pahlavi autocracy, 75, 96, 102
Pahlavi dynasty, 16, 70, 80
Pahlavi, Mohammad Reza Shah, 48, 62, 74, 76, 78, 119, 155
Perso-Islamic, 61, 88
Pitts, Jennifer, 4, 40, 147, 167
pluralism
as ethical doctrine, 53
as fact, 53
as secular politics, 55–58
political Islam, 41, 63, 70, 104, 105, 106, 108, 117, 118, 121, 136
postcolonial societies, 9, 21
pseudo-modernism, 81, 82, 84, 96

Qajars
capitulation agreements, 49
despotism, 37, 38
elites, 65
the state, 29
Qanun (periodical), 1, 24, 34, 37, 38, 104, 153, 161, 166

Rasoulzadeh, Mohammad-Amin, 46
rationalism, 35, 85, 86, 149
Rawls, John, 53, 143, 144, 167
regime change, 67
representative government, 3, 15, 23, 39, 41, 50, 51, 52, 126, 133, 140
revolution of 1979, 79, 102
Reza Shah, 16, 23, 41, 48, 71, 72, 74
Russia, 16, 41, 63, 66, 69, 75
Russian Caucasus, 12
Ryan, Alan, 4, 17, 26, 35, 58, 128, 143

Saba, Hossein, 46
Sahabi, Yadollah, 117, 119
Said, Edward W., 45, 86, 148
Salam (periodical), 130

174 Index

SAVAK, 77
Scott, James C., 7
self-determination, 17, 28, 43, 137
self-government, 18, 27, 49
Shabestari, Mohammad Mojtahed, 54,
104, 127, 130, 166, 168
Shadman, Seyyed Fakhroddin, 63
on pseudo-modernism, 82–85
Shariati, Ali, 63, 88
critique of economism, 89–90
Islamic revivalism, 88–91
Shariatmadari, Mohammad Kazem, 113
Shiism, 3, 16, 50, 68, 88, 99, 103, 109,
129, 156
Shirazi, Mirza Hasan, 66
socialism, 3, 13, 17, 88, 148
Society of Humanity, 39
Soroush, Abdolkarim, 21, 54, 104, 126,
127, 129, 132, 160
Islamic democracy, 132–139
sovereign rights, 42, 43, 44, 47, 48
Spencer, Herbert, 40
standard of civilization, 3, 15, 40, 44, 61, 87
state-building, 13, 16, 18, 23, 29, 41, 48, 76
Students Following the Line of the
Imam, 113
Sur-e Israfil (periodical), 34

Tabatabaie, Mohammad, 68
Tajzadeh, Mostafa, 130
Talebof, Abdul-Rahim, 23, 31, 32, 41, 95,
96, 153, 169
Taleqani, Mahmoud, 117, 119
Tamir, Yael, 5, 45
tanzimat reforms, 1

Taqizadeh, Hassan, 30, 39, 46, 48,
155, 169
Taylor, Charles, 56, 145, 147, 169
Teymourtash, Abdol-Hossein, 41
theocracy, 27, 36, 128
Third World, 43, 54, 77, 89, 153
Tobacco Régie, 65
toleration, 3, 5, 10, 27, 54, 100, 117, 123,
125, 126
towhid, 89, 90, 112, 116, 129
traditionalism, 30
Tudeh Party, 75, 92, 109, 114, 118,
119, 128
Turkey, 33, 72, 164

University of Tehran, 73

velayat-e faqih, 99, 102, 109, 112, 113, 116,
118, 123, 124, 126, 133, 134

Western imperialism, 3, 7, 9, 22, 28, 39, 41,
48, 64, 87, 94, 96, 114, 148, 149
Westernism, 20, 61, 63
Westernization, 17, 70, 92
Western modernity, 2, 20, 60, 61, 62,
64, 74, 81, 82, 83, 84, 85, 86, 87,
89, 96
Westoxication, 61, 62, 63, 70
definition, 61
White Revolution, 62, 78, 155
World War II, 62, 74, 119

Yousefi-Eshkevari, Hassan, 54, 104, 130

Zia-Ebrahimi, Reza, 33, 34, 45, 170

Lightning Source UK Ltd.
Milton Keynes UK
UKHW020042031220
374536UK00004B/53